Ideology and Welfare

Ideology and Welfare

Gary Taylor

Sheffield Hallam University

palgrave
macmillan

© Gary Taylor 2007

First published 2007 by
PALGRAVE MACMILLAN
Houndmills, Basingstoke, Hampshire RG21 6XS and
175 Fifth Avenue, New York, N.Y. 10010
Companies and representatives throughout the world

PALGRAVE MACMILLAN is the global academic imprint of the Palgrave
Macmillan division of St. Martin's Press, LLC and of Palgrave Macmillan Ltd.
Macmillan® is a registered trademark in the United States, United Kingdom
and other countries. Palgrave is a registered trademark in the European
Union and other countries.

ISBN-13: 978-0-333-92928-5   hardback
ISBN-10: 0-333-92928-4   hardback
ISBN-13: 978-0-333-92930-8   paperback
ISBN-10: 0-333-92930-6   paperback

This book is printed on paper suitable for recycling and made from fully
managed and sustained forest sources.

A catalogue record for this book is available from the British Library.

Library of Congress Cataloging-in-Publication Data

A catalog record for this book is available from the Library of Congress.

10   9   8   7   6   5   4   3   2   1
16   15   14   13   12   11   10   09   08   07

Printed in China

Contents

Acknowledgements

I have benefited greatly from conversations with friends and colleagues. In particular, I would like to thank Anthony Arblaster, John Schwarzmantel, Tony Taylor, Malcolm Todd, Rob Sykes, Alan McGauley, Helen Hawley and the late Bob Pearson (I miss you Bob). My thanks also to Catherine Gray and the editorial team at Palgrave and to the anonymous referees for their comments, observations and critique. Finally, my family has been brilliant and patient in the extreme. Thank you Karen for reading and commenting upon the manuscript and for keeping our children entertained as I approached the deadline. Matthew and Laurie, I can play now.

1

Introduction

The aim of this book is to outline a variety of ideological perspectives on welfare and to consider how these ideas are reflected in a range of social policies. It is important to realise at the outset that ideas have an important part to play in setting the tone and defining the parameters of political activity and that when governments develop their policies they often do so within constantly changing ideological frameworks. Ideologies do not stand still, nor do they develop in isolation of the policies and debates engineered by governments. Ideologies develop as a result of successes and failures of government initiatives and in response to circumstances that can sometimes appear beyond the control of government. This book looks at ideological debates about the role of the state in tending to the general welfare of the citizens and concentrates, in particular, on the development of ideas and policies in such areas as the benefits system, housing, health care and education. Ideologies provide us with numerous interpretations of economic, social and political life. We can pose questions about who should be responsible for financing health care and to what extent the state should provide benefits, subsidise housing or provide education. It is often the case that the answers to these questions owe more to our ideological assumptions about the character of humanity than to distinct views on social issues. Each ideology has its own distinctive way of viewing human characteristics, of interpreting economic and social affairs, of considering the legitimate functions of the state and of challenging and changing the way we live. By looking at ideologies, we have access to a range of critical perspectives on contemporary society and a broad spectrum of possibilities for the future.

The nature of ideology

Ideologies are often thought to have descriptive and prescriptive features because they describe social reality and suggest ways to change it. Their descriptions of reality, however, will be formulated in accordance with the principles they value. Socialists, for example, have traditionally concentrated upon the effects of society upon the working class, whereas liberals are more likely to focus upon the rights and potential of the individual. The slant they place upon describing social reality thus provides a springboard for their proposals and a clue to their visions of how society should be. It is apparent that they only put forward solutions to the problems they identify and that a conservative vision of how society should be organised is not designed to remedy problems identified by liberals or socialists. In some ways, ideologies are attempts to create a self-contained vision of how society is and how it should be. Each ideology identifies a limited number of problems and a limited number of solutions. Whereas Marxists identify key problems with capitalism and look for ways to undermine what they consider to be an unjust system, conservatives will focus upon its strengths and seek to find ways to stabilise capitalism. The solutions offered by ideologies make sense only when considered alongside their views on existing society. It has been argued that the core of an ideology lies in its particular image of how society should be transformed. From this stems a practical programme that identifies what needs to be done to unite image and reality. Ideologies, therefore, provide us with a way of understanding and influencing the world in which we live (Eccleshall, 1984a, pp. 7–8). It would be wrong, however, to reduce any ideology to a simple wish list constructed by people discontent with the status quo. Some ideologies seek to preserve rather than to engage in radical change.

We can gain considerable insight into ideologies by uncovering their divergent views on the purpose of life, rather than by comparing policy recommendations on such issues as the state or the economy. Although it is important to understand practical proposals, those subscribing to different ideologies may well share some policy recommendations but for different reasons. Some conservatives, for example, are critical of the welfare state for sapping the will and initiative of the individual and for draining the nation of resources (see Chapters 3 and 5). Some Marxists have also been critical of the welfare state. They have argued that it props up and prolongs the life of the capitalist system by providing a safety net to be used during times of economic hardship, thus taking the wind out of revolutionary sails (see Chapter 7). Given these vastly different agendas, it makes sense to view policy recommendations in the light of broader ideological structures.

The development of ideologies

Ideologies are developed in a variety of ways. At a basic level, people construct their own ideological makeups by developing their own philosophies of life. This is a process that might draw upon the ideas of others and one that is often driven by the need to place our own experiences into some broader context. We often draw conclusions about our nature and about the nature of other people in society. We also have economic views, relating perhaps to the work we do and to the incomes we have, even if these views do not run to detailed knowledge of macro-economic policy. Attitudes towards social policy likewise develop through our own experiences of the education and health systems, through the way we view our own housing needs and perhaps as a result of our own or our family's experience of the benefits system. The importance of this basic level of understanding should not be underestimated. Those who devour weighty theoretical texts may well dismiss such views as undeveloped or even as uninformed, but this fails to recognise the importance of such views in influencing the way we vote, moulding the for-mation of policy (particularly in a more pragmatic political climate) and in affecting the kinds of literature we choose to read. Ideological perspectives often have fairly simple foundations. They tend to rest upon a particular view of life, and one that can be heard in a variety of places and expressed by a broad range of people. It is not necessary to be an expert in politics to understand and appreciate the importance of ideas in society and to recognise the relevance of ideology.

Ideologies are also developed by theorists who, at various stages in their writings, attempt to grapple with the defining characteristics of society and work towards building programmes of reform. It is worth remembering that many of the great theorists of the modern age have written, more often than not, in response to immediate and specific events. The conservative philosophy of Edmund Burke, for example, developed in response to news about the French Revolution of 1789 and because he was worried about the potential appeal of revolutionary ideas in Britain. At the other end of the conventional political spectrum, Marx developed many of his ideas by taking note of the political programmes and activities of the nineteenth-century labour movement and through his intensive study of the capitalist economy. Marx rarely outlined his vision of the future, yet these are the sections that often feature in discussions on socialist and Marxist ideologies. Key theorists in the development of political ideologies do not necessarily regard themselves in this way. Theorists often make a range of contributions, only some of which survive their lifetimes and influence other theorists. It is clear, moreover, that theorists fall in and out of favour. Socialist theorists like William Morris and Edward Carpenter, who concentrated upon the ethical and aesthetic features of socialism, wrote during the 1880s and were 'rediscovered' in the second decade of the twentieth century and during the 1960s. The way we view their contributions to socialism will in turn change over time. This shows, among other things, that ideologies are not stable or unchanging streams of thought. The way that ideologies are interpreted will depend upon the questions being asked and, to some extent, on the current intellectual climate. The idea of socialism, for example, is constantly redefined by theorists, practitioners and commentators in the hope of either promoting or defeating its dominant features.

Social and political movements are also important in the development of ideologies. Practitioners, by working out and responding to policy initiatives, play a key role in adapting theoretical perspectives to practical problems, in showing the limitations of any particular theory and in creating new possibilities for theoretical developments. Developments in conservative and new right ideas, for example, owe a great deal to conservative parties throughout the world. Indeed, it could be argued that conservatism has no great need for detailed theoretical backing given that its primary aim is to conserve rather than to change. Conservatives have traditionally shunned abstract political theory, claiming that it distracts practitioners from the serious business of managing society (see Chapter 3). Similar reservations about the value of theory have also been expressed by advocates of the third way (see Chapter 6). In both cases, these reservations influence the nature of their respective ideologies rather than do away with the need for ideology itself.

In discussing ideologies, it is necessary to recognise that they are not necessarily tied to party politics. The liberal ideology, for example, is not necessarily applied and developed solely by liberal parties. Liberalism can appeal to members of the Liberal Party in Britain and to the Democratic Party in America as well as to members of other right or left wing parties. The same applies to the other ideologies. When we look at ideology, we are concentrating upon systems of thought that encompass entire philosophies of life rather than mere party programmes. Political parties, indeed, can pull from a variety of ideologies when developing their policies and when constructing their rhetoric to appeal to the electorate. It is not necessary for us to accept or reject any particular ideology in its entirety. Something of value can be found in most ideologies and, by combining and refining ideas drawn a range of sources, we are able to develop our own perspectives on politics and on life. These perspectives might owe more to one ideology than to another, but without access to diverse ideological debate our own political understanding is likely to remain stunted. We do not have to agree with ideologies other than our own, but we should at least be aware of them.

Welfare

The concept of welfare is far from straightforward. It is often used as a shorthand term to describe the benefits system but this is an extremely limited view of what welfare entails. O'Brien and Penna point out that welfare can mean 'well-being' and thus can refer to such things as the economic prosperity, health and personal security of the population. It can also refer to the institutions of the welfare state that many believe are necessary to promote individual and collective welfare. Finally, it can be viewed as a discourse (of social welfare) through which we understand the world (O'Brien and Penna, 1998, pp. 7–8). Ideological perspectives on welfare go far beyond discussing the arguments for and against the benefits system. Although some politicians might use fairly restrictive definitions of welfare, many social and political theorists are aware that our welfare consists in a number of interrelated things.

Welfare (or well-being) rests upon a number of foundations. Tony Fitzpatrick ties it to such things as long term happiness, degree of security, whether our needs and preferences are being satisfied or stifled, whether we get what we deserve and how we compare with others. Rather than see welfare as something that can be measured objectively, it is important that we take into account its subjective features because it relies upon the way we view our own well-being (Fitzpatrick, 2001, pp. 5–11). Our welfare thus exists not only in the possession of good health, good education, secure and decent housing and sufficient money and resources to live a decent life, but also in our appreciation of these things. The value of a university education, for example, can be expressed in objective and subjective terms. Its objective value can be measured by comparing the incomes of graduates and non-graduates, while its subjective value is found in the impact it has upon our quality of life and in the value we place upon education. The more we value our existing levels of education, health or housing, the greater our sense of well-being.

Structure of the chapters

This volume recognises that ideologies develop through theoretical speculation and through political practice. Rather than concentrate solely upon theoretical developments, an attempt has been made to produce a blended approach that uses theory and practice to illuminate the distinctive features of each ideology. While each chapter has a theoretical backbone, this is often supplemented with a variety of policy examples. It is important to recognise that ideological perspectives are developed internationally. Although each nation might formulate and apply ideas to suit its own particular needs, these nations contribute towards a rich and sprawling ideological tapestry of international dimension and significance. While it is beyond the remit of this book to cover the international system as a whole, an attempt has been made to infuse a comparative element that allows us to look beyond any one particular country. In drawing comparisons, special attention has been given to perspectives developed by theorists and practitioners in Britain and in the United States. Some reference is also made to certain policies developed and implemented in other European states, Asia and New Zealand. It is hoped that this broad approach will give the reader access to a multitude of alternatives that cast light not only on the nations concerned but also on the international importance of ideologies.

An attempt has been made in this volume to view each ideology on a number of levels and to identify a series of interrelated layers. It is argued that in order to understand the policy recommendations of the various theorists and ideologies, it is necessary to take into account how these recommendations rest upon economic, social and political foundations. Each chapter is organised so that the foundations are covered first and are followed by a discussion of areas of policy. In the hope of assisting readers to navigate their way through the issues and to allow for comparisons to be made, a standard format has been used for all of the chapters. Following a brief introduction, each chapter is divided into the following sections:

- Economy
- Social values
- State and welfare
- Welfare and social policies.

It should be appreciated that these sections are by no means self-contained. The sections on state and welfare will also refer to social policies and these individual examples of social provision also overlap to some degree. When discussing health, for example, it is quite possible that the benefits system and housing will have some bearing on the topic. This study acknowledges and reinforces the view that welfare issues are interconnected and that, if we want to deal with problems in one area, we need to take into account how these problems are influenced by and impact upon other areas of social life. Let us now take a closer look at the areas outlined above.

Economy

All of the ideologies covered in this volume include an economic dimension, so much so that the economy is often seen as a key foundation for social policy initiatives. The capitalist economy rests upon private ownership and control of the means of production. The capitalist ethos allows for individuals to prosper by either selling their labour or by purchasing the labour of others and extracting a profit. This method of buying and selling of labour power is commonplace in modern Western economies and carries with it significant ideological baggage about the way that individuals relate to each other through a cash-nexus. In a capitalist system, we operate within a variety of markets. We equip ourselves to compete in the labour market, the housing market and even in what we choose to buy and how we choose to display it.

The economy provides a framework for the development of social policies. Apart from anything else, it generates wealth and thus creates the material resources that can be distributed or withheld from diverse sections of society. The capitalist system and its sophisticated methods of production, distribution and exchange needs workers who are healthy, educated and housed. Fluctuations within the business cycle will often create problems of unemployment and therefore make it necessary for us either individually or collectively to find ways to protect ourselves from the ravages of unemployment and from the perils of poverty in old age. Capitalism, moreover, relies upon the existence of inequalities and the desire to succeed economically. Such inequalities, especially when they are extreme and unregulated, can pose a serious threat to social order. Given these factors, it makes sense to ask what can be done to regulate or transform the economy so as to maximise the common good. Contemporary ideologies and political movements vary in the degree to which they are willing to use the state to intervene in the economy and to redistribute the wealth. These debates on the role of the state in the economy do indeed have a central place in the modern ideological landscape.

Social values

In addition to an economic dimension, ideologies also contain social values. These social values include such things as freedom, equality, justice, responsibility and so on and are important for a variety of reasons. In particular, they express views about the relationship between individuals and establish a conceptual framework within which politicians and policymakers operate. Economic and social policies in Western democracies often rest upon and influence the type of freedom that citizens expect in society, or the extent of equality or social justice deemed appropriate in the modern age. As long as these policies are not imposed regardless of popular opinion, policymakers will make assumptions about the way that the citizens of their particular society view freedom and equality and, if they are ambitious, how these values can be altered or strengthened. Social values can be seen scattered through policy documents and have an extremely important place in ideological debates. Social and political theorists, indeed, use social values as part of their theoretical currency. It could be argued that social policies in particular rarely have value in themselves and that they are evaluated more often than not according to their contribution to levels of freedom or equality in society.

As we will see, there are many different interpretations of freedom. Freedom is not a single definable entity but something that people from different ideological backgrounds seem to value. Attempts have been made over time to distinguish between different types of freedom and to create categories within which different views can be housed. Perhaps the most widespread and to some extent useful distinction can be found in the work of Isaiah Berlin (1969), who argued that freedom could be viewed in terms of a distinction between negative and positive liberty. Negative liberty consisted in the right to do as we wish, unrestrained by others in general and by the state in particular. Positive liberty, on the other hand, relied upon us listening to our better selves and doing what we should do. This latter view of freedom gave considerably more scope to the state to intervene in the lives of citizens. Although this distinction was not meant to capture all forms of freedom for all time, it is useful when looking at ideological debates, and we will find that many of the ideologies covered in this volume advance notions of freedom that resemble the categories outlined by Berlin. For many of the leading theorists of these ideologies, establishing a suitable combination of freedom and equality is of fundamental importance.

Debates over the value of equality also have an important place in many ideologies. Just as freedom cannot be defined as a single entity, so it is with the idea of equality. Once again, it might be useful to begin with a distinction between different types of equality. Although there are undoubtedly many types of equality, it is often the case that social and political theorists use the term to mean either equality of outcome (in which goods could be distributed equally) or equality of opportunity (where the emphasis is on allowing people to compete on equal terms). It should be clear from what has been said already that equality of outcome is incompatible with the ethos of capitalism because capitalism relies upon the existence of economic incentives and even on the fear of failure and destitution. Equality of outcome would clearly disrupt these fears and incentives and threaten the vitality of the capitalist system. Although equality of outcome is incompatible with capitalism, there are other economic systems that it might suit, most notably the communist and perhaps other communal systems. Equality of opportunity, on the other hand, is compatible with capitalism. Indeed, it could be argued that equality of opportunity would make capitalism more vibrant and efficient by attracting a broad range of suitable workers and innovators.

In addition to using the ideas of freedom and equality, theorists often use other concepts to capture and characterise their particular cocktail of values. Of particular importance are concepts like social justice, paternalism, patriarchy or a spiritual view of life. In each case, these ideas add to the range of social values used by ideologies and provide ways to combine potentially conflicting values. They help us moreover to recognise differences between the ideologies far more so than if we were to rely solely upon identifying different philosophies of freedom and equality. The account of social values contained in this volume is by no means exhaustive. Rather than attempt to list the values promoted in the various ideologies, an attempt has been made to make some contribution to our understanding of the relationship between freedom and equality and to show how this debate influences the social content of the ideologies contained herein.

State and welfare

Having outlined and identified the economic and key social dimensions of the ideologies selected for the volume, we will move on to consider the role of the state in a little more detail and concentrate in particular on the role of the state in the provision of welfare. We are accustomed in the West to look to the state to satisfy at least some of our fundamental welfare needs and it is clear that the welfare state has had an important role in the development of modern society. Numerous commentators have attempted to grapple with the nature and importance of the welfare state. Asa Briggs sees it as a means by which people are granted a minimum level of security against unstable market forces (Briggs, 1969, p. 18). Commentators have argued that the welfare state is an essential feature of capitalist industrialisation and it provides a way for the system to allocate resources and establish order. It has been described as a system of 'citizenship stratification' and it is thought that this system competes with and even replaces our class position (O'Brien and Penna, 1998, p. 140). The welfare state does not simply exist on the sidelines of contemporary Western societies. It is often the case that welfare states are embedded in the entire economic and social structure. This makes attempts to deprive the welfare state of its functions potentially distastrous for national economies.

When looking at the state and welfare, it is important that we begin by taking note of how the various ideologies view the state. The term state is used to refer to the agencies of central government. It is recognised that these agencies will often operate and apply policies by using local government or other organisations, but it is clear that central government still has a major role in governing society. As we shall see, some of the ideologies are hostile towards the state because they want the capitalist system to regulate itself. For more radical spirits, the state is too tied to the interests of capitalism to be trusted to legislate in the interests of all sections of society. Between these extremes, there are those who wish to use the state to reform the capitalist system and more often than not to attend to the common welfare. It should be noted that the present volume is by no means dedicated to theories of the state but that an attempt has made to say something about ideological perspectives on the state as a foundation for broader discussions on the role of the state in the provision of welfare.

Welfare and social policies

Once we have seen how each ideology regards both the nature of the state and the role of the state in welfare provision, each chapter will then look at specific policy examples. It is argued in this volume that welfare means considerably more than the provision of income support in the form of unemployment benefit, child allowances or retirement pensions and that our welfare as individuals relies upon a variety of factors. The list could of course be extensive. If we held onto an all-encompassing view of welfare, we could no doubt include such things as job satisfaction, the ability to participate fully in the democratic process or even personal factors relating to our friends, families and social circles. Although these factors are no doubt important, this volume looks at welfare in the light of a range of social policies that cover the benefits system, housing, health care and education. By making use of these policy examples, it is hoped that we can gain a better understanding of the practical dimensions and implications of the ideologies outlined and discussed herein.

When dealing with these policy areas, special attention will be paid to the social roles of the state. Although there are many other interesting issues that could be covered, giving due attention to the role of the state in the selected areas of social provision will assist us in establishing connections between the policy examples and the sections covering the economy, social values and the state and welfare. Each chapter will discuss the way in which state provision is viewed and attempt to ascertain whether the proposed state intervention is adequate to deal with the problems highlighted by each ideology. For some ideologies, state intervention in these policy areas is enough to compensate for the instabilities of the capitalist system. For others, the problems created by the existing system are too extreme to be treated by such palliatives. As we will see, the ideologies covered in this volume will tend to veer one way or the other.

It is worth taking note that most of the successful governments in Britain, the United States, Northern Europe and Scandinavia in the years since the Second World War in particular have accepted the need for some government intervention in either the provision or direction of benefits, housing, health and education. The welfare state has become part of the contemporary political landscape, even if some political factions want to prune it beyond recognition. As Chapters 2–6 of the current volume will show, debate in the political mainstream has tended to look at the extent to which the state should intervene in such areas rather than whether the state should intervene at all. These ideologies have influenced and reflected the policies of successful Western governments. The chapters on liberalism, conservatism, social democracy, neo-liberalism and the third way will attempt to provide an insight into both the theoretical dimensions of the ideologies and the ways in which social policies have been applied in a variety of countries. Although special attention will be given to developments in Britain and in the United States, examples from other countries will also be used.

This book will also include chapters on radical critics of the welfare state. The attention to policy developments in these chapters will necessarily be rather different from the chapters covering the political mainstream. Marxists, feminists and the Greens are treated as radical voices because influential sections of these ideologies and movements reject capitalism and are therefore less than convinced that the welfare state can do anything significant to cater to the general welfare of both the individual and society. For these critics, government intervention in the provision and direction of key areas of social policy is of limited value. They are certainly important in articulating radical views and some of their ideas at least have impacted upon the political mainstream, but as yet there are no examples of their ideas being applied in full in any of the countries dealt with in the current volume. When dealing with the social policies of these critics, attention will be given to their critiques of existing social provision and, where appropriate, to the kind of alternatives they choose to offer.

Conclusion

The chapters contained in this book have been structured so as to allow the reader to travel through different layers of the ideologies concerned. The foundations of the ideologies are covered in sections on the economy and on social values. The sections on state and welfare and on welfare and social policies build upon these foundations and explore the social content of the selected ideologies. We should bear in mind that ideologies contain a multitude of dimensions. The detailed examination of social issues could be replaced by a discussion of ideological perspectives on the economy, crime or international affairs, and indeed any of the issues covered could have been explored in greater detail. The issues have been selected because each in its own way contributes towards our understanding and appreciation of human welfare. It is argued throughout the volume that our welfare depends upon a range of social issues that include access to benefits, housing, health care and education and that, in order to understand the ideological perspectives on these policy areas, we need at least some appreciation of the economic and social foundations of the various ideologies. By approaching the subject in this way, it is hoped that we can gain some understanding both of the ideologies and of their plans for the enhancement of human welfare.

2

Liberalism

The term liberalism can be used in a variety of ways and can attract people with extremely different views. The left and the right sometimes use the word liberal as a term of abuse. In both cases, liberals can be condemned for displaying weakness in their attempts to balance conflicting interests in society rather than side with capital (the right wing perspective) or with labour (the left's preference). We should bear in mind, however, that there are different types of liberals. The classical liberals of the late eighteenth and early nineteenth centuries were arch defenders of capitalism and ardent critics of an interventionist state. It was not until the late nineteenth century that liberals began to engage with social problems in a way that allowed the state to increase its functions. The term social liberal will be used when referring to these pioneers of the modern welfare state. This chapter will have something to say about both these forms of liberalism. Given that we are primarily interested in welfare issues, greater attention will be given to the social liberals and to their sensitive handling of social issues. In a later chapter (Chapter 5), we will look at attempts to revive the spirit of classical liberalism and repackage it in the form of neo-liberalism. For now, the discussion of classical liberalism will draw upon the ideas of Adam Smith, Tom Paine, Herbert Spencer and the ever-changing John Stuart Mill. The ideas of T.H. Green, L.T. Hobhouse, John Maynard Keynes and John Rawls will be used to illustrate some of the key features of social liberalism. Material on these theorists will be supplemented by some examples of policies introduced by key liberal regimes including the 1906–1914 Liberal governments in Britain and the Democratic administrations of Roosevelt and Johnson in the United States.

Economy

It could be argued that liberals defend the interests of capitalism and of the capitalist class because they believe that capitalism is capable of serving the public good. Whereas a feudal system based upon inflexible class divisions allowed relatively little social mobility for the talented and the desperate, many liberals regard capitalism as an open system in which people from a variety of backgrounds can aspire to success and pursue their own interests. This promise or potential touches the very heart of liberalism and provides the individual with a way to make him or herself distinctive and unique. Indeed, for liberals it is essential that individuals be allowed room to grow and to prosper.

There are of course many fine liberal economists that could be used to illustrate the liberal approach to the economy. The great enlightenment thinker Adam Smith certainly has longevity on his side. His monumental study *The Wealth of Nations* (1776) inspired generations of liberals and is still one of the finest examples of classical liberal reasoning. The classical liberals were advocates of laissez-faire. In their view, it was necessary to keep the state out of economic affairs and to allow the economy as far as possible to regulate itself. Working upon the assumption that individuals are primarily motivated by prospects for material gain, they felt that making use of the free market was the best way to ensure that the capitalist system produced what people wanted and that it provided a range of opportunities for those who strived to excel in their working lives. Adam Smith (1776) believed that people are apt to pursue their own interests rather than deliberately set out to promote and enhance the public good. This does not mean, however, that the public good is undermined. Indeed, he believed that the free market economy was capable of serving the public good and that individual self-interest can in turn benefit the wider community. Smith believed that by attempting to maximise individual profit, individuals will also contribute towards the economic progress of society and that the individual is effectively '... led by an invisible hand to promote an end which was no part of his intention' (Smith, 1776, p. 572). In Smith's view, the public good is advanced to a far greater extent by individual self-interest than by acts intended to serve the public good. Indeed, Smith claimed that he had '... never known much good done by those who affected to trade for the public good' (Smith, 1776, p. 572). Free market economics evidently serves the interests of the capitalist class. Its advocates want the economy to be left to the activity, vision and entrepreneurial skills of the minority rather than rely upon the state taking an active role in the coordination or management of economic affairs.

For many liberals, however, such profound levels of trust in the workings of the free market seem inconsistent with social compassion and with guaranteeing that all people have the opportunity to excel. Even John Stuart Mill (1836, 1852), a theorist who shared and articulated the classical liberal fear of the state, argued that free market economics was too harsh in its scientific formulations and that there should be room for at least some state intervention in the economy to ensure that the common good is not ignored and submerged under the dominance of self-interest. Social liberals of the late nineteenth century onwards were also among those who argued that an economy that relied too heavily on self-interest would have no effective way of securing common advantage. Hobhouse (1911) claimed that the idea of laissez-faire was far too optimistic in promoting the view that a natural harmony can develop from individuals pursuing their own interests and that leaving individuals to their own devices can benefit society as a whole. He claimed that although economic individualism has created great wealth, this was often done at the expense of the majority of citizens. Hobhouse was adamant that wealth had a social dimension and that it could not be attributed solely to the outcomes of individual effort, for property rights would be unstable without the protection of society.

Liberal economics changed considerably in the twentieth century with the further development of social liberalism. Although liberals continued to maintain a firm commitment to liberal social values, it was recognised increasingly that the classical liberal free market economy could not be relied upon to secure the common good and that the state might be needed to intervene to manage capitalism and to strengthen its long-term vitality. The ideas of John Maynard Keynes (1936) were particularly important in this regard. While he defended the right of capitalists to make their profits, he argued that there were significant gaps in classical liberal economics that needed to be filled. Although he did not want the state to assume direct control over the means of production, he believed that there must be room for the state to cooperate with the private sector in the interests of creating and maintaining a stable economy. In particular, he argued that the state should be willing to pump money into the economy in the interests of stimulating demand and thereby helping to secure full employment (Keynes, 1936, pp. 374–381). The ideas of Keynes had a tremendous impact upon the way that liberals, conservatives and social democrats view the relationship between the state and the economy. Indeed, Keynesian economics provide a foundation for many of the ideologies that seek to stabilise the capitalist system.

Such recognition of the limitations of free market economics became one of the dominant features of liberal political economy during the twentieth century. Echoes of this can be discerned in political debate in the United States. Franklin Roosevelt (1932), for example, argued against unrestrained capitalism but feared state paternalism. He respected that all Americans required the right to life, liberty and the pursuit of happiness but justified government intervention in social and economic affairs on the grounds that it can create opportunities for all individuals to reach their potential (Roosevelt, 1932, pp. 302–304). Liberals in the United States continue to praise the free market because it is consistent with individual freedom and equality of opportunity. However, it is also recognised that markets do not always satisfy all needs and that state intervention in the economy can assist in improving the efficiency of the capitalist economy and in maintaining decent levels of employment (see Rawls, 1999, pp. 240–245). From a liberal point of view, such intervention does not necessarily detract from the social values they hold so dear.

Although many liberals might want to support free market economics, partly because the free market provides an arena in which individuals can grow and pursue their potential, their faith in such arrangements is often predicated on the belief that the free market can benefit all people. This faith, however, can be undermined by the instability of the free market and by the conspicuous absence of Adam Smith's 'invisible hand'. Under such circumstances, social liberals in particular become willing to embrace the state as a potential ally and as an instrument that can be used to protect and even humanise the capitalist system. If capitalism was fair and everybody experienced similar levels of freedom and opportunity, then liberals might shy away from using the state in this way. The precarious free market, however, cannot be relied upon to respond to and satisfy the increasingly complex needs articulated in modern society. Given this, the state is recast as a guardian and promoter of the common good.

Social values

Freedom is undoubtedly the dominant social value within the liberal tradition. From a liberal point of view, individuals should be left to pursue their own interests. This is thought to help both the individual and the community for '... self interest would be tempered by reason and a natural benevolence that would deter people from engaging in anti-social behaviour' (Perry, 1993, p. 216). Liberals are firm believers in education, reason and science and believe that the individual can prosper if freed from tyranny and oppression. This oppression can take many forms. From a liberal perspective, religion, custom and deference are potentially dangerous to the mind of the individual. We are called upon to find our own way through life, to develop our own ideas and not to rely too heavily upon the received wisdom of previous generations. Liberals recognise the importance of tolerance and are generally arch defenders of freedom of speech and religious freedom. A liberal world is one where individuals are free to explore their own interests, while respecting the freedom of others.

The liberal tradition has spawned many great theorists of freedom. One of the most influential must surely be John Stuart Mill. Mill (1859) feared that governments and public opinion were potentially oppressive and he warned of the so-called 'tyranny of the majority' through which the majority, or those who represent the majority, can often stifle individual liberty and in turn create a conformist and mediocre political culture. In his view, it is important that individuals have as much independence as possible in matters that concern themselves solely. According to Mill, the adult individual should have sovereignty over his or her own mind and body. He believed that in order for us to be free we need liberty of conscience, thought and feeling, liberty of lifestyle and the freedom to unite with others. Indeed, our freedom was thought to depend upon all of these being respected and observed. For Mill, it was important for us to remain free from the undue influence of others. Given this, Mill was clearly an advocate of negative liberty in which liberty is equated with the absence (rather than with the possession) of something.

Not all liberals view freedom in this way. The social liberals of the late nineteenth century onwards have viewed freedom as far more than the absence of restraint. T.H. Green (1888), for example, claimed that freedom is not simply doing as we wish, but doing something that is 'worth doing' in cooperation with others. Freedom is said to contribute towards the progress of society by encouraging people to make the best of their lives. According to this line of reasoning, freedom should not be enjoyed by the minority at the expense of the majority, as had been the case in ancient society, but it relies upon people making the best of themselves and in so doing making a positive contribution to the common good. L.T. Hobhouse (1911) argued that it is useful to distinguish between unsocial freedom and social freedom. Unsocial freedom was said to allow for the free reign of self-interest without regard for the interests of others. According to Hobhouse, this form of freedom was 'antithetic to all public control' (Hobhouse, 1911, p. 91). Social freedom, on the other hand, relied upon freedom being distributed throughout the community and upon imposing some forms of restraint to ensure that individuals do not harm others (Hobhouse, 1911, pp. 91–94). This view that freedom should be distributed or redistributed in the community does create room for the state to engineer levels of freedom in society. For those who believe in positive liberty, the state can intervene in social life without detracting too much from the freedom of the individual. Indeed, it is argued that state intervention is necessary to enhance the freedom of the individual and to secure the good of the community.

Liberals in America have likewise placed a high value upon the social dimensions of freedom. Michael Sandel (1996) points out that the American case for the welfare state rests upon a deep respect for freedom rather than upon communal obligation and that American liberals are apt to point out that individual freedom cannot be achieved unless granted to all members of society and that everybody needs freedom to develop (Sandel, 1996, p. 280–281). Consider, for example, the way that Rawls views freedom. John Rawls (1996,

1999) argues that all citizens in a democratic society should have equal rights to a range of liberties including the right to participate in the democratic process as well as to freedom of thought and person. He recognised, however, that these liberties might not necessarily be of equal worth to different sections of society and that members of the poorer sections of the community might have the same right to liberty but have less ability to use this right to fulfil their potential (Rawls, 1996, p. 5; 1999, pp. 178–179). For social liberals, the freedom of significant sections of society needs to be enhanced. There is a general recognition that capitalism creates inequalities and that for freedom to mean anything something needs to be done to reduce these inequalities.

For many liberals, equality of outcome is considerably less attractive than equality of opportunity. As defenders of capitalism, even if in a moderated form, liberals generally have no interest in attacking all inequalities. Hobhouse (1911) argued that inequality in society was legitimate as long as it served the common good and that this applied even to extreme economic inequalities. He did however argue in favour of equal opportunities and he believed that the state should provide such things as free education to ensure that people can benefit from their freedoms (Hobhouse, 1911, pp. 32, 131). John Rawls (1996, 1999) likewise concentrated his attack on inequalities that he considered to be unjust. He argued that if we were asked to choose the starting positions we have in life behind a 'veil of ignorance' that obscured our own personal wealth and status, we would chose to begin in a position of equality with others. Although Rawls could be seen as one of the great advocates of egalitarian thinking, he supported the existence of inequalities as long as these inequalities were tied to positions of responsibility. For Rawls, it was essential that inequalities were fair. He was a firm believer in equality of opportunity and he believed that this equality should extend as far as possible in the economy and in access to education and culture. Rawls would only tolerate inequalities to the extent that they mirrored our contributions to society and as long as they did not relegate any section of society to permanent hardship and failure. In his view, a notion of 'justice as fairness' could go a long way to harmonise the values of freedom and equality. It was thought to recognise our right to basic liberties and to equality of opportunity. He believed that it should be possible to gain public support for a conception of political justice as long as individuals were left to determine the relationship between this notion and their own philosophies of life. He was adamant that we must respect diversity in society and that governments should avoid attempting to create social unity by imposing a single philosophy of life.

Liberal social values are anchored in a deep respect for individuality and for maintaining a personal space within which individuals can grow. For many liberals, it is important that we have room to develop, for without this freedom our senses become duller and our potential contributions to society could be stifled. From a liberal perspective, it is individuals that make history and the sovereignty of the individual must be protected as far as possible from the intrusive powers of the state. This does not necessarily mean that we need to strip the powers of the state to the minimum. The state can and does have a dramatic impact upon the economic and social welfare of society. Rather than deny the state the ability and power to serve the common good, liberals are more inclined to look for ways to gauge whether state intervention will allow enough room for the ambitious and enough tolerance for eccentric, radical or dissident spirits. It is clear that liberals want to enhance opportunities for all to benefit from the fruits of capitalism. If this means that the state must intervene, then so be it.

State and welfare

Liberals are often cautious in the way they view the state. As we have seen, their preoccupation with the freedom of the individual means that they are often fearful of the state assuming too much control and power over the life of the individual. It is argued that the state poses a potential threat to the freedom of the individual and that the state needs to be limited in what it does. The value that liberals are willing to place upon the state depends a great deal upon how its activities impact upon the freedom of the individual. For liberals, the state ceases to be useful or welcomed as soon as it places unnecessary limits upon what individuals do. There are of course variations in the way that liberals view the state. Making use of the distinction between classical and social liberals will allow us to understand at least some of these variations.

Classical liberals tend to be suspicious of the state and regard the state as a necessary evil at best. They are wary of organised collective power and are therefore critical of the state extending its jurisdiction into the private affairs of the individual. Mill (1859) was a firm believer in a private sphere that should be protected from public intervention. For this reason, he drew a distinction between self and other-regarding actions and argued that our freedom should be restricted if our actions pose a definite threat to other people. Although he believed that we should be free in issues that concern us solely and that we need the freedom to judge what is best for ourselves, he pointed out that we are not isolated beings and that many of our actions can impact upon the freedom of others. Where this happened, the state could intervene to prevent the spread of harm. For classical liberals, the state is often seen as a useful force that can be used to ensure that individual rights are not infringed by other individuals and groups. According to this line of thought, it would be foolish and counter-productive to give the state too much power for it too could undermine our freedoms.

A less critical view of the state is often put forward by social liberals who tend to look for ways to balance the interests of the individual with those of the community. They recognise that freedom should be as widely dispersed as possible, rather than restricted to a minority, and that the state can assist in the development of freedom by providing opportunities for the vast majority. Liberals believe that the state can compensate for the volatility of the capitalist economy and that prudent levels of intervention can help to stabilise the economic system and make inequalities in outcome and opportunity less extreme. L.T. Hobhouse (1911), for example, believed that society is an organism and that this has significant implications for the way we view the relationship between individuals and society, the way we understand what could be regarded as the 'collective life' of society and the way that society can and does develop. According to Hobhouse, each of us is influenced by society and by interacting with our fellow citizens. All parts of society were regarded as interdependent to such an extent that '... nothing of any import affects the social life on one side without setting up reactions all through the tissue' (Hobhouse, 1911, p. 248). Although he rejected the view that society has a personality distinct from the people in that society, he argued that society has a 'collective life and character' that rests upon and is informed by the myriad of ties between people. For Hobhouse, fruitful social reform cannot take place in isolated pockets of society because each of these pockets is far from isolated and is connected inextricably to other parts of the social organism. In his view, the individual parts of society should develop and be reformed in a way that '... tends on the whole to further the development of others' (Hobhouse, 1911, p. 136). According to this view of society, there is plenty of room for the state to intervene to harness the energies and nurture the social organism. Indeed, the state could be seen to have a duty to legislate in the interests of the social organism rather than simply to protect the rights of the individual.

Classical and social liberals have very different views on the role of the state in the provision of welfare. Whereas classical liberals are more prone to believe that individuals should look after their own welfare needs, new liberals are aware that whatever happens to the individual also happens to society. Poor health, for example, affects not only the person who is sick but also the rest of society. Illness can be passed on in a direct way and can also contribute towards social malaise. By viewing society as an interconnected whole, new liberals see the state can have an important role in alleviating poverty and in freeing people from the horrors of poor housing and sickness. For Hobhouse (1911) it was important to define individual rights in terms of the common good and to recognise that the common good depended upon the welfare of all members of society. Hobhouse believed that the state had a responsibility to maintain hospitals, provide a decent system of education and to make provision for the poor. In his view, the function of the state was '... to secure conditions upon which its citizens are able to win by their own efforts all that is necessary to a full civic efficiency' (Hobhouse, 1911, p. 158). This meant that the state had a duty to regulate the economy in such a way as to prevent widespread destitution and to dedicate resources to fighting and preventing harsh levels of poverty. Indeed, he argued that the state must '... secure the conditions of self-maintenance for the normal healthy citizen' (Hobhouse, 1911, p. 174). For American social liberals likewise, the state was seen to have a potentially important role in the provision of welfare. Lyndon Johnson's 'war on poverty', for example, was designed to attack poverty on a variety of fronts. His administration recognised that poverty does not consist in a single thing but stems from a variety of factors including unemployment, poor health, poor quality housing and inadequate or inappropriate education. The solution involved setting up a series of local programmes to provide aid to schools, training for adults and decent housing for all. He recognised that people were trapped by poverty and that these circumstances were passed down through the generations. It was argued that if poverty was to be defeated, it required a reasonable level of community participation. Johnson waged his war on poverty not only for the poor sections of society but also to stimulate the moral and economic well-being of the American nation (Johnson, 1971, pp. 69–87).

It should be appreciated that modern social liberals have had an important role in the development of the welfare state, especially in Britain and in the United States. The foundations of the British welfare state were laid by the Beveridge Report of 1942 and were couched within a social liberal framework. In the United States, the Democratic Party in general and the administrations led by Roosevelt and by Johnson have been extremely important in establishing a range of state funded and directed welfare services. Some of these measures will be discussed in more detail in the next section, but for now it is important to recognise that social liberals will often view the state as a potential ally in the battle against the obstacles to individual freedom and that this will often involve some role in the provision of a range of welfare services. The welfare state envisaged by social liberals is one that exists alongside a regulated capitalist system and one that seeks to enhance positive liberty and equality of opportunity. It does not attempt to supplant capitalism or remove all inequalities. Rather, the welfare state is seen as one of the mechanisms that can be used to stabilise capitalism and to remove at least some of the inequalities created by the system.

Welfare and social policies

Liberals are well aware of the importance of social policies in the promotion of the common welfare. Liberal theorists have been at the forefront of those who argue that the state should assume at least some responsibility for protecting and advancing the economic and social security of the citizen body. Although at times sceptical about state intervention, liberals have still seen that the state can have an important role in providing benefits, housing, health care and education. If the state is neutral and can be used to implement progressive policies, then it makes sense from a liberal point of view to use its power in an attempt to eradicate or at least minimise social problems in the knowledge or belief that this proactive approach can help to stabilise and prolong the life of the capitalist system.

Benefits

Many liberals recognise that the state could and should have a role in the provision of benefits. In the closing stages of the eighteenth century, classical liberals in Britain helped to place the alleviation of poverty on the political agenda. Tom Paine, for example, believed that there should be some assistance available for the underprivileged. In particular, he was in favour of retirement pensions, family allowance and maternity pay. Writing passionately about the wretched living conditions of the poor, he complained that the poor are raised without morals and without prospects and that social reform aimed to reduce poverty would be of benefit to the nation as a whole (Paine, 1792). Classical liberals did not necessarily want to leave the poor without any protection. Despite all of the rhetoric about the importance of individuals being responsible for themselves, wide-scale poverty is still recognised by classical liberals as a social problem that requires at least some government intervention.

Social liberals have likewise been active in their support of a benefits system. Consider, for example, the ideas contained within the Beveridge Report. One of the aims of the Beveridge Report was to establish a system of benefits to assist the unemployed, the sick and the elderly (Beveridge, 1942). These proposals were made, however, on the assumption that families would stay together, that the majority of men would work, that the majority of women would stay at home and that people would only receive pensions for a short period given that the majority of people did not live long beyond retirement age. The Beveridge system also relied upon government developing policies to prevent mass unemployment. Unemployment benefit would only be paid as an unconditional right in the short term. Thereafter, receiving benefit was to be made contingent upon looking for work or training. The

Beveridge Report pointed out that the costs of unemployment benefit could become heavy and 'insupportable' and that it was therefore necessary to fight against unemployment, which increased spending on benefits and deprived the state of income. A war was thus declared on mass unemployment and against prolonged unemployment for individuals. The Beveridge plan involved the 'abolition of want' through redistributing our incomes through different stages in our lives (Beveridge, 1942; BBC2, 23.10.1997). The aim was certainly not to make us dependent upon welfare but to provide a safety net that all workers helped to construct and maintain. This safety net would be there for times of hardship and for when our working lives are over. It was envisaged, however, that the benefits system would operate under conditions of full employment and that it would not be available as a long-term resting place for those who chose not to work. In more recent times, liberals have recognised the need to adapt the benefits system to the changing nature of work. Charles Kennedy (2001), for example, argued that governments should recognise that many people no longer work nine-to-five and that the benefits system needs to be reformed so that people do not lose their entitlement to benefits if they take on part-time work. This shows that liberals are aware that the benefits system needs to be designed so that it is not confined solely to those who are without any type of work.

In addition to providing some of the theoretical backbone for the post-war welfare state in Britain, liberal governments have had an extremely important role in creating the benefits system in Britain. Most notable of all was the Liberal government of 1906–1914, which was responsible for a batch of welfare legislation that included such important reforms as pensions, national insurance, child labour and minimum wage acts. The Old Age Pensions Act of 1908 gave pensions to all people over 70 as long as their annual incomes did not exceed £31.10 shillings. Those who had previously refused to work, been in prison in the previous ten years or had been denied the right to vote under Poor Law regulations were disqualified. This left the so-called 'respectable poor'. The issuing of pensions, however, was instrumental in showing that poverty had social roots. Indeed, the character test imposed upon prospective recipients of a pension undermined the view that the pension was a universal rather than a selective right (Pearson and Williams, 1984, p. 164). The Liberal government also made some provision for the unemployed. The National Insurance Act of 1911 made employers and employees responsible for paying a weekly insurance stamp. This money was meant to finance a system of unemployment benefit and health cover for those who paid into the system. This was a compulsory form of insurance, which was thought to benefit the individual and serve the common good. As employers and employees shared responsibility for paying the insurance, it was thought to reinforce mutual obligations in society, encourage cooperation between the classes and be a force in moral education. The architects of the act were said to believe that they were '... not restricting liberty but enlarging it, using one form of compulsion to prevent greater infringements of individual liberty' (Pearson and Williams, 1984, p. 166). According to Asa Briggs, national insurance was introduced in the interests of the medical profession and he claims that it should be seen in relation to '... the history of hidden pressures from established interests and a sectional demand for an enlargement of professional freedom' (Briggs, 1969, p. 25). National insurance gave working people access to medical treatment and some security in the event of being made unemployed. This was not a universal form of social security, but a way for workers to insure themselves against some misfortunes.

Liberals have also stamped their mark upon the development of the benefits system in America. Roosevelt's Social Security Act of 1935 introduced a range of benefits into American society and went part of the way to supplement previous philanthropic relief. Retirement pensions were introduced and states were encouraged to initiate some form of unemployment insurance. This unemployment insurance did not aim to overcome all hardship but attempted instead to address the problems of involuntary unemployment. Benefits were to be given to those who had contributed to the scheme and were thus deemed to have 'earned' their right to relief during times of unemployment. The 1935 Social Security Act also created a programme of Aid to Dependent Children, also known as the ADC system, through which benefit was paid to families in poverty to help towards the maintenance of their children (Clarke and Fox Piven, 2001, pp. 27–28). It is notable that the ADC system sought to give relief to children rather than to those adults who had not contributed towards unemployment insurance. This was in character with the tone of the New Deal, which deliberately set out to reward the hardworking and to deter the feckless.

Liberals tend to approach the benefits system rather hesitantly, as if it draws attention to the failings of capitalism. Classical liberal views on the benefits system show that they are willing to provide a safety net for those who are unable to adapt to the needs of the free market. For social liberals, it was assumed that only a minority of those of working age would need benefits because the state would also have an active role in managing the economy and in creating jobs. Although liberals want the benefit system to be there for those in need, it is certainly hoped by many that capitalism (whether free market or planned) could cater for the needs of the vast majority. Although the benefits system might be a necessity, liberals would argue that there are many other alternatives that can be explored by public and private interests to ensure that capitalism works efficiently and that the need for a benefits system is minimised.

Housing

Liberals have often been reluctant to allow the government to intervene too directly in the ownership and management of housing. If we were to employ the logic of classical liberalism, it could be argued that housing is too personal to allow for extensive government intervention. This argument would be perfectly compatible with the liberal distinction between the public and private spheres, which attempts to keep the government out of the private lives of individuals. Herbert Spencer (1884), for example, was extremely critical of government intervention in housing. Spencer argued that the British government had introduced too many housing regulations and that these were deterring private investors and penalising private landlords unnecessarily. As the private sector turn away from investing in housing, greater pressure would be exerted on local government to provide housing and to increase taxes to finance its intervention (Spencer, 1884, pp. 57–58). Although classical liberals might be opposed to government intervention, social liberals are far more prone to recognise the value of government intervention in housing. For modern liberals like Charles Kennedy (2001), the government can assist in the development of decent housing if it adopts a holistic approach to community development. Kennedy points out that a sensible approach to housing consists not so much in investing in more housing but in investing in struggling communities where there exists plenty of empty housing stock and in attempting to improve environmental conditions in the inner cities (Kennedy, 2001, pp. 57–58). This approach shows that government intervention in housing should not be seen in isolation of other economic and social policies. From a liberal perspective, there is room for both private and public initiatives. This can be illustrated by reference to the housing policies supported by the Liberal Democrat Party in Britain and the Democratic Party in the United States.

The Liberal Democrat Party in Britain supports the extension of private ownership alongside a safety net of public or social housing. In the party manifesto in 1992, the Liberal Democrats argued that housing relief should be available for people in owner-occupied and rented accommodation and that restrictions placed on local authority house building, introduced by the Conservative government during the 1980s, need to be lifted so as to allow local councils to enter into partnerships with housing associations and to encourage the development of tenant cooperatives. The Liberal Democrats argued that local councils should be made responsible for housing the homeless, that short-term rented accommodation should be made available and that all 16–18 year olds should be given preferential status on council house waiting lists (Liberal Democrat Party, 1992). The Liberal Democrats have been particularly active in calling for the creation of sensible partnerships between the public and private sectors. In their 1997 election manifesto, for example, they claimed that councils should be allowed to approach the private sector for help in financing social housing and that the money raised from the sale of council housing in the past should be used to build up the stock once more (Liberal Democrat Party, 1997, p. 29).

The Democratic Party in the United States has addressed the problem of housing but has done relatively little to challenge the dominance of private sector provision. Roosevelt failed to deal effectively with poor housing conditions. In many areas, especially where there were defence plants during the war, people often lived in temporary shacks, trailers and tents (Burns, 1970, pp. 52–53). The Johnson government in the 1960s was a little more proactive and it pledged its support for a massive programme of slum clearance and inner-city regeneration. Johnson believed that a comprehensive housing programme was necessary as part of a general attempt to increase the aspirations of the poorer sections of the community. In his view, slums were '… a breeding ground of human failure and despair, where hope is as alien as sunlight and green grass' (Johnson, 1971, p. 330). The Johnson administration introduced the Model Cities Act in 1966 that forced cities, with the aid of federal grants, to embark upon inner-city reconstruction. This was followed in 1968 with the National Housing Act that envisaged the building of 26 million new homes, again with federal assistance, over a ten-year period. Although the administrative machinery was established to implement this programme, it was abandoned because of the costs involved and because of a significant rise in interest rates (Johnson, 1971, pp. 329–332).

For social liberals, the government can have a role in the ownership and control of housing but they believe that this should not usurp the role of the private sector and the innovative activities of the voluntary sector. It is often the case that liberals will lend support to the public provision of housing when the private sector is unable to meet the housing needs of the nation rather than out of principle. Liberals in the twentieth century and beyond recognise that the government should assume at least some responsibility for housing, even if that role is to facilitate and coordinate the activities of different private and voluntary sector groups. Liberals would argue that playing an active part in addressing the housing needs of the nation does not mean that the government must own housing stock, as long as there are feasible alternatives at hand. Although housing might be seen as a personal issue, liberals have shown that they are willing to allow the government to intervene when the private sector fails to provide suitable housing.

Health

Liberals have earned the reputation of supporting government intervention and investment in health care. Health could be viewed as a purely personal possession, but many liberals are aware of the social context of health and of health care. For social liberals like Kennedy (2001), the health care needs of the nation cannot be satisfied by a private sector motivated by the desire to make profit. In his view, all citizens need equal access to the National Health Service. This, indeed, was regarded as '... vital for securing individual liberty' (Kennedy, 2001, p. 104). Although Kennedy wants significant government intervention in the provision of health care, he harboured severe reservations about the virtues of centralised control and he argued that the control of the National Health Service should be decentralised to the regions of Britain and opened up for patients to be involved in decision making. In this way, the health service could be made more accountable and responsive to the needs of the citizen (Kennedy, 2001, p. 118). Even if liberals support the principle of government intervention in social provision, their fear of the authoritarian and centralised state control means that they are often likely to favour the administration of schemes in a way that makes use of local skills and knowledge.

Liberals in Britain, especially in recent years, have tended to be supportive of direct and quite extensive government involvement in health care. The Liberal Democrat Party in Britain claims that it supports the original aims of the National Health Service, which purports to provide free health care financed through direct taxation and available according to the needs of the patient. The Liberal Democrat Party argued during the 1990s that it was against the application of market principles to the health service, which had been introduced by the Conservative government (see Chapter 6), and favoured long-term funding arrangements between the various branches of health care. It claimed that although the National Health Service was efficient and cost-effective, shifting more resources into primary health care and into preventative services could make improvements. It argued that the National Health Service concentrates too much upon curing illness and that more time should be spent on preventing people from becoming ill by helping them take responsibility for their own states of health. Extra funds would be raised for health care by increasing taxation on cigarettes which, it was hoped, would also reduce the numbers of people smoking and the levels of smoking-related illnesses (Liberal Democrat Party, 1992, 1997; Wallace, 1997, pp. 94–97). In many ways, the Liberal Democrats have shown themselves to be quite collectivist in the way they approach health care and considerably more aware than the Conservative Party of the social origins and context of poor health.

The most notable American liberal programme on health care was introduced by the Johnson administration, though vested interests blocked attempts during the 1960s to socialise health care and led to a compromise in which health care was subsidised for those in need. Medicare was established as a system of social security for the elderly and was introduced by the Johnson government in response to the mounting costs of illness faced by people in old age. Medicaid was also established to assist the poor, but this was plagued by the stigmas attached to public assistance packages. Aware that medical professionals might resist the measures, given their history of resistance to 'socialised medicine', Johnson played an important personal role in gaining the support of health workers. His administration introduced 40 new bills on health care and increased annual federal spending on health from $4 billion to $14 billion. Johnson claimed that these measures helped to show that '... good medical care is a right, not just a privilege' (Johnson, 1971, pp. 220, 212–221; Ginsburg, 1992, p. 131; Clarke and Fox Piven, 2001, pp. 30–31). Although American liberals have recognised the social dimension of health care and that the government should have a role, the systems they have introduced continue to reflect class differences and fall short of supporting 'socialised medicine'.

Liberal perspectives on health care reflect a diverse range of views. While some liberals are against the state intervening to any great degree, others consider it an essential feature of modern social policy. For many liberals, health policy needs to take into account the social context of health and they recognise that a lot can be gained from paying attention to the views and needs of patients. Simply having a well-funded health service is not enough in itself to guarantee that high levels of care are available where the need is the greatest. Liberals are well aware that the most vulnerable sections of the community are often virtually invisible to centralised government departments and that a more democratic and decentralised system of care is often warranted.

Education

Liberals have long been aware of the need for some state involvement in the provision of education. Even Adam Smith (1776), the arch defender of the free market and of limited government, argued that the government should invest in education because the division of labour in industrial enterprises was apt to stupefy the modern worker. Smith called upon the government to establish district or parish schools and to invest something alongside parental contributions. He was particularly keen on people having the ability to read, write and to have some numerical skills and he believed that geometry and mechanics were particularly useful areas of study because they could be applied in the industrial setting. Although this education was deemed necessary for the development of the citizen body and was therefore of intrinsic value, Smith was careful to point out that the state benefits from developments in education because educated people are less likely to be guided by ignorance and superstition, less swayed by sedition, less opposed to the government and more respectable and respectful of their social superiors (Smith, 1776, pp. 987–994). In this early vision of a state-assisted education system, it was recognised that education can have an important role in transmitting safe value-systems and that if the state is not involved in the provision of education it can leave a gap for other more critical movements and causes to fill. A state that is interested in establishing an intellectual consensus could do far worse than invest in a centrally controlled education system.

It could be argued that education is also necessary to further other parts of the liberal agenda. As we have seen, liberals place a high value upon individual freedom and upon individuals deliberating on public matters. A liberal society relies as heavily upon our ability to distinguish between our own interests and those of other people, as it does upon us scrutinising and challenging those who would seek to deprive us of our liberty. For social liberals like J.A. Hobson (1974, 1998) intellectual liberty was of paramount importance and he believed that without this liberty all other freedoms were damaged. In his view, true intellectual liberty could not be achieved unless education was made available to all sections of society. He was extremely critical of elitist education and he was condemning of the power wielded over education by the church and by wealthy patrons because such control would inevitably tinge the education made available with subservient values. Hobson recognised that the employers wanted the workers to have nothing more than a technical education that would serve the interests of the employers rather than the interests of the workers. Concessions towards working class education were thus often meagre and offered with ulterior motives and with a distinct lack of grace. Hobson was scornful of such education and he doubted whether the workers could be educated in this limited way without liberating their minds to other possibilities. Hobson believed that the state had a duty to provide free education to all, financed through general taxation, because the alternatives outlined above retarded intellectual development. He claimed, indeed, that if '… intellectual liberty in the sense of free access to disinterested culture is to become the common heritage of all, public ownership and control of the instruments of this education is indispensable' (Hobson, 1974, p. 111. See also pp. 109–113 and Hobson, 1998, pp. 55–57, 186–191). For social liberals, we all have (or should have) an interest in protecting and promoting the freedom of the individual. Such an aim, it could be argued, cannot be furthered by sentencing sections of society to perpetual ignorance and by leaving the business of education to market mechanisms.

The Liberal Party in Britain has been active in campaigns to ensure the involvement of the state in educating the British people. The coalition government during the First World War, which was established by and dominated by liberals, extended state education for children up to the age of fourteen and began to develop plans to expand provision for children under the age of five. In addition to wanting the state to assume greater responsibility for education, liberals have often opposed the use of education to promote a specific religious creed. This was shown, for example, in the way that the Liberal Party attempted to overturn the Conservative's Education Act of 1902 because it gave state support for Anglican schools at the expense of other faiths. Although the House of Lords and the Anglican Church crushed attempts by the Liberal government of 1906–1911 to reduce the power of the church over the education system, the aspiration to create a free and inclusive education system remains a hallmark of liberal education policy (see Cross, 1963; Lawton, 2004). For many liberals, state involvement in the provision of education must always be tempered with a healthy respect for intellectual and religious diversity. Education is not always a progressive force and, as liberals are inclined to point out, it can often be used to enslave the minds of people.

Liberals in the United States have likewise found it difficult at times to expand government provision of education without falling foul of powerful religious groups. Lyndon Johnson, who had been a schoolteacher three decades before becoming president of the United States, placed education at the heart of his social programme in the election campaign of 1964. Central government in the United States had always found it difficult to deal with education effectively because of long-standing antagonism between the church and the state and the constitutional separation of these two institutions. Given the importance of religious freedom in America and the extreme diversity of religious beliefs practised in America, the federal government was unable for many years to provide aid to state schools for fear of being accused of meddling with the curriculum and thus, inadvertently or otherwise, promoting one religious creed over another. The Catholics in particular had been critical of federal involvement and had effectively scuppered J.F. Kennedy's plans for education. Johnson chose to woo the leaders of a variety of religious communities and passed a bill that allowed for federal aid to state schools to be used for employing extra teaching staff and buying audio-visual equipment. This was seen as part of a programme to extend educational opportunities to the poorest sections of the nation (Johnson, 1971, pp. 206–212; Taylor and Hawley, 2003). Liberals in the United States seem acutely aware of the need to respect diversity, even if this limits the scope of their broader social programmes.

It is apparent that for many liberals, education is of supreme importance. Whereas benefits, housing and health care help to provide a foundation for individual life, education creates prospects for individual development and is therefore clearly indispensable for the achievement of broader liberal social aims. The liberal thirst for freedom is motivated in part by the belief that giving people access to education and to realistic opportunities can help to prepare us for autonomy and for responsible citizenship. It could be argued indeed that liberal aspirations would fall flat unless accompanied by at least some commitment to educational provision. Even classical liberals have been willing to suspend their mistrust of the state in order to allow it to have a role in cultivating the intellect of the many. What, it could be asked, is the value of freedom without education? For a liberal, the two are intimately connected.

Conclusion

Central to liberalism is the belief that capitalism can benefit all citizens. We have seen that for some liberals, capitalism should regulate itself and the individual be left with as much freedom as possible. For these classical liberals, the state might still have some role in providing basic education and even a minimal benefits system. But what happens if the market fails and if the opportunity to live a free and prosperous life is restricted to the few? Once liberals realised that capitalism is too unstable to guarantee sustainable employment and opportunities, they turned towards the state and helped to draw the state into social programmes designed to bring balance to the system. Social liberals believe that all citizens need access to freedom and to equal opportunities. They focus far more than classical liberals on community development and call upon the state to intervene alongside the private and voluntary sectors in social provision. These liberals have been extremely important in developing welfare states (especially in Britain and the United States) and in addressing with considerable skill the need to find a way to reconcile individual and collective interests. It would seem quite likely that social liberalism will continue to have a future for as long as the capitalist system needs to be tamed. Although the policies introduced by some liberal administrations are sometimes regarded as too interventionist, liberal attempts to balance individual and collective interests seem to have almost perennial significance. Although it is clear that many liberals fear too much state intervention, they have some interesting things to say about the vibrancy of civil society and about the role of the state in facilitating individual and social development. It could be argued, however, that liberal social philosophy, which recognises the importance of civil liberties and human rights, is likely to survive long after their designs for the welfare state have been redrafted beyond recognition. They leave the curious, however, with some salutary lessons about the nature and importance of freedom.

3

Conservatism

Conservatives are less prone than social liberals to rely upon the state to address and solve social problems through direct intervention in the economic and social systems. Whereas some liberals have put forward reasonably radical proposals, conservatives talk about the importance of preserving what we have and protecting our cherished traditions from unfamiliar and untried political schemes. This is not to say that conservatives are against all change. Conservatives often argue that slow and methodical social reform is necessary to preserve the fundamentals of the existing order and to reduce the appeal of revolutionary ideas and movements (see Kendall, 1963; Macmillan, 1966). Although this chapter will make use of some international examples, it will concentrate in the main on conservative ideas and movements in Britain and the United States. We will take a look at the ideas of theorists from the eighteenth and nineteenth centuries including Edmund Burke, Thomas Carlyle, John Ruskin and Matthew Arnold. Key British conservatives like Iain Gilmour, Harold Macmillan and Lord Hailsham will have a central place in the chapter alongside some American theorists. In addition to covering these theoretical developments, key conservative administrations will be discussed. These include the Macmillan governments in Britain and the Eisenhower, Nixon and George W. Bush administrations in the United States.

Economy

Although it might be tempting to believe that conservatives are arch defenders of the capitalist system, there is a deeply ingrained sense of scepticism (and almost disdain) for the capitalist cash–nexus in significant strands of the conservative tradition. Many of the more traditional conservatives wish to conserve social hierarchies and they often hold culture and national characteristics in far higher regard than the mere pursuit of profit. Cultural conservatives of the nineteenth century were particularly critical of capitalism and of its liberal defenders. John Ruskin (1862) was convinced that liberal political economy paid too little attention to our non-economic needs and focussed our attention far too much upon the accumulation of riches. For Ruskin, we should be more mindful of the qualitative nature of real wealth and be willing to sacrifice 'economic success' in the interests of enriching our spiritual lives. For Thomas Carlyle (1843) politicians should, in the interests of social order and of restoring a natural balance to society, seek to cultivate benevolent relations between workers and management. In his view, the political economy of the classical liberals was inhumane and needed to be tempered by compassion, understanding and benevolence. Although these observations might seem rather quaint and were certainly at odds with the hard-nosed business ethics of the nineteenth century, they captured at least some of the conservative dissatisfaction with the profit motive and with reducing politics to the defence of an amoral economic system.

Although modern conservatives might want to distance themselves from such levels of disdain for capitalism, there are still signs of conservatives being guarded in their support for free market economics. Whereas classical liberals believed that a largely unregulated free market system could serve the public good, modern conservatives have argued that the state should assume some responsibility for coordinating the economy. The great British conservative Harold Macmillan (1966) argued in favour of a mixed economy that combined private enterprise and state planning. In his view, this movement towards 'planned capitalism' provided an opportunity to produce a new synthesis of capitalism and socialism and to avoid the dangers and disruptions created by extreme measures. The Macmillan governments of the 1950s and 1960s showed that they were willing to use the state to regulate the economy and, in an attempt to secure social peace, to involve workers and management in economic planning in the National Economic Development Council (see Morgan, 1992; Sked and Cook, 1984). In the USA, the Nixon government likewise favoured active intervention in the economy in the hope of achieving greater levels of stability and undermining unemployment and inflation (Siciliano, 2002). For such administrations, failure to use the power of the government to tame the excesses of capitalism would have been seen as politically irresponsible.

It is clear that for many conservatives a willingness to use the government to regulate the economy does not diminish their commitment to capitalism. Indeed, state intervention in the economy is often seen as a way to protect the capitalist system. Gilmour (1978) argued that capitalism has distinct advantages and that it rests upon a supposed instinct for property and a deep-seated desire that many people have to work for themselves and to control their own economic destinies. He was particularly keen to preserve what he could of a market economy because he believed that markets were efficient and libertarian in their operations and considerably better than a more coercive command economy (Gilmour, 1978, pp. 149, 233). Although Gilmour was generally in favour of the freedom and flexibility that capitalism can offer, he was still willing to concede (like many of the more traditional conservatives) that government intervention in the economy and sensible cooperation between government and industry were at least sometimes necessary. He believed that post-war British governments had intervened too much in the economy and that, while intervention should not be viewed as a sacred principle, it was often expedient (Gilmour, 1978, pp. 232–236).

Although this form of traditional conservatism became less influential in conservative administrations during the 1980s, it still attracted support from those who were critical of Thatcher's defense of the free market. In his influential and emotively entitled book *Dancing with Dogma* (1992), Gilmour pointed out that Thatcherism anchored itself in dogma and thereby deviated significantly from the more pragmatic features of the conservative tradition. He argued that the influence of classical liberal economics on conservatives ran counter to the protectionism championed by conservatives in the nineteenth century and the conservative support for Keynesian methods in the post-war period. In Gilmour's view, state intervention in the economy was necessary to make markets work and to '... make capitalism more or less tolerable for the mass of people' (Gilmour, 1992, p. 12). Although conservatives are often associated with the interests of the business class, there remains a deep sense of unease with the ethically barren profit motive and a firm commitment (at least among some) to use the state to render capitalism safe and stable for the vast majority.

Traditional conservatives often place economic success and profit maximisation into a broader social context that allows some room for benvolence and for considering the common welfare. According to this line of thought, unrestrained capitalism is potentially dangerous and is unlikely to serve the interests of the majority. For those who argue in this way, it makes sense for the state to assume a protective role in regulating the economy and in ensuring that those lower in the social hierarchy are not left at the mercy of market forces. Driven in many cases by compassion, the state is sometimes called upon to assume at least some of the responsibilities once discharged by the privileged few. As we can no longer rely upon being protected by those at the top of the economic hierarchy, conservatives have turned their attention to the political hierarchy and called upon public servants to assist in building a unified social and economic system in which the poor are protected from the self-interest and avarice of entrepreneurs.

Social values

Conservative social values give considerably higher priority to social order
than to individual freedom. From a conservative point of view, liberals have
too much faith in humanity and they fail to understand the benefits of maintaining hierarchical relations in society. Conservatives believe that individuals
are bound and ultimately civilised by shared allegiance to the nation and to a
common moral framework. Conservatism is not a doctrine of multi-culturalism,
innovation and social engineering. It is one that attempts to reaffirm our ties
with the nation and with the past. Conservatives tend to believe that human
nature is flawed and that society will forever remain imperfect. For conservatives, we live in a selfish and corrupt society because humans are made that
way. If we believe this, it makes little sense to devise sophisticated plans for
radical social change. The pursuit of social justice and equality is pointless if
humans are incapable of transforming themselves into people who are capable of making a significant contribution to society. Rather than advertise a
utopian vision of society in which we are all capable of participating fully,
conservatives ask us to accept our limitations and recognise that we need, as
a species, to be supervised and disciplined rather than liberated.

From a conservative point of view, liberals vastly overstate the value of
individual freedom. Matthew Arnold (1867) held that freedom for the 'ordinary self' was ultimately of less worth than freedom for our 'better selves' and
that it was therefore right that we should be prevented from pursuing our
selfish interests and encouraged to develop our higher and more noble capabilities. It is not that conservatives are antagonistic towards all types of freedom, but they do object to the way that the rights and liberties of the
individual are considered of primary importance. Gilmour (1978) complained
that there had been too much emphasis upon the individual in the nineteenth
century and too much upon state authority in the twentieth century. In his
view, it was important to find ways to preserve freedom and to recognise that
many freedoms evolve over time and are enshrined in traditions rather than
in sometimes wild declarations of rights and liberties (Gilmour, 1978, pp.
146–148). For conservatives, it is important to accept the status quo and to
recognise that the way that society is organised has evolved over time and that
it should not be tampered with in the name of abstract principles. This is
apparent in the way that conservatives regard freedom and in their general
opposition to egalitarian policies.

Conservatism is based upon a belief in inequality and it is argued that a
minority should be responsible for guiding the majority. The conservative
vision is one of a hierarchical class society in which the rich have authority over
the poor. Conservatives believe in inequality because they claim that human

beings are unequal in their possession of skills and energy and because they believe that egalitarian policies contain the seeds of authoritarianism. Inequality, which is thought to benefit the rich and the poor, is considered necessary to ensure that society is run by the wise and that the economic system is in the hands of those who display superior skills and initiative. For many conservatives, an egalitarian system would stagnate both economically and politically (Eccleshall, 1994b, p. 90). Lord Hailsham, for example, claimed that '... in a free society the incentives to make oneself unequal are a necessary part of the mechanism of creating new wealth and therefore new welfare' (Hailsham, 1959, p. 112). Hailsham argued that the trend towards imposing equality and reducing economic diversity in society, which he associated with the social democratic policies of the Labour Party, should be resisted because the wealthy have an important role in providing welfare through charity work. He believed that individuals are more innovative than the state and that individuals must be free to provide for themselves rather than having to rely solely upon services provided by the state (Hailsham, 1959, pp. 112–114). This line of argument suggests that inequality is both natural and beneficial to society. The existence of a hierarchy is thought to fuel ambition and spur people to greater levels of success. It would be wrong, however, to assume that conservatives are always in favour of a meritocracy. As we shall see, some conservatives favour preserving the existing hierarchy as opposed to encouraging upward mobility.

Conservatives are even more prone than liberals to attack equality of outcome. According to the American conservative Willmoore Kendall (1963), conservatives should oppose egalitarianism rather than equality. Kendall points out that equality is enshrined in the American Declaration of Independence and refers to an equal right to justice and to the idea that we are born with equal rights. Egalitarianism, on the other hand, is seen as a liberal imposition that attempts to convince people that they have a right to be 'made equal' through a plethora of government measures that undermine self-reliance and encourage people to 'learn to play the angles' (Kendall, 1963, p. 18). British conservatives are likewise critical of equality of outcome. Iain Gilmour (1978) not only rejected the ideals of absolute equality and those of a classless society but also the notion of equality of opportunity which, in his view, was impossible to achieve without undermining the influence of family ties. In Gilmour's view, government policies that promote equality merely harm liberty and ignore the importance of providing people with realistic incentives to do well for themselves and their families. This does not mean, of course, that conservatives are unmindful of the problems caused by harsh inequalities. Indeed, Gilmour argues that governments should attempt to diminish extreme inequalities and help the less fortunate (Gilmour, 1992, pp. 128–130, 150–151). It is evident, however, that such help is offered out of benevolence rather than to maximise levels of equality in society. Conservatives usually want to maintain existing inequalities and existing structures of authority. This is often justified on the grounds that benevolent authority, or paternalism, enriches relationships between people who occupy different positions in the hierarchy. Indeed, there is a strong paternalistic thread running through the conservative tradition. If individuals are weak, as many conservatives believe, then it is important that they are protected from the unscrupulous.

The paternalistic features of conservatism can be illustrated by reference to the ideas of the one nation conservatives in Britain (see Macmillan, 1966; Pym, 1984). Like some social liberals, the one nation conservatives argued that society should be seen as an interconnected whole and that all people have a duty to perform functions corresponding to their place in the social hierarchy. This form of conservatism, which is modelled upon a rosy interpretation of the medieval social system, confers upon the rich the obligation to 'protect' and 'discipline' the poor. In the twentieth century, it has become associated with idea of using economic planning to alleviate poverty and unemployment. The one nation conservatives have always been concerned with protecting the capitalist system from instability and from the challenges of more radical ideas and movements. They argue that society has to be reformed and justice seen to be done if the existing inequalities and social divisions are to be preserved. The aim should be to create one nation in which everybody knows their place rather than allow society to remain fractured by competition and self-interest. This might involve allowing the state some power to intervene in social life. For many conservatives, those with wealth, power and/or moral understanding have a responsibility to ensure that the weak are not victimised by the strong and that each of us is aware of the functions we have in society (see also Eccleshall, 1994b).

The social values championed by conservatives view individuals within the context of social hierarchies. Rather than talk about the individual as if a neutral entity making his or her way through life, conservatives are more prone to want to locate the individual in the class system. Conservatives do not generally believe that all individuals are capable of freedom and they tend to argue that egalitarianism is incompatible with the human makeup. They point out that individuals have different capabilities and that not all are destined for greatness. Lying beneath this view is the firm conviction that human nature is fairly grubby and that virtue is something we learn rather than something that we are born with. For conservatives, we need to find ways to civilise society and to ensure that those who have taken the time and invested their energies into cultivating civilised virtues have the opportunity to lead and serve society. Instead of leaving individuals to the mercy of market forces, these leaders can be among those who find ways to protect the weak and stabilise the system. This might mean using the state and other agencies to ensure that the common welfare is attended to.

State and Welfare

Conservatives tend to view the state as important for the preservation of social order and for maintaining the essentials of the status quo. Traditional conservatives do not have a reputation for being great democrats. There is very little in their makeup to suggest that they have faith in the judgements made by the average citizen. Sometimes this apparent contempt for 'common people' flows freely. Edmund Burke (1774, 1791) believed that the political system should be under the control of an enlightened minority for only a minority could possibly have sufficient wealth and leisure time to cultivate civilised virtues and to thus have the temperament necessary for political wisdom. According to Burke, the aristocracy was best placed to represent the nation and he urged these people to use their judgement rather than cave in to the private interests of their constituents. For Matthew Arnold (1867) it was important that political leaders had the courage to ignore what he described as the 'ordinary self' of individuals in favour of responding and helping to develop the 'better self' of the citizen body. It was considered the responsibility of political leaders to maintain social order and Arnold acknowledged that this might often be at the expense of freedom. From a conservative point of view, governments should govern and make important judgements rather than pander to the pressures of public opinion.

Although conservatives are willing to grant greater powers to an enlightened and probably privileged minority, many conservatives want to limit what the state does in economic and social life. A considerable number of conservatives would want to avoid the laissez-faire model advanced by classical liberals, but often want the state to do less than the majority of social liberals. Iain Gilmour (1978) was generally sceptical of the powers that can be weilded by the state. Although he acknowledged that the state is necessary for the maintenance of freedom and social order, he warned that state power '... should not be used to coerce its citizens but to prevent their coercion by anybody else' (Gilmour, 1978, p. 155). In terms reminiscent of John Stuart Mill, Gilmour claimed that it was necessary to keep the state from intervening too much in the private life of the individual. He was critical of the state imposing compulsory moral codes and he believed that such a morality would be of limited value. According to Gilmour, freedom is harmed where individuals are coerced in their private lives. In his view, if we want freedom in our political lives we must understand that such freedom is invariably based upon a healthy respect for freedom in the private sphere (Gilmour, 1978, pp. 157–158). As we will see, the state is not there to tell us what to do in all areas of our lives but to help stabilise an inherently unstable economic system and to head off radical social change by humanising the system.

For many conservatives, the welfare state is seen as a mechanism for looking after the population and for creating stability in the system. Conservatives are aware that social and economic systems that allow for extreme inequalities in wealth and opportunities are unstable and fragile in the long term. Conservatives, who tend to value social stability and design their policies to conserve important values and traditions, tend to believe that a healthy society is one in which all people contribute towards the common good by working in accordance with the character and tempo of their society. According to this outlook on life, the common good is threatened by radical schemes that either ignore or minimise the importance of the national character or seek to undermine conventional approaches to social and economic affairs. The wealth of the nation is seen as something that has been accumulated through the hard work of previous generations and through our own prudent guardianship. Although it is accepted that the state can assist members of the population in fulfilling their functions, by providing a range of welfare services, conservatives are rather cautious in granting powers to the state. The responsibilities adopted by those welfare states heavily influenced by conservative principles thus tend to be quite limited.

Conservative principles have had some impact upon the welfare state in Britain. The one nation conservatives in particular were responsible for managing the welfare state in the period between 1951 and 1964 and to a less extent between 1970 and 1974. One nation conservatives respond to problems created by the capitalist system and have no real interest in overturning this system or in radical change for its own sake. Instead, they see reform as a way to make the system work more efficiently and in the interests of the nation as a whole. Lord Hailsham (1959) was emphatic that conservatives share with socialists a hatred of what Beveridge called the five 'giant evils', but part company with socialists over their understanding of the origins of these social problems. Hailsham claimed that capitalism was not to blame. Indeed, capitalism was said to provide society with the resources to tackle '... part of the primeval slime from which it is the business of civilization to emancipate itself' (Hailsham, 1959, p. 126). Although one nation conservatives defend capitalism, it is clear that they have little regard for the self-interest praised by classical liberals. It would seem that for many of these more traditional conservatives, the world of industry, commerce and production for profit is far from appealing. The aristocratic background shared by many of this group made them a little suspicious of grafters. While acknowledging the importance of wealth creation, these conservatives pay more attention than classical liberals to the ways in which wealth is created and to the responsibilities that social leaders have to ensure that the fruits of industry serve the national interest rather than fortify the position of entrepreneurs at the expense of everybody else.

Although conservatives have been willing to support the establishment and maintenance of the welfare state, their general alliance with the business community has often meant that their support is somewhat tempered by their concerns over any negative impact that the welfare state might have upon business. Gilmour (1978) was generally in favour of the welfare state and he believed that it was perfectly compatible with conservative principles, Indeed, Gilmour described the welfare state as a 'thoroughly conservative institution' (Gilmour, 1978, p. 152). He believed, however, that state welfare in Britain had gone too far and that it often prevented individuals from satisfying their own needs. He believed moreover that it was '... prohibitively expensive, damaging to the economy, socially harmful, and a threat to freedom' (Gilmour, 1978, p. 152). According to Gilmour, it was necessary to find ways to prune the welfare state and to reduce its bureaucratic and authoritarian features (Gilmour, 1978, pp. 152–154). A pruned welfare state, however, would still satisfy the needs that many conservatives feel they have to tend to the welfare of the poorer sections of the community. Conservative leaders since the fall of Mrs Thatcher have been at pains to prove their credentials as compassionate and caring politicians. John Major, Iain Duncan-Smith, David Cameron and even Michael Howard have expressed views, while stopping short of the full force of one nation conservatism, nevertheless emphasising that the government does at least have some responsibility for the welfare of society and for social provision (see Preston, 1999; Taylor, 2001a; Hencke, 2006).

Conservatives in America have likewise been willing to support some aspects of the welfare state. As we will see in later sections, the Republican administrations of Nixon (and to a less extent, Eisenhower) were important in maintaining and developing social provision in the United States. For some contemporary conservative theorists, conservatism has a moral dimension that allows for greater levels of state intervention than granted by neo-liberals (see Chapter 5). Lawrence Mead (1991), for example, believed that attempts to cut social expenditure during the 1980s did little to energise people and that sections of American society had been lulled into apathy and disaffection. In his view, a new paternalist form of conservatism was needed to address the problems associated with dysfunctional families and poor levels of motivation in society. According to Mead, the government should have a positive role in stimulating people out of lethargy through educational reform and workfare programmes (Mead, 1991, pp. 111–116). Traces of this moralistic strain of conservatism can be seen in the policies of George W. Bush. Bush has been described as a 'compassionate conservative' who is interested in devising ways to create an inclusive society. It is argued that whereas Reagan wanted to 'curb government', Bush wants to use government intervention to 'enable citizens to assist themselves' (McSweeney, 2002, p. 44). This involves, for the Bush government, using the power and resources of federal government to empower and coordinate voluntary sector provision. Rather than rely upon active intervention by federal government, Bush (2004) believes that extending the social functions of religious organisations in such areas as relieving poverty and providing help for families with children can strengthen the community.

The paternalistic features of the conservative tradition give due recognition to the ways in which we are all interconnected and to the belief that what happens to each of us will have repercussions on society at large. From a paternalist point of view, it makes sense for the state to provide a basic framework of welfare services and for these services to be supplemented by private philanthropic endeavours. This tradition believes that a minority should be responsible for advancing the common good and that this minority is defined and selected according to its ability to see beyond its own private interests. It is recognised, however, that seeking to protect the existing system will benefit disproportionately the existing holders of social, economic and political power. Conservatives, indeed, often adopt cautious views in reaction to more radical alternatives. As Asa Briggs (1969) points out, this form of welfare state was originally constructed to postpone class war and to undermine the appeal of social democracy. Many conservatives accept that the state should have some role in either the coordination or provision of welfare services. Their deep sense of responsibility for the common good, and for preserving the essentials of the existing system, often pushes them to accept that the state (alongside private philanthropy) should look after and defend the poor. Although conservatives are more likely to allow the state to intervene than many classical liberals, it is clear that conservatives prefer the state to have a fairly limited role. Conservatives are more apt to talk about the state having a coordinating role, in which it attempts to guide the private sector towards socially useful projects. Rather than leave people to fend for themselves, conservatives want everybody to have a place in society and for the state and the private sector to be benevolent in their dealings with people. This approach to welfare policy is, in many ways, an extension of the charitable ethos in which the poor are granted concessions rather than given social rights.

Welfare and social policies

Conservative social policies aim in the main to promote the common welfare by ensuring that the poor are not at the mercy of the rich and that all citizens are treated with respect. There is something distinctly disarming about many features of the case for conservatism. Conservatives will try to convince us that the existing system, perhaps with a little more attention being paid to benevolence and to rewarding loyalty and service, is in no need of far-reaching and fundamental change. Instead, they would argue that the common good is best served in a system that is stable, tried-and-tested and familiar. For many conservatives, social policies are designed to protect the vulnerable and in so doing shield the system from the insidious influence of radical ideas.

Benefits

The paternalist tradition of conservatism recognises the need to make provision for people when they are unemployed. The paternalist rationale can be seen clearly in the views expressed by Iain Gilmour (1992) who argued that in the majority of cases, it was pointless to blame individuals who found themselves unemployed or in poverty and that it was necessary for governments to recognise and respond to the myriad of social factors that contribute towards unemployment and to deprivation. In his view, attempts to cut access to benefits do little to reduce dependency and merely transfer it from the state to dependency upon family or charities. For Gilmour, governments should be responsible for maintaining a decent benefits system and for managing the economy in such a way as to minimise unemployment and poverty by promoting economic stability and employment opportunities (Gilmour, 1992, pp. 144–171). For such conservatives, benefits were to be given out of compassion and in the recognition that if the state failed to provide, the burden would likely be transferred onto other organisations. Although conservatives are willing to concede that some people might need access to benefits at certain stages in their lives, they do not as a rule believe that people have a social right to these benefits. If the state can maintain a benefits system, then conservatives are apt to regard this as an act of compassion rather than as a central obligation for the government.

The British one nation conservatives have been particularly cautious in their support for the benefits system. It should be remembered that the benefits system in Britain had been established by a Liberal government prior to World War One and expanded by a social democratic government following the Second World War. Although British conservatives were never particularly active in the campaign for unemployment benefits, Macmillan was in favour of increasing unemployment benefit and pensions during the depression of the 1930s but argued that these increases should be in the form of essential foodstuffs (Macmillan, 1966, pp. 360–361). This illustrated the way in which British conservatives tend to regard the benefits system as a last resort. Lord Hailsham (1975) blustered against what he considered to be the fallacies of the benefits system. He believed that keen advocates of universal benefits were still fighting 'imaginary evils' that had existed during the 1930s but had been vanquished, or at least diminished, in the post-war period (Hailsham, 1975, pp. 168–171). It should be noted that if the benefits system is regarded as a concession rather than as a right, it will often lose out in a trade-off with the essential and life-enhancing provision of health care and education.

The Republicans in the United States have also been cautious in their support for the benefits system. In response to pressure from right wing sections of the Republican Party to reject some features of the legislation introduced in the New Deal, Eisenhower is reputed to have told his brother that any party that attempted to abolish social security or unemployment insurance would not be heard from again. Eisenhower increased the number of workers covered by social security and argued that, although he wanted to reduce public expenditure, social security was an indispensable feature of modern American society (Damms, 2002; Pach and Richardson, 1991). For many Republicans, the benefits system is a part of the political culture they inherited from the Democrats rather than something valued in its own right. Nixon believed that it was important for the government to provide incentives and encourage those in receipt of unemployment benefit to become more self-reliant and less dependent upon the state. He believed that work is necessary for a person's dignity and self-respect and that the benefits system must be reformed because it penalised people in work. Indeed, he declared that welfare reform was 'one of my highest priorities' (Nixon, 1971d). Nixon's reforms included pumping more resources into training, increasing public sector employment and increasing the financial penalties imposed upon those who did not comply with their responsibilities to find suitable employment (Nixon, 1971c, 1971d).

For many conservatives, the benefits system is a necessary if unattractive feature of the welfare state. Conservatives who aim to create a sense of unity or 'one nation' are aware that the benefits system is necessary so that people do not fall into unacceptable levels of poverty. Whereas the development of two nations consisting of the rich and the poor might be the acceptable outcome of the market economy, at least for its more ardent supporters, it is clear that many conservatives are uncomfortable with such harsh extremes. Many conservatives accept the need for at least some state intervention to assist in maintaining levels of employment and provide at least some form of relief for the unemployed. Conservative administrations have been instrumental in introducing benefits in other parts of Europe, most notably in Germany and in Italy where benefits have traditionally been given in recognition of the service given by workers to their place of employment (Esping-Andersen, 1990; Wilson, 1993; Fargion, 2001). For conservatives, the benefits system tends to be supported out of necessity rather than because it provides a way to minimise levels of inequality between the classes. Because of this, conservatives are likely to want to place severe limitations on the amount of benefits made available by the state.

Housing

Conservatives traditionally defend private property and, perhaps more so than any of the other mainstream political factions, support the privileges that owning property confers upon the owners. We should remember that modern conservatism began in most countries as a defence of privilege and inequality and that it has always stood against attempts to apply abstract political principles. Conservatism has a deeply situated pragmatic thread that recognises that privilege cannot be sustained in the long term by denying others the chance for social and economic advancement. This has pushed many conservatives towards using the state to assist the poorer sections of the community and has led conservatives to accept that the government should be involved, at least to some degree, in the provision or coordination of housing. Some conservative theorists have illustrated why some state intervention in housing is at least potentially beneficial to wide sections of society. When Gilmour (1978) argued in favour of spreading home ownership and allowing council tenants to buy their own homes, he did so in the belief that this would be good for individual freedom and would represent a significant blow against socialist principles (Gilmour, 1978, p. 149). When the Thatcher government pursued such policies, Gilmour became more convinced of the need for social housing. Gilmour (1992) was critical of the way in which the Thatcher governments had gone about undermining social housing and he was convinced that the private sector would not be able to satisfy all housing needs and that '... government intervention in housing has for a long time been seen to be necessary in most civilised countries' (Gilmour, 1992, pp. 176–177). Once again, the emphasis appeared to be on the government using its discretion and adapting to social needs rather than embarking upon a crusade to establish social justice.

British conservatives have tended to allow the state to intervene in the provision of housing. Macmillan believed that the allocation of rented housing should be directed by a National Housing Board and governed by '... considerations of the size of the family to be accommodated rather than only by the ability of the wage earner to pay rent' (Macmillan, 1966, p. 367). When he became

Minister of Housing in the 1951 Churchill government, Macmillan launched what he called his 'housing crusade' that involved setting up regional boards to expedite the building of houses and to act as a coordinating body in the allocation of resources. In Macmillan's view, housing should be 'taken out of politics' and he set about reducing the stringency of local authority regulations on house building. He was in favour of selling council house stock and of making it easier to build affordable houses for people to buy. He claimed that whereas Labour policy aimed to make the state a 'universal landlord', the conservative government supported the 'widest distribution of property' (Macmillan, 1969, pp. 395–406). For British conservatives, social housing was to be one of many alternatives open to the people; but it is clear that it was never the preferred option.

Conservatives in America have tended to be rather less enthusiastic about direct government involvement in housing, though there are notable exceptions. Eisenhower was particularly interested in the government helping to clear slums and regenerate urban areas and he was adamant that these reforms should not be restricted by budgetary issues. The Truman government had tried to push for an extensive programme of constructing public housing, but this had been curtailed by the war in Korea. When Eisenhower took office, he revived the Truman plan by establishing a system of grants and loans to help renovate older properties and provide finance to build 140,000 new houses over a four-year period. Eisenhower had originally intended to support a more extensive package of public housing but was blocked by right wing members of the Republican Party who argued against direct federal involvement (Eisenhower, 1963; Damms, 2002). Republican housing policy, indeed, has tended to rely to a far greater extent upon the private sector. Nixon, for example, argued that the federal government should do all that it could to eliminate discrimination in housing and encourage developers to build housing suitable for low-income and moderate-income families. He was clear, however, that the Department of Housing and Urban Development (HUD) should not itself own land or build houses. Instead, he argued that HUD should provide guidance and assistance to those involved in planning and community development. Although Nixon was certain that the federal government should not assume direct responsibility for providing housing, he recognised that the government could play a role as a facilitator and catalyst for the private sector through policy leadership rather than by building, owning or managing housing itself (Nixon, 1971e). George W. Bush, finally, has argued that federal government should encourage private initiatives to deal with problems in housing. Bush believes that federal government should support private charities dealing with the problems of homelessness and give taxpayers financial incentives to donate to charity. Private developers could also be encouraged to redevelop poor areas through a generous system of tax credits (Bush, 2000). Although the federal government could have a role in encouraging the development of affordable housing for the poor, it would seem that Republicans want this to stop short of direct government provision. Social housing, indeed, seems to be the dream of relatively few conservatives in the United States.

The conservative approach shows that the government can help in expanding the provision of housing in a variety of ways. In particular, conservatives recognise that a completely free market in housing is liable to favour the affluent and exclude, to a large extent, the working class. Modern conservatives have been willing to intervene to a limited degree in the direct provision of housing but are far more likely to use government policy to help direct the private sector towards an inclusive approach to housing provision. Private property is valued so highly by many conservatives that it would be unthinkable for conservatives to invest too much in the public provision of housing. Conservatives are more likely to support a housing policy that allows for great diversity than one that aims to secure more uniform levels of accommodation. It could be argued, indeed, that the choices we make in our housing reflect the place we occupy in the social hierarchy.

Health

The role of the state in the provision of health care is a controversial issue and has long been the site of numerous battles between conservatives and liberal opinion. Apart from anything else, there would seem to be a great deal of money to be made from the provision of health care and conservatives have often been some of the more consistent supporters of private practice. Conservatives are, of course, faced with the problem of reconciling their instinctive support for hierarchies within the health profession and the need to find a way to meet at least some of the needs of the poorer sections of society. This commitment seems to be heartfelt. Consider, for example, Richard Nixon's claim that the nation's wealth consisted far more in its health than in its material goods and that, as a healthy nation is also potentially a productive nation, the health of each person is of social concern. He believed, like many of the one nation conservatives in Britain, that we have responsibilities towards each other and that '... in carrying out its responsibilities in this field, a nation serves its own best interests, even as it demonstrates the breadth of its spirit and the depth of its compassion' (Nixon, 1971a). There were therefore some good reasons for the state to take an interest in health care.

The conservative tradition is by no means dominated by supporters of extensive state involvement in the provision of health care. Such levels of state involvement usually attract only moderate support among conservative factions. Ian Gilmour (1992), although no advocate of a state monopoly in the provision of health care, admitted that there were limits to what the private sector can provide. He argued that the private sector relied too much on the payment of private insurance premiums and that these premiums tend to be set at a level that effectively excludes most people who are not relatively young, gainfully employed and healthy. As such, private provision was seen as an insecure foundation for a national Health policy. According to Gilmour, attempts to undermine state involvement in the provision of health care are likely to backfire as health professionals might be less inclined to serve an organisation driven by the stark calculations of the business mind. Health is not, he claimed, a commodity to be bought and sold and left in the hands of market forces. Indeed, he believed that governments need to recognise that our health needs fluctuate and that they are likely to be more acute precisely when we are least able to afford private care (Gilmour, 1992, pp. 184–197). A case for state involvement in health care is thus made in response to the perceived failings of the private sector and in the belief that there are limits to what can be left to the free flow of market forces.

Conservative governments have shown, however, that they are willing to intervene when necessary. British conservatives inherited a National Health Service from the 1945–1951 Labour government and found that they were unable to do much to challenge what had become a very popular institution. Winston Churchill, leader of the Conservative Party and of the wartime coalition government, supported plans to create a National Health Service as early as 1943. Many in the Conservative Party, however, had reservations about the way the Labour government established the National Health Service. In particular, conservatives believed that the nationalisation of hospitals amounted to a compulsory seizure of property and forbidding General Practitioners from selling their medical practices was a blatant restriction of trade. According to Hogg (1947), the Conservative Party would have been content in 1945 to use existing administrative structures and to avoid alienating significant sections of the medical profession who evidently felt bullied by the reforms introduced by the Labour government (Hogg, 1947, p. 255). Despite these criticisms, however, the Conservative Party did very little to transform the health service when it was back in office in the period 1951–1964. When research showed that the National Health Service was efficient and value for money, the government was unable to justify any significant cuts (BBC2, 9.07.1995; Klein, 2001, p. 32). It also considered introducing charges for people staying in hospital but decided that, because some people would have to be exempt, it would be too expensive to administer. This is said to provide '... an example of ideology yielding to administrative expediency' (Klein, 2001, p. 30). British conservative support for the National

Health Service seems to be justified on fairly pragmatic grounds rather than because it is an area that conservatives want to be under the long-term jurisdiction of the state.

American conservatives have likewise been a little cautious in their support of government intervention in providing health care. The health system in the United States has traditionally relied upon private health insurance and, although American conservatives have done relatively little to challenge this system, some leading conservative politicians have recognised that this method of finance needs to be supplemented with government funding. Eisenhower had hoped to establish a federal fund to support health insurers, who agreed to extend their coverage to the poorer sections of the community, but his plans were attacked as an attempt to introduce 'socialised medicine' and they failed to gain the support of Congress (Damms, 2002). Richard Nixon was a little more successful in pushing through his reforms. Nixon's conservative approach to health care is interesting for a number of reasons; not least because his administration introduced a range of policies that seem to resonate quite well with the third way approaches of Clinton and Blair (see Chapter 6). In February 1971, Nixon launched his National Health Strategy that promised to improve access to health care for the poor and increase investment in (and the supply of) decent health care facilities. Although he believed that the federal government should be one of many partners in health care provision, Nixon felt that health care should still be financed through an insurance system. While people in paid employment were to be covered by National Health Insurance financed by contributions from employers and employees, the needs of the unemployed and the working poor were to be covered by a government-funded Family Health Insurance Plan. This mixture of public and private financing was considered preferential to a nationalised system because it took into account the important contribution that could be made by the private sector and because it encouraged competition between providers and gave the consumer greater freedom of choice. Nixon believed that health insurance should be available not merely for sickness but also for the development of health. He supported the growth of Health Maintenance Organisations, which would concentrate upon preventing sickness and treating the early stages of illness. Just as doctors in Ancient China were paid to keep their patients healthy, so American doctors were to be given a fixed-price contract for all health care that would effectively provide them with an economic incentive to promote the long-term health of their patients (Nixon, 1971a). For the Nixon administration, those who provide health care should be given an incentive to improve levels of health rather than respond constantly to sickness. As we shall see, this has become a dominant feature of contemporary health policy and it is supported by a variety of ideologies.

Conservative policies on health care tend to suggest that, while health is of social concern, limits should be placed upon direct government provision of health care. Conservatives display a natural bias towards private provision and tend on the whole to be sceptical about the role of the state in health care. Conservative welfare regimes in Germany, Italy and in Japan illustrate that even where the state does have a role in health care it is often limited and that the private sector is still considered of primary importance (Wilson, 1993; Fargion, 2001; Uzuhashi, 2001). But even the most weathered of conservatives find it difficult to resist the argument that state intervention can help to secure and maintain a healthy workforce. Faced with a business case for government involvement, conservatives will often be willing to concede that the private sector is often too expensive for many of the poor and that some state intervention is needed regardless of the pressures exerted by the powerful medical lobby. From a conservative point of view, the health service is too important to be left solely in the hands of private sector organisations.

Education

Conservatives have often adopted a reasonably elitist attitude towards education. Traditionally, possession of an education distinguished the rulers of society from the labouring poor and the class system, especially in Britain, was often justified on the grounds that only a few had sufficient education and culture to rule society (Burke, 1774, 1791). Although conservatives tend to protect this gateway to privilege, they have historically played an important role in the expansion of public education. Disraeli's conservatives did not make education compulsory, but they made sure that children between the ages of 10 and 14 could not work unless they had reached a certain educational standard or unless they continued some form of part-time education (Pearson and Williams, 1984, pp. 96–98). Conservatives do not, however, have a reputation for being egalitarian in their views on education. During the 1930s, Harold Macmillan acknowledged that class differences in education helped to breed snobbery and alienation but he argued that the 'public mind' was not ready to provide a common programme of education for all classes (Macmillan, 1966, pp. 64–65). Conservatives are more prone to see education as part of a social filtering process rather than as something that can transform the social fabric.

Conservatives are often quite suspicious of the state's interest in the education system. They recognise, along with many of their political opponents, that the education system can potentially be misused by zealots and that attempting to provide the same education for all people might be inappropriate and futile. Quinton Hogg (1947) argued that conservatives should support equality of opportunity rather than 'identity of opportunity' and that families should be given freedom from the overarching power of the state to choose the right kind of education for their children. He defended vehemently the right of parents to send their children to public school even if this resulted in creating a 'generation of little snobs' and he was against identity of opportunity because he believed that this would undermine standards by 'levelling down' rather than 'levelling up' education. In Hogg's view, identity of opportunity was also inappropriate given the multi-cultural and multi-faith character of Britain. He believed that the state should concern itself with secular instruction and avoid imposing a single set of moral and religious values upon pupils (Hogg, 1947, pp. 144–146). He remained convinced, however, that any attempt by the state to control the 'intellectual content' of education was incompatible with the basic tenets of freedom and that he was '... profoundly antagonistic to the enthusiasts of the left who try to make the educational machine a vehicle for social engineering' (Hailsham, 1975, p. 139). For many conservatives, education should provide a mark of distinction rather than a way to obliterate differences between people.

Although conservative administrations have supported the view that the state should assume some responsibility to educate its citizens, this support has often been tempered by a commitment to maintain social inequalities. The 1951–1964 Conservative governments in Britain were particularly vocal in their support for extending grammar school provision, though many local authorities did not share this preference and argued in favour of the comprehensive system in education. Lord Hailsham complained that he was '... completely contemptuous of those who decide to force comprehensive schools as a single pattern for all secondary education' (Hailsham, 1975, p. 140; Todd, Ware and Taylor, 2002, p. 7). When Hailsham (Quinton Hogg) became Minister of Education in Harold Macmillan's government, he used this position to give greater state assistance to denominational (especially Catholic) schools and to create the foundations for the development of polytechnics. For all of his high-minded conservatism, Hogg was quite critical of the university sector because of its tendency to teach subjects regardless of the needs of society. He saw polytechnics, on the other hand, as democratic institutions that supplied education according to need and gave mature students (and those who could only afford to study part time) greater access to higher education. In his view, polytechnics understood and showed with clarity and conviction that there was 'more than one route to the top' (Hailsham, 1975, p. 148). Although it might sometimes appear that conservatives want to preserve educational opportunities for the few, it is more likely to be the case that they are interested in protecting differences in the types (and quality) of education offered by the state and other providers.

American conservatives have likewise declared their commitment to maintain differences between people and have tended to be reluctant to extend the role of federal government over the education system. This stems, in part, from recognising that American society is so diverse and that there are great differences between the various states in terms of culture, economic position, ethnic mix and even educational needs. President Eisenhower increased federal support for education, especially in the sciences, but this assistance did in no way threaten the local control of schools. In his State of the Union Address to Congress in 1960, he claimed that education was 'a local and personal responsibility' that could not be assisted greatly by federal government intervention (Eisenhower, 1960; Pach and Richardson, 1991). American conservatives seem to prefer federal government to assist local states rather than usurp their powers. Richard Nixon, for example, was interested in finding ways to widen access to higher education. He set up the National Foundation for Higher Education to review the higher education needs of the population and created the National Student Loan Association as an additional provider of student loans in the hope that it would encourage greater numbers to enter higher education (Nixon, 1971b). George W. Bush (1998), finally, has argued likewise that local states, rather than federal government, must determine the curricula because it is foolish to believe that one size fits all. He pointed out that although the education system must recognise and respect local differences, it is essential that the education system pays serious attention to the transmission of moral values and that it teaches the importance of people fulfilling their civic responsibilities. This belief that the education system has a moral function to perform is one of the key features of conservative thinking on education.

In many ways, conservatives are advocates of diversity in education and in educational provision. As supporters of the class system, they argue that different types of education are needed for different strata in society. This does not mean of course that they are supporters of a closed caste system. Conservatives understand that education can be an important tool in allowing for mobility between the different sections of society. What they are clearly against is the tendency or desire to view education as a way to equalise or blunt the differences between the various social classes. From a conservative point of view, social differences are important and should as far as possible be maintained. Because of this, conservatives are often worried about the government playing a central role in educational provision and tend to be critical of attempts to impose a uniform brand of education on all people. Rather than see education as a way to transform society, conservatives are apt to believe that the function of education should in part be to conserve and maintain the existing social order.

Conclusion

It should be appreciated that many conservatives feel ill at ease with the modern capitalist system. Capitalism can be harsh, unless it is tempered by some benevolence and ethical appreciation of human worth. For conservatives, we must assume some responsibility for each other and if employers fail in this regard, then the state must intervene. Like social liberals, conservatives want capitalism to work and they are willing to use the state to compensate for market failures and even to plan capitalism for the common good. Social policies are offered as concessions to the less fortunate rather than to challenge or reform the social hierarchy. These policies are often put into effect in the interests of dampening more radical plans for social reform and in an attempt to stablise the system. Conservative ideas and policies have been important in shaping social provision in Britain, the United States and in other parts of the world. They show, among other things, the importance of compassion in the development of social provision and how the charitable ethos can be adapted and reworked by an interventionist state. The aim of the conservative welfare state is to conserve rather than to revolutionise existing society. It could be argued that this more traditional form of conservatism has had its day. It rests upon an old class system and relies upon people displaying deference and being willing to slot into hierarchies in society. It might be that this class system is no longer in evidence in Western society and that there is far greater mobility between the classes. Although the stability longed for by many conservatives might have existed in the past, it is now challenged constantly by the spread of further and higher education and by global communications. The appeal of conserving, however, is not tied to any particular period in history. New class systems develop and it is quite conceivable that a new generation of conservatives could campaign to protect the system from rampant individualism on the one hand and radical schemes on the other. Conservatism is a frame of mind, not only a political ideology. Stripped of some of its more archaic features, the conservative insistence that the state should coordinate the private sector in the interests of the public good could still make a positive contribution to the future of welfare.

4

Social Democracy

Social democrats are primarily interested in finding ways to reform capitalism out of existence. Unlike many Marxists, they favour gradual change rather than the chaos created by revolutions and believe that the capitalist state can be used against the exclusive interests of the capitalist class and made to serve the common good. Social democrats tend to want to use social policies to create a more egalitarian society. Like social liberals and many conservatives, they often subscribe to an organic theory of society in which society is seen as an interdependent organism that evolves over time and influences the character of the citizen body. It is argued that society has a life of its own and that individuals have a responsibility to nourish the social system. Sidney Webb (1889), for example, pointed out that we all have social functions to perform and that individuals develop by contributing towards the social good rather than by acting in ignorance or indifference towards the good of society. What follows on social democracy will draw heavily upon British social democratic theorists including the Fabian Society, Ramsay MacDonald, Tony Crosland, R.H. Tawney, T.H. Marshall and Aneurin Bevan. Special attention will also be given to the policies introduced by the Labour Party in Britain and international examples will be used for comparative purposes.

Economy

Social democrats tend to be critical of capitalism and believe that capitalism can and should be eroded and replaced by a more humane and just economic system. The extent to which they are willing to attack capitalism and to promote a socialist economy will of course vary. What they tend to share is the conviction that capitalism is unjust and that conservative benevolence is too discretionary and patronising to be relied upon to usher in a stable alternative. It should be recognised at the outset that social democratic views on the economy have a great deal in common with those of social liberals. Where social democrats differ from many liberals is in the extent to which they are willing to use the state to secure greater levels of equality and social justice.

Social democrats have often argued that the state must have a significant role in the economy. For many, this was seen as preferable to the scenarios developed by revolutionary socialists. Rather than wait for socialism to happen through some sudden and complete change of heart or through a catastrophic revolution, social democrats have argued that if the state can gradually increase its role in the economy, then the foundations of socialism could be built within capitalism (Webb, 1889, 30–61). Ramsay MacDonald (1905) described capitalism as the economic stage of civilisation, whereas socialism was referred to as the moral stage during which selfish interests were to be subordinated to the general interest and it was assumed that people would become more likely to be moved by their heads rather than simply by their material wants and desires. He argued that under socialism, the state could help to unify society by nationalising industry and redistributing the fruits of industry in accordance with the common good.

The British Labour Party in the years immediately following the Second World War was instrumental in applying social democratic ideas in Britain. Although the Labour Party never created a purely social democratic society, it was certainly willing to use the state to manage significant sections of the British economy. The Labour governments of 1945–1951 nationalised approximately 20 per cent of the British economy. Special emphasis was placed upon gaining control over the raw materials and basic industries necessary for capitalism to function. Coal, steel and the railways were among the industries placed under national ownership, each of which could be seen as playing pivotal roles in British manufacturing. When pushed out of office in 1951, the Labour Party began its retreat from these ideals. Believing that nationalisation was unpopular, the more moderate elements in the party began a campaign to disengage the Labour Party from its commitment to use the state to circumvent the capitalist system (Dutton, 1991; Cairncross, 1992; Callaghan, 1989). For the so-called 'revisionists' in the Labour Party, the existence of the welfare state and a mixed economy rendered it unnecessary to pursue more revolutionary routes to socialism. Tony Crosland (1956), for example, argued that British society had entered a post-capitalist era because Labour Party policies on nationalisation, full employment and the welfare state had helped to alleviate the problems of poverty and mass unemployment and that, under these conditions, the Labour Party should avoid nationalising other segments of the economy and concentrate instead upon the continued pursuit of social equality. In his view, it was important that reforms aimed to maximise the common welfare rather than attempt to undermine and transform beyond recognition the existing economic system. From 1918 until the mid 1990s, the British Labour Party remained committed (at least on paper) to a programme of nationalisation. Clause four of the Labour Party constitution promised Labour administrations would work towards establishing a system of common ownership of the means of production. Although it is no doubt possible to interpret this clause in a variety of ways, for the majority of the Labour Party this came to mean that the party was committed to the nationalisation of at least key industries (Benn, 1980, pp. 39–42).

It would be wrong to assume that all social democrats are critical of the private ownership of the means of production and in favour of widespread nationalisation. In his contribution to the 1984 edition of *Fabian Essays in Socialist Thought*, Alan Ryan argued that private ownership of the means of production was compatible with personal freedom, innovation and personal security. He believed moreover that socialists should consider seriously the problems that can arise from the state attempting to manage industry and look instead at ways to make industrial management more open to worker participation in the managerial process (Ryan, 1984, pp. 101–112). David Marquand (1988, 1993) was likewise critical of nationalisation. He argued that public ownership and control of industry had proved to be inefficient and difficult to manage. In his view, social democrats should be willing to use the state to assist and to regulate the private sector. He pointed out that this notion of a 'developmental state' had been applied with a great deal of success in Japan, Germany, Sweden and France and he believed that it was possible to get cross-party support for such intervention.

Not all social democrats believe that the state is capable of reforming society in a fundamental and far-reaching way. Social democrats in Sweden, for example, stopped short of open support for the nationalisation or socialisation of the means of production. According to Esping-Andersen (1985), the strength and vitality of social democracy relies upon the state having the ability and power to regulate the economy by helping to maintain full employment, high levels of investment and by helping to control the business cycle. By creating high levels of economic stability and by assisting in the development of the economy, it was argued that the basis for the 'social citizenship state' could be established. Esping-Andersen admitted, however, that this places social democrats in a strange and ambiguous position as defenders of the capitalist system. (Esping-Andersen, 1985, pp. 35–36, 107, 192–193, 271–273). Social democracy can indeed be regarded as an ideology designed to preserve the long-term interests of the capitalist class. Even in Britain, where 20 per cent of the economy was nationalised, the remainder of the capitalist system remained in tact. As we will see in the later chapter on Marxism, social democracy can be viewed as an illusion perpetrated to protect capitalism.

Within social democratic thought, there is a definite sense that capitalism is far from the last feasible economic arrangement and that underlying much of what they have to say is the belief that we will one day wake up and be resolute in our desire to overcome the instabilities of capitalism. This is shown in the way that social democrats regard capitalism as somehow grubby and in desperate need of state intervention to free us from our greed and our willingness to exploit others for our own gain. There is of course a definite moral dimension to all of this. From a social democratic point of view, some form of socialism (even in a diluted form) is morally superior to capitalism and thus worthy of support from people of good faith. For social democrats, state intervention in the economy does not necessarily mean that the state has to take over the ownership and control of industries. It could mean regulating the economy and promoting alternatives to free market economics. What is clear is that social democrats are often willing to go further than conservatives and liberals in granting to the state overall responsibility for the health of the national economy. Whereas conservatives and liberals can be viewed as defenders of capitalism, social democrats seem to have severe reservations about the value of capitalism and its long-term future.

Social values

Social democrats tend to be openly egalitarian and believe that freedom is not a purely individual possession but something that resides in the community. While classical liberals are famed for wanting to free the individual from the constraints of others, social democrats believe that freedom depends upon there being at least some measure of equality. Inequality is thought to stand in the way of freedom. For many social democrats, our freedom depends upon us having guaranteed social, economic and political rights. It is argued that we need rights against authoritarian state activity and against material hardship and that any infringement of these rights takes place at the expense of our liberty (George and Wilding, 1994, p. 98). The classical liberal preoccupation with negative liberty is attacked because it effectively reduces all social issues to questions about the interests of the individual. Barry Hindess, for example, argues that the freedom of individuals to do as they please should by no means take precedence over all other values. He complains that the idea of negative liberty concentrates far too much upon intentional barriers to human freedom, and thus fails to take into account the harm caused by poverty, illiteracy and unemployment. For Hindess, and many other theorists on the left, economic inequality poses a severe threat to liberty and should therefore be countered by the state redistributing wealth (Hindess, 1990, pp. 9–13). Rather than wait for a revolution to smash capitalism, social democrats are convinced that the state can be used constructively to promote both freedom and equality.

Although social democrats are moderate in the sense that they value slow, methodical and piecemeal change, they differ significantly from many liberals and conservatives by challenging the very foundations of the capitalist system. Whereas liberals and conservatives attempt to balance the needs of the economic system with the welfare of the whole, social democrats argue that this welfare cannot be guaranteed and sustained in a society that requires the maintenance of inequality. Although social democrats dress from the same conceptual wardrobe as many liberals and conservatives, they criticise capitalism for subordinating the general welfare to the profit motive and they often place far more emphasis on the importance of pursuing policies to maximise levels of equality and social justice. According to Andrew Gamble, equality became important to socialists and social democrats because they recognised that '... the ideals of liberalism could only be fulfilled if individuals were given not just civil rights (the right to free speech, free association and free trial), and political rights (the right to vote), but also social rights' (Gamble, 1981, p. 181). Social democrats indeed often appear to be the self-appointed guardians of our social rights.

Social democrats argue that freedom and equality are compatible. By defining freedom as the opportunity to fulfil ourselves and to be free from economic deprivation, they see that some measure of equality is necessary for the individual to experience true freedom (Goodwin, 1987, p. 108). This can be illustrated by reference to the ideas put forward by R.H. Tawney in his 1931 study *Equality*. Tawney denied that freedom and equality were mutually exclusive and he believed that there must be a 'large measure of equality' to secure true freedom. In his view, 'economic liberty' required '... the absence of such economic inequalities as can be used as a means of economic constraint' (Tawney, 1931, p. 168). True freedom was said to rely upon expanding the range of alternatives open to people and increasing the capacities of people to follow their own preferences. He implied that this is liable to increase as a result of reducing inequalities and he claimed that society is free to the extent that '... its institutions and policies are such as to enable its members to grow to their full stature' (Tawney, 1931, p. 235). Expanding the range of opportunities open to people therefore '... not only subtracts from inequality, but adds to freedom' (Tawney, 1931, p. 135). Tawney's analysis shows that freedom and equality can go together, as long as we subscribe to a positive conception of freedom. Throughout his account, he condemns the narrow (negative) definition of freedom because it neglects the importance of expanding opportunities for self-development for the many and does little more than preserve the arbitrary rights of the few.

It should be appreciated that while many social democrats want to increase levels of equality in society, this does not mean that they want to secure equality in all things. Many fear that the pursuit of total equality of outcome would lead to excessive state intervention and that this could harm the freedom of the individual. Social democrats tend to be a little cautious in their support for equality. T.H. Marshall (1949) believed that 'equality of status' is more important than 'equality of income' because he believed that equality of status could serve as a foundation to attack gross inequalities while leaving some inequalities intact. In his view, the welfare system should aim to bring about '... a general enrichment of the concrete substance of civilised life, a general reduction of risk and insecurity, an equalisation between the more and the less fortunate at all levels' (Marshall, 1949, p. 40). Social democrats (and some liberals) believe in equality of worth. This feeds into demands for equal opportunities and is expressed in the belief that people deserve to be treated with respect and not prevented deliberately from reaching their potential. For many social democrats, as for many liberals and feminists, governments should assist people in achieving their goals in life. It is believed that barriers should be broken down and that people should be given the chance to succeed (Commission on Social Justice, 1993, pp. 54–58). This involves, among other things, using the state to promote the welfare of the people.

The social values advanced by social democrats recognise that individuals live and develop in communities. Rather than see the individual as an isolated being, social democrats are apt to consider people in their broader social context and to regard freedom as something that can only be achieved for the vast majority in a well-ordered and collectivist society. While individual rights remain important, social democrats look at the social rights and the benefits we should accrue from being members of a community. When they look at society, they see at least some of the numerous social barriers that stand in the way of individual fulfilment and they deliberately look for ways to improve the life chances of the majority by seeking to undermine a range of inequalities. A social democratic world is not necessarily one where there is total equality of outcome, but it is clear that social democrats are critical of capitalism for either creating or increasing social divisions and that they often want the state to foster harmony and reduce levels of inequality. This shows that social democrats have more ambitious plans for the state than many liberals or conservatives.

State and welfare

Although social democrats are critical of both capitalism and the capitalist state for helping to perpetuate inequalities, this does not mean that they are willing to abandon using the state altogether. As we saw in the section on the economy, many social democrats are in favour of the state playing an active role in the management of economic affairs. For social democrats, taking control of the state provides one of the key ways to usher in social-ism in a gradual, piecemeal and peaceful way. If socialism is about giving people what they deserve and alleviating the hardship experienced by the poor under capitalism, then it has to involve more than the state taking over industries and wielding them for the common good. Although many social democrats are in favour of extending the state ownership of industry, it is recognised that this is of little value unless accompanied by decent levels of social provision. Socialism, it should be remembered, relies upon the quali-tative enrichment of people and socialists often want to establish a society based upon cooperation rather than upon competition. They recognise that such cooperation is more likely to occur in a society where material goods and opportunities are distributed according to principles of social justice, rather than in response to market mechanisms.

Social democrats played an extremely important role in the development of the welfare state in Britain. The Labour governments of 1945–1951 set about regenerating the post-war economy and society by introducing sig-nificant measures to regulate the economy and to provide the population with a batch of welfare measures that were designed to cushion them from the harsh realities of capitalism. As we will see later in the chapter, the Labour government showed that it was willing to extend the role of the state in social provision and lay the foundations for the post-war welfare state. It was recognised and acknowledged that this involved applying liberal ideals and finding ways to compromise with the needs of the capitalist system. Richard Crossman (1952), for example, was willing to admit that the wel-fare state had its limits and that it could be seen as a monument to the way that capitalism has adapted to the pressure exerted by the labour movement. In his view, the policies and achievements of the 1945–1951 Labour gov-ernments in Britain represented '... the climax of a long process, in the course of which capitalism has been civilised and, to a large extent, recon-ciled with the principles of democracy' (Crossman, 1952, p. 6). For some of the most influential social democrats, the welfare state was of central impor-tance to their political creed. Tony Crosland (1956) believed that the wel-fare state reflected significant changes in the British mind. For him, the idea of collective responsibility and the willingness to use the state constructively had helped erode the appeal of laissez-faire and had helped to establish a more just system in a peaceful and incremental way. Even if the welfare state was seen as a compromise with the interests of capitalism, it was regarded as a considerable and worthwhile achievement that benefited society as a whole and helped to avoid the chaos of both free market capitalism and violent revolutionary activity.

In addition to saving society from the ravage of extremes, social democrats recognise the positive value of the state intervening to provide welfare services. Social democrats tend to see the welfare state as a mechanism for reducing inequalities and for cultivating a sense of cross-class solidarity. Esping-Andersen (1985) argued that welfare states are important because economic insecurity and lack of education are bad for full participation in the social democratic state and because it was foolish to believe that the market can distribute resources in a way that can create social solidarity. In his view, the welfare state should embrace and support the building of social unity by undermining income differentials, by reducing the influence of divisive market mechanisms and by attempting to diminish conflict and differences within the working class. In order to build solidarity and social unity, Esping-Andersen thought that people need to recognise that they should have a right to welfare and that such rights were not contingent upon means testing or acts of benevolence (Esping-Andersen, 1985, pp. 147–159). It is evident that state provision of welfare can be viewed as one of the ways to engage citizens in the life of the nation and to ensure that everybody feels that they have a stake in society. Seen in this way, the welfare state might help to enrich democracy and protect it from anti-democratic movements.

For social democrats, the state is there to be captured and used for the good of all. Rather than use the state to protect the interests of the capitalist class, they argue that the power of the state can be mobilised to alleviate social injustices and to create a more harmonious and unified system. It is recognised that the state would need to attend to the needs of the working class in a way that did not alienate unduly the more prosperous sections of the community. This is perhaps one of the great things about the welfare state. By providing a range of services, it could be argued that all sections of the community can benefit. Although the middle class might be less dependent upon the benefits system and on the social provision of housing, there is still a lot of room for the middle class to gain advantage from state involvement in the provision of health care and education. The welfare state can be sold to different classes for different reasons. Social democrats are aware of this and have therefore been generally supportive of the state playing an active part in social provision.

Welfare and social policies

Social democrats have traditionally relied upon a string of social policy initiatives to maximise the welfare of individuals and of society. Rather than

1e operations of the free market or to the benevolence of
democrats argue that progressive forces need to gain control
d to use it to tackle social need and to establish a more egali-
1. As we have seen, social democrats tend to support the welfare
ely to a great extent upon the state responding constructively to
oui   1 needs.

Benefits

Social democrats tend to be far more supportive of the benefits system than
the majority of liberals and conservatives. The logic and force of the social
democratic argument can be seen clearly in the ideas of T.H. Marshall.
Marshall (1970) was a firm believer in us having a social right to unemployment benefits and to a pension once we were beyond working age. In his
view, this right was '... underpinned and sustained in modern democratic
and welfare societies by social rights attached to the status of citizenship'
(Marshall, 1970, p. 190). Marshall believed that it was the responsibility of
the state to oversee and to run this system to ensure that people's social rights
were respected and that a harsh regime of means testing did not threaten
these rights (Marshall, 1970, pp. 189–190). From a social democratic perspective, the benefits system should be made available as a right rather than
as a concession. Whereas supporters of capitalism are inclined to believe that
the capitalist economy can provide a range of opportunities for people who
want to work, social democrats recognise that such opportunities are not
necessarily spread equally through all sections of society and that a civilised
economic and social system should recognise the existence of social as well
as individual rights.

The British Labour Party supported the provision of benefits for much of
the post-war era. It applied the recommendations of the Beveridge Report
and introduced a system of national assistance (unemployment benefit) in
1946. Although there were some changes to the way in which these benefits were administered, the Labour Party tended to regard access to such
benefits as a right. Labour Party election manifestos in 1959 and 1964 argued
that the Conservative government was intent on destroying the benefits system and the Labour Party promised to increase and stabilise entitlement of
unemployment benefits. In 1970, the manifesto talked about the economically vulnerable having a right to share in the nation's economic prosperity
and in 1983 a pledge was made to secure a right to receive long-term unemployment benefit (see Dale, 2000, pp. 97, 169, 170, 260). The tone of these
manifestos showed that the Labour Party saw the unemployed as victims
of the economic cycle and that they deserved better than the insecure
and precarious existence offered by the benefits regimes established and

promised by the Conservative Party. For the Labour Party, unemployment was seen as a social and economic problem rather than something that people voluntarily chose for themselves.

Social democrats in Scandinavia have been extremely influential in helping to establish a benefits system in their countries. The Swedish benefits system had two main sources: the liberal ideas of Beveridge and the conservative ideas of Bismarck. It is said to combine the universal benefits feature from Beveridge and the income-related insurance features characteristic of the German system (Olsen, 1999). Sweden introduced a range of insurance measures including sickness benefit as early as 1891, followed by old age and invalidity insurance in 1913 and occupational injury insurance in 1916. Universal benefits included a rudimentary social assistance package (1914) and pensions for people over the age of 67 (1946) that were topped up by an earnings-related contribution scheme known as ATP in 1959. Bryson points out that although this addition appears to undermine the commitment to equality, it was considered necessary to prevent the more affluent members of the community from pouring resources into private insurance (Bryson, 1992, p. 112). Both Norway and Sweden have two-tier benefits systems that provide additional cover for the middle classes, financed by an earnings-related insurance scheme. This was introduced in the hope of maintaining '... the degree of political consensus required to preserve broad and solidaristic support for the high taxes that such a welfare state model demands' (Esping-Andersen, 1990a, p. 161). Swedish social democrats have thus shown an interest in gaining cross-class support and in reconciling conflicting interests. They have illustrated quite effectively that the welfare state can be used to further the interests of different classes and that the welfare state is not there simply to support the poor.

The maintenance of a decent benefits system would seem to be an important feature of the social democratic case. For those who believe that society is an interdependent organism, it makes perfect sense to cater for the needs of those who are unable to work at any particular time. Rather than blame the unemployed, social democrats recognise that the roots of unemployment are systemic and need to be tackled through state intervention. Social democrats have, however, found it difficult to maintain this defence of benefits in the face of concerted attacks on the welfare state by neo-liberal forces (see Chapter 5). In Germany, social democratic governments increased unemployment insurance contributions and attempted with only limited success to place restrictions on access to benefits (Clasen, 2000). French social democrats were rather more resilient, as shown in 1991 when the Rocard government introduced a 1.1% levy on income to finance welfare reforms (Beland and Hansen, 2000). For social democrats, state provision of benefits is an important feature of the welfare state and essential to ensure that the working class in particular are not trampled on and marginalised by the needs of the capitalist system.

Housing

For many social democrats, the state should be actively involved in the provision and management of housing. This could be justified on the grounds that housing is seen as a fundamental social right in the West and that without decent housing the rest of their egalitarian programme would crumble. Recognising that not all people are in a financial position to buy their own homes, social democrats tend to see the state as a potential provider of decent and reasonably priced housing for rent. This is in part responding to the needs of the working class. According to Esping-Andersen (1985), it is important for the government to have a significant role in the provision of housing partly because the working class and the population at large place housing high on their list of priorities (Esping-Andersen, 1985, pp. 179–188). It is clear that without state provision, the working class in particular is potentially at the mercy of private landlords.

Social democrats are by no means in favour of nationalising the provision of rented accommodation. Instead, they recognise that the state can have a number of roles in the provision of housing and in the coordination of housing policy. Tony Crosland (1974) argued that a sound housing policy should be a central feature of a social democratic programme because it was necessary in the fight against poverty and squalor. In his view, housing not only affected the individual but also the local area. He believed that access to decent housing should be regarded as a basic right of citizenship and that it was a significant landmark in the journey towards social equality. According to Crosland, the free market could not guarantee decent housing for all citizens so '... the government must bear a final responsibility for the overall housing situation' (Crosland, 1974, p. 118). It could do this by providing social housing and by encouraging housing cooperatives, housing associations and other voluntary groups to provide housing and increase choice for tenants. For Crosland, it was important to develop a mixed economy of housing in which the state was an important but not sole provider of rented accommodation (Crosland, 1974, pp. 131–143). This shows quite clearly that although they believe that there should be limits to state intervention, social democrats want the state to assume responsibility for housing and to intervene when necessary and to compensate for the shortcomings of private provision.

The Labour Party in Britain has tended to rely quite heavily upon government intervention in the provision of housing. Whereas conservatives are often reluctant to allow the state too much power in this field, mainly because they place positive value on owning property, social democrats have been motivated by the desire to provide the working class in particular with decent housing. Aneurin Bevan, who was the Labour government's Minister of Housing 1945–1947, was instrumental in extending the provision of social housing in Britain. He believed that communities were 'castrated' by sharp divisions between local authority housing and private dwellings and that housing policy should attempt to integrate communities by building towns where different social classes could live alongside each other. He claimed that if local authorities were to provide housing, attention should be paid to the aesthetics of an area. Bevan was critical of the working class being deposited into bleak dormitory areas and urged town planners to think about the impact of their designs upon working class life. The Labour government of 1945–1951 initiated a massive programme of house building and when the Labour Party returned to office in the 1960s, it continued to invest heavily in social housing. Some of the decisions made, especially to pursue a policy of building high-rise flats, proved to be unpopular and did little to endear many tenants to the virtues of state planning (Foot, 1973, pp. 60–81; Morgan, 1992, pp. 39–41; Todd, Ware and Taylor, 2002, pp. 8–10; Lund, 2005, pp. 172–174). It should be noted, however, that these developments were a far cry from the original vision of social housing.

The state has also played an extremely important role in the provision of social housing in Sweden, largely because social democratic governments in Sweden have seen it as one of many ways to increase cooperation between the classes. Following the Second World War, the Swedish social democrats initiated plans to expand state provision of social housing. The central state delegated considerable powers to local governments, which controlled the supply of land and determined the kind of accommodation that was to be built. The state provided preferential low-interest loans for building contractors, many of which operated as non-profit organisations. A National Federation of Tenants also represented the opinions of tenants and this helped the government understand and respond to the needs of the population rather than plan according to some preconceived and ill-informed agenda. These policy initiatives helped to create a large social housing sector in Sweden. In the period prior to 1990, when the Social Democrat government left office, the amount of social housing as a percentage of housing stock increased considerably and continuously. It could be argued, indeed, that Sweden continued its social housing projects long after many Western countries had abandoned using the state so extensively (Doling, 1997, pp. 94–96, 115–117, 180–198; Kemeny, 1992, pp. 120–149).

State provision of decent social housing can be justified and supported by social democrats on the grounds that such intervention is necessary to eradicate squalor and help to create the foundations of an integrated and harmonious community. When the state intervenes, however, there is no guarantee that it will provide what people want. Some of the problems that developed in social housing programmes in Britain would tend to suggest that the state could make serious mistakes when it fails to listen to or elicit the opinions of tenants. Government investment in large-scale social housing is by no means supported by all social democrats. Social democrats in Australia, for example, have shown very little interest in social housing and have tended to favour tax incentives to encourage private ownership of housing (Bryson, 1992, p. 95). Even if the state does intervene, social democrats are careful to point out that it will never be at a level that threatens either private ownership or the private provision of rented accommodation.

Health

The state provision of health care is clearly compatible with many features of social democratic theory and with the social policy agenda of many social democratic parties. According to Bevan (1952), equal medical treatment should be provided to all people regardless of class and the National Health Service was surely a '… triumphant example of the superiority of collective action and public initiative applied to a segment of society where commercial principles are seen at their worst' (Bevan, 1952, p. 85). Tony Crosland (1957) argued in favour of high levels of investment in the National Health Service to a level comparable with the private sector in health care. He believed that the National Health Service provided an important social supplement to the income of the nation and that it could in its own way help to nurture social unity and equality. According to Crosland, if all people used the same providers of health care this could be '… an immensely important influence in creating a sense of social equality and lack of privilege' (Crosland, 1957, p. 143). State intervention in the provision of health care has often been defended by social democrats with passion and this intervention is not supported on pragmatic grounds but because of its potential role in creating a more egalitarian society.

The Labour government in Britain transformed the provision of health care when it created the National Health Service in July 1948. The National Health Service Act of 1946 established a new Ministry of Health with the remit of working towards providing free health care for everybody in England and Wales. The first Minister of Health Aneurin Bevan looked to combine under national ownership the old elitist voluntary hospitals and the poorly financed municipal hospitals. Understanding that this was likely to be opposed by key interests in the health care profession, Bevan struck a deal with the powerful consultants in which they were allowed to continue treating private patients in National Health Service hospitals and were given significant financial inducements to support the formation of the National Health Service. At first the National Health Service covered all branches of health care, but charges were introduced in the early 1950s for visiting opticians and dentists in response to the particularly heavy demand for these services. Convinced that this was the thin end of the wedge, Bevan resigned from office in disgust that his socialist vision was being diluted. Labour policy on health care left many inconsistencies, which future Labour governments had to deal with. In seeking the support of consultants, Bevan had perpetuated inequalities between consultants and General Practitioners and had allowed for the continuance of pay beds in National Health hospitals. The Labour government of 1964–1970 had to placate the General Practitioners when they threatened mass resignations over pay and conditions. Attempts were also made during the 1974–1979 governments to reduce the power of consultants by removing pay beds, but this campaign was ultimately unsuccessful (Taylor, 1999, p. 106). Although the National Health Service in Britain might seem like a socialist experiment, it has never been able to remove all traces of privilege and inequality in access to health care.

Health care in Sweden has also been heavily influenced by social democratic ideas. For much of the post-war period, the Swedish health system was run predominantly by the state and there was a consensus across parties on the need for the state control of health care. Workers in Sweden were also covered by a generous system of national insurance, paid for by the employers, in which they were guaranteed 90 per cent of their salaries in the event of sickness. Good intentions aside, Swedish social democratic governments during the 1980s were unable to maintain levels of service within the health system and so began to ration access to some services. The social democrats favoured an increase in investment in health care, while liberals and conservatives pushed for the expansion of the private sector. The Swedish health system was eventually transformed during the 1990s by the introduction of market principles and by doctors taking control of their own budgets (Gould, 1993, pp. 189–195). As we shall see in Chapter 5, these ideas were originally developed by the neo-liberals and signalled at least the temporary suspension of a social democratic health service in Sweden.

Social democrats have tended to be quite generous in the resources that they are willing to give to state health care. They recognise that the insurance-based systems established by liberals and conservatives often exclude significant sections of society, either because the insurance is tied to paid employment or because the premiums are too expensive for the less affluent to afford. In the hope of overcoming these inequalities, social democrats look to the state and suggest that access to health care should be viewed as a social right. It could be argued that social democrats take it quite literally that the state should be responsible for the health of the social organism. Although there are a variety of ways in which the state could tend to the nation's health, social democrats have tended to favour direct state ownership and control of health care facilities. Once again, this would not mean the end of private practice. Individuals would still have the right to purchase private health care and in so doing help to relieve the pressure on state provision.

Education

Social democrats have argued that the state should find ways to undermine privilege in education and to use the education system to inspire and to liberate people. For some, access to education was one of our fundamental social rights. Tony Crosland (1974), for example, argued that we have a variety of rights as citizens. We have certain personal liberties, we have democratic rights and even a rather more fragile 'right to welfare'. In his view, the right to 'educational equality' needed to be added to the list. He recognised that true equality of education could not be introduced by a single act of parliament because its success relied upon a broader social revolution which involved such things as eliminating sub-standard housing. However, he was certain that '... so long as we choose to educate our children in separate camps, reinforcing and seeming to validate differences in accent, language and values, for so long will our schools exacerbate rather than diminish our class divisions' (Crosland, 1974, p. 204). For Crosland, the state was not only responsible for educational provision but also for ensuring that this provision helped to reduce inequalities in society.

For much of the post-war period, the Labour Party in Britain looked upon education as a way to enhance the prospects of the working class and to assist in the erosion of the traditional class system. When it came to power immediately after the Second World War, the Labour Party extended the provision of state education by raising the school leaving age to 15. This education system was, however, rife with divisions between the relatively privileged grammar schools dominated by the middle classes and the less academic secondary schools, where the working classes were expected to learn the skills necessary to move into manual work. Students were segregated at the age of 11 following their 11 plus exams, which were thought to favour children from the middle classes because of the support they often get from their parents. When Crosland became Secretary of State for Education, he began a concerted attempt to introduce and impose a system of comprehensive education. Grammar schools were gradually phased out in some areas in Britain and comprehensives introduced to cater for children of mixed ability. Labour governments also presided over the expansion of higher education and to encouraging adults to return to education with such brilliant initiatives as the Open University (Crosland, 1974; Bochel, 2005). Labour governments promoted the view that education was a life-long process and that our aspirations should not be sealed once and for all at the age of 11.

Social democrats have also had a significant impact upon the education system in Sweden. The Swedish education system developed considerably in the post-war period as a highly centralised social service. The social democrats presided over an increase in compulsory schooling and the expansion of higher education. The government assumed responsibility for the character of the education delivered and a deliberate attempt has been made to foster democratic ideals and to enhance citizen identity (Fleisher, 1956; Erickson, 2000). This is a recurring feature in social democratic thought and initiatives. The state is called upon to intervene in the interests of reducing inequalities and of improving levels of social unity. Social democrats in both Britain and Sweden recognise that education can help to reduce class divisions and create a more coherent citizen identity.

The social democratic view of education can be viewed as a form of social engineering. Rather than see the education system as a place where people are graded according to skills they acquire and where inequalities in provision are not only allowed but also encouraged, social democrats see education as a way to undermine old-fashioned views and to form a new, confident and egalitarian citizenship. But even social democrats are aware that the state can be too authoritarian in its handling of the education system. The Rocard government in France, for example, turned against the centralising tendencies of French social policy and attempted to increase the independence of schools and teachers from the influence of government (Izbicki, 1989). But the value of state intervention depends upon who controls the state. It is evident that social democrats are happy to use the state to push forward their own agenda, but state intervention in itself is not valued unless it has a beneficial impact upon the social transformation of society. For social democrats, this is measured according to the extent to which class divisions and inequalities are subject to erosion.

Conclusion

Social democrats want to find ways to reduce the influence of capitalism and, in many cases, to explore alternatives to capitalism that can be introduced in a peaceful and gradual way. Social democrats do not trust the free market and therefore have very little interest in protecting its operations and gaining the active support of its defenders. For social democrats, the economy and society need to be transformed. Social democrats want to use the state in the economy, whether to coordinate it or to place it under public ownership and control. The state would also have increased jurisdiction in social affairs. Social democrats hold egalitarian views. They consider equality of opportunity, and in some cases equality of outcome, as a desirable and practical aim. Because of this, they hope to use the state to create a more equal society by guaranteeing our social rights to benefits, decent health care, suitable housing and education. By guaranteeing these rights, the social foundations of the capitalist system would be overturned and a new scale of values introduced. Although social democracy was one of the key ideologies in post-war Europe, many people seem to believe that it failed to achieve its aims and that many of its aims are no longer attractive. It should be recognised that social democracy rested upon a certain view of the class system and that it gained a lot of its support from the working class. It could be argued that traditional class divisions have been undermined by a range of welfare services and by an expansion in educational and employment opportunities. This belief that class divisions are becoming blurred has encouraged many social democrats to reinvent themselves as advocates of the 'third way'. As we shall see (in Chapter 6), the third way has allowed social democrats to redesign their ideas in response to perceived changes in the economic and social systems.

5

Neo-liberalism

With the rise of neo-liberalism, debates on the social responsibilities of the state changed direction. The ideologies covered so far attempted to varying degrees to defend, and in many cases advance, the notion that the state should be involved in the provision of a range of social services. There is of course a vast difference between Republican presidents like Eisenhower and Nixon and passionate socialists like Aneurin Bevan, but social liberalism, conservatism and social democracy shared the view for much of the post-war period that the state has at least some responsibility for the common welfare and that this welfare can be advanced by using social policies. This view is attacked mercilessly by neo-liberals. The neo-liberals, and the new right regimes they inspired, believed that the apparent consensus on the economy and on welfare had increased the power of the state to such an extent that individuals were being swamped and subjugated in the interests of the common good. For the neo-liberals, it was important to remind ourselves of the wisdom and insight contained in the thoughts of the classical liberals. It was argued that individuals need to be made responsible for their own welfare and that the state should withdraw as far as possible from economic management and social provision. This can be interpreted as a right wing reaction to the centre (and in some cases, centre-left) ideas and policies of social liberals, conservatives and social democrats. Key theorists involved in this reaction included Freidrich von Hayek, Milton Friedman and Robert Nozick. Administrations influenced by and participating in this reaction included the Thatcher governments in Britain and the Reagan governments in the United States.

Economy

Neo-liberalism consists, in part, in an attempt to revive the spirit of classical liberalism and to strip the liberal tradition of the reliance on state intervention in the economy. As we saw in the chapter on liberalism, the social liberals of the late nineteenth and early twentieth centuries argued that the free market was too unstable and that some state intervention in the economy was both prudent and necessary to protect the capitalist system. So great was their influence, that liberalism came to be associated with both the state management of the economy and with a well-funded welfare state. For the neo-liberals, this went too far and allowed for socialist-type policies to be introduced in the belief that capitalism needed to be saved from itself. It seemed to the neo-liberals that social liberals had failed to understand the value of the lessons offered by Adam Smith and that they had been far too willing to use the state to minimise the occurrence and effects of slumps in the economy. Apart from anything else, these slumps could be seen as necessary for capitalism to evolve and for the creation of the conditions under which forward-looking entrepreneurs could take advantage of the cheap labour that makes new and risky ventures possible.

For the neo-liberals, it was time to allow capitalism to regulate itself and for employers to have the freedom to make a profit. It was argued that state intervention in the economy ran against the natural order and did far too much to increase the power and jurisdiction of the state. In his passionate study *The Road to Serfdom* (1944), a book dedicated to 'socialists of all parties', Hayek argued that granting governments the power to plan the economy could lead to totalitarianism and that it gave governments power over all aspects of life because the ability to plan and control the economy '... is not merely control of a sector of human life which can be separated from the rest; it is the control of the means of all our ends' (Hayek, 1944, p. 92). For Hayek, economic freedom does not consist in being free from economic needs (a position approached, albeit timidly, by social liberals and social democrats) but in the freedom to pursue our own economic interests (Hayek, 1944, p. 100). For neo-liberals, the instabilities of capitalism are invigorating and should be welcomed. State intervention in the economy, on the other hand, was seen as a threat to freedom and harmful to the fortunes of the economy. They argued that economic progress relied upon giving free rein to the capitalist class. Nozick (1980), for example, defended capitalism and complained that Marxists in particular had failed to give sufficient weight to the entrepreneurial abilities of the minority. He balked at the injustice of people expecting to share in the successes of the capitalist class while not being willing to share in the failures (Nozick, 1980, pp. 255–262). The neo-liberals, indeed, are willing to champion the successes and the failures of capitalism in the belief that more can be gained from the operation of the economic cycle than from the authoritarian meddlings of the state.

The ideas of the neo-liberals provided governments, especially during the 1980s, with a new philosophy to counter and challenge the widespread tendency of governments to use Keynesian techniques to regulate the economy. In Britain, Margaret Thatcher attempted to recapture the spirit of classical liberalism and to promote the virtues of the free market. In her view, it was more important to encourage production rather than attempt to redistribute wealth between the affluent and the poorer sections of society. She believed that if production could be encouraged, then all would benefit as a result of a 'trickle down effect' whereby the affluent spend their money thus creating jobs for the poor. The Thatcher governments argued that enterprise was stifled in Britain by progressive taxation, deemed necessary by many liberals and social democrats to finance the welfare state. The Thatcher governments, in order to reduce taxation, deprived the state of many of its economic functions, privatised many of the nationalised industries and left unemployment to find its own level (Durham, 1989, p. 63; Heywood, 1992, p. 84; Kavanagh, 1990; Gamble, 1988). A similar degree of faith in the free market, and hostility towards government intervention in the economy, can be discerned in the ideas and policies of the Reagan governments. The Reagan administrations set out to reduce government intervention in all areas of economic and social life. Rather than seeking to manage the economy or redistribute resources through egalitarian taxation policies, the Reagan administrations hoped to remove as many of the supposed barriers to capitalism as possible. It was hoped that the business community would recognise the potential for profit and increase levels of investment, once freed from the shackles imposed by interventionist governments (Spulber, 1989). These examples go to show how neo-liberal ideas revived not only the spirit of classical liberalism but also impacted upon Conservative and Republican governments, respectively, and in so doing steered conservative ideas in a new direction.

For neo-liberals, capitalism is championed because it generates wealth and allows room for talented entrepreneurs to exercise their skills in the market place. It is also thought to serve the common good by creating more wealth and by providing a broader range of incentives. For those who think in this way, the alternative of getting the state to regulate and redistribute a relatively small and stagnant pool of resources seems rather less exciting. Neo-liberals consider it unwise and counter-productive to rely too heavily on the state to manage the economy. For them, it makes more sense to accept that the self-interest of the business class is the key motivating force behind economic activity. By helping to fuel economic growth and prosperity, capitalism can be seen as a system that will guarantee the long-term welfare of all. Armed with this renewed faith in the capitalist system, governments showed that they were willing to pull the plug on the mixed economy and allow capitalists room to expand and, if need be, to stumble and fail.

Social values

For neo-liberals, the social values supported by many social liberals, conservatives and social democrats overemphasise the importance of reducing differences and inequalities between individuals. As we have seen, these ideologies often view the individual in terms of his or her place in a social organism and argue that society needs to be moulded in a pre-determined way to improve the chances of the individual. This is believed to be a faulty approach to social issues. Indeed, the logic of neo-liberalism is that if we want to improve society we must start by liberating the individual. It could be argued that society is made up of individuals and that it has no existence of its own. Those who believe this will often be less than charitable in the way they view those who wish to use the state (or for that matter any other organisation) to mould society in accordance with some pre-conceived social model. From a neo-liberal perspective, the character of society is determined by the way that individuals behave.

Neo-liberals are often committed to the freedom of the individual, though the freedom they value is closer to Berlin's negative liberty than to any notion of positive liberty. According to Milton Friedman (1962), freedom should be the dominant value we use when considering and judging social affairs. In his view, it is not for the state or society to determine how individuals use their freedom (as long as they act within the confines of the law) as this should be left to the realm of ethics and for the individual to judge. He admitted, however, that absolute freedom to do whatever we wish was not feasible and he noted half-regretfully that anarchy would be an attractive philosophy were it not for human imperfections (Friedman, 1962, pp. 12–25). From a neo-liberal point of view, the more the government does the less free we become.

This approach to freedom can be seen in the rationale used by Conservative and Republican governments in Britain and the United States, respectively, during the 1980s. The Thatcher and Reagan governments pulled out of the economy to a large extent and argued that this was in the interests of promoting individual freedom. It is clear, however, that both governments sought to place greater limits on individual lifestyles in their broader campaigns to restore (or reinvent) family values (Pemberton, 1998; Jagger and Wright, 1999; Evans, 2004). It would appear that neo-liberals were rather more tolerant than many of their more conservative followers. Neo-liberals, like the classical liberals before them, are committed to expanding a broad range of human freedom and are suspicious of the state intervening to control the life of the individual. Such intervention can be regarded as meddling with both the sovereignty of the individual and with natural differences between people.

Neo-liberals defend the inequalities that capitalism both allows for and relies upon. It is often considered right that some people have more material wealth and social power than others. Like the classical liberals of the eighteenth and nineteenth centuries, neo-liberals place a positive value upon the existence and maintenance of inequality. Nozick (1980) believes that inequalities should be accepted even if they do not operate to everybody's advantage. He complained that egalitarians are too willing to argue that equality is a good thing and that it should always feature in theories of justice. According to Nozick, people are often critical of inequalities in income and position precisely because they see that these inequalities are earned and deserved and because this can harm their self-esteem. He considered it futile to attempt to equalise self-esteem simply by giving people equal positions in society. In his view, self-esteem is personal and varies considerably between individuals and he felt that this made attempts to equalise society unrealistic and guaranteed to fail (Nozick, 1980, pp. 241–245). This approach to inequality is designed to cast doubt upon the wisdom of using the state to blunt or eradicate the inequalities prevalent in the capitalist system.

For neo-liberals, it makes no sense for the state to promote social justice. Such ideas are thought to run counter to the natural order of things and tend to be designed by those who have very little understanding of the values embraced by their fellow citizens. Hayek (1944) was adamant that the government should not attempt to impose distributive or social justice upon its citizens. He argued that to secure such a state of affairs, the government would need to treat people differently and that it should always aspire to treat them the same. He pointed out moreover that it would be virtually impossible to secure a sufficient level of agreement on the scale of values and principles needed to secure social justice. In his view, such justice could only be achieved if absolute equality was established between citizens. However attractive this might sound, Hayek was convinced that such an aim was both unrealistic and lacking support from the majority of people (Hayek, 1944, pp. 79, 109). Neo-liberals consider it dangerous to give the state the power to discriminate against sections of the community through deliberate intervention. It was considered more prudent and just to leave things to the free flow of market forces.

Neo-liberal social values attempt to recapture the spirit of individualism and self-help and to save us from what some regard as misguided social engineering. Neo-liberals place the individual at the centre of their analysis and have little time for those social values that require the government to act in a positive way to redistribute resources and opportunities to those who 'fail' in the free market system. Collectivism is rejected firmly in favour of a neo-liberal vision of individuals competing with each other to advance their own prospects and in so doing help to keep society vibrant and alive. For neo-liberals, it is foolish to underestimate the importance of individual self-interest and to penalise the rich in the interests of bailing out those who (for whatever reason) are unable to compete successfully. They warn us of the dangers of 'dumbing down' and of attempting to appeal to the masses with promises of equality and social justice. A neo-liberal world is one where individual freedom is placed above the apparent desire to make us similar (or even the same) and one where the functions of the state are severely curtailed.

State and welfare

Given that neo-liberals extol the virtues of economic efficiency and low taxation, it should come as no surprise that they tend to be critical of the state playing a major role in the provision of welfare. Neo-liberals have been critical of supporters of the welfare state for concentrating too much upon trying to solve social problems. These problems are said to result largely from personal failings rather than from solvable economic fluctuations. Neo-liberals have criticised the broad sociological approach that looks to the state to solve problems faced by the individual and have argued that this approach has harmful effects upon the economy and will ultimately fail to achieve its goals (George and Wilding, 1994, p. 20). From a neo-liberal perspective, the state is an outsider that lacks sufficient understanding of the natural ebbs and flows of the capitalist economy and the need to provide people with incentives to do well.

Neo-liberals, like the classical liberals of the late eighteenth and nineteenth centuries, are quite fearful of the state. Nozick (1980), for example, was in favour of a minimalist state in which the state concentrated upon such things as enforcing contracts and protecting citizens from crime. He was critical of attempts to give the state a wider range of social and economic functions and he believed that attemps to establish distributive justice allowed and encouraged the state to go beyond its legitimate and limited functions. According to Nozick, the state had no right to redistribute wealth and opportunities according to some pre-conceived plan because such endeavours would result in violating the rights of individuals (Nozick, 1980, pp. ix–xi, 230, 238, 172–173). For neo-liberals, individuals need to be protected from the power of government and this applied especially to when the government took it upon itself to mess with the impersonal and largely rational operations of the free market.

According to neo-liberals, the welfare state poses a significant threat to the freedom of the individual. As we have seen, neo-liberals are firm believers in individual responsibility and in natural inequalities. The logic of their argument states that freedom and independence are required for dignity and self-respect and that interventionist governments undermine these virtues. It could be argued that attending to our entire social needs, the welfare state can deprive us of the need to use our initiative and make us dependent upon the state. According to this line of thought, it was inappropriate to expect the state to intervene in such ways. Hayek (1959) argued that interventionist governments harm liberty because, by redistributing resources, the government discriminates against some people in favour of others. Rather than intervene in such a coercive way, Hayek believes that the state should restrict itself to providing for the physical security of the population and that it should provide public amenities like parks, museums, theatres and sports facilities (Hayek, 1959, pp. 92–94). Neo-liberals do not talk about people having the right to welfare because this right would appear to be at the expense of other people. Instead, for neo-liberals, it is important that individuals find ways to improve their own circumstances and attend to their own needs.

The logic of neo-liberalism can be seen quite clearly in the social policies of the Thatcher and Reagan governments during the 1980s. Thatcher is famed for reminding us that there is 'no such thing as society' and for advancing the view that we are simply individuals pursuing our own interests. In the hope of cutting into the foundations of the so-called 'dependency culture', she reduced direct taxation (and the revenue that these taxes provided for the welfare state) and told the British people to take care of their own welfare. Rather than rely upon the state, the British people were asked to work within their own families and look out for their neighbours. This was considered better than receiving help from the state (Kavanagh, 1990; Evans, 2004). The Reagan governments likewise did what they could to reduce state expenditure on social services and justified this on the grounds that welfare provision undermined individual responsibility and the stability of families (Sandel, 1996). For these Conservative and Republican governments, attempts to reduce the scope of state provision was regarded as necessary to strengthen the resolve of the individual to survive and do well in the capitalist system.

For neo-liberals, the welfare state runs counter to their most cherished social values. Instead of allowing individuals to reap the rewards of their own labour, the welfare state could be seen as compensating (and even rewarding) people for their failings. Neo-liberals, and many of their conservative followers, want the state to withdraw as far as possible from the provision of social services. Conservative administrations in Japan, New Zealand and to a less extent Germany instituted significant cuts in welfare provision (see Bryson, 1992; Leisering, 2001; Davey, 2001). In a neo-liberal world, individuals would be left to provide for themselves and their families and they would certainly get considerably less from the state. The welfare state would be replaced, at least in theory, by a thriving entrepreneurial culture that would operate largely unfettered by the state. Instead of responding to and providing for our social needs, the neo-liberal state would have limited functions and limited resources at its disposal. Taxes would be reduced and individuals would be left with more of their own income to spend. The welfare state would not, of course, disappear altogether. Like the classical liberals, the neo-liberals recognise that the state would have to assume some responsibility for the common welfare. This responsibility, however, would be limited to intervening only when necessary rather than because it is in the interests of social justice.

Welfare and social policies

Neo-liberals are actively committed to reducing the role of the state in the provision of social services. From a neo-liberal perspective, the state is clumsy, wasteful and thoroughly unreliable in its handling of economic and social matters. Given this, they argue that attempts should be made to reduce the scope of what the state does and to intervene only when necessary. Individuals are asked to take more control over their own lives and provide for themselves rather than rely upon a benevolent state or (from a neo-liberal perspective even worse) a state committed to reducing inequalities and remoulding society according to some utopian plan.

Benefits

For neo-liberals, unemployment benefit is the least attractive and most problematic feature of the welfare state. By providing benefits for people who are not in paid employment, the unemployment benefit system runs counter to the capitalist ethos. As the success of the capitalist system relies upon individuals being willing to work, payments given to those who do not work could be seen to be counter-productive. The tone of neo-liberal views on unemployment benefits can be discerned in Hayek's study *The Constitution of Liberty* (1960). Hayek argues that although the unemployment benefit system should remain in some form or another, it should aim to reduce poverty rather than be used to further the egalitarian aims of centre-left governments. A firm believer in self-help, he claimed that the more the state provides benefits the less people are inclined to provide for themselves and that this has a disastrous effect upon individual initiative. It was considered wrong, moreover, for the state to attempt to impose left-wing ideas of social justice upon society because this involved the state making value judgements about what people deserved and using coercive measures to reshuffle the social deck. Rather than attempt to engineer a state of social justice,

Hayek claimed that the state should as far as possible reduce some of its social functions and that it was far more important for the government to find ways to reduce the problem of unemployment than to provide more money for people when they are unemployed. Whereas Keynes believed that the state had a responsibility to alleviate unemployment by managing demand in the economy, Hayek believed that the free market should be left to find its own level and that the state should assist the market by curtailing the power of the unions and by making sure that the availability of unemployment benefit does not act as a deterrent to work. The aim was to produce a new generation of flexible workers, willing to engage with market forces. Although the benefits system would not be disbanded, its aim would be to provide a basic level of income to alleviate poverty rather than to redistribute income. All benefits would be meanstested to ensure that only people in need would qualify for assistance. The benefits system was to be divorced from all notions of social justice and be reformed to provide no more than a safety net for the very poor (Hayek, 1960, pp. 45, 258–305).

Echoes of this theoretical position can be seen in the policies of conservative administrations in the 1980s and 1990s. Conservative governments in Britain and Republican administrations in the United States were active in their campaigns to toughen regulations on access to benefits. Like Hayek, the Thatcherites argued that poverty could be overcome by encouraging economic growth rather than by redistributing income through progressive taxation. They argued that absolute poverty no longer existed in Britain and that the poor were benefiting from the so-called 'trickle-down effect'. According to this line of thought, the poor will not be made appreciably better off by taking money from the rich and that those who create wealth (primarily, the entrepreneurs) deserve the lion's share. Thatcherites attempted to wean people off the benefits system. This involved making it more difficult for them to receive benefits, by reducing the real value of benefits and by encouraging self-help. Although the Thatcherites attempted to cut back on benefits, spending on unemployment benefit continued to rise during the Thatcher era. The large-scale unemployment that accompanied the Thatcher years made it virtually impossible to cut unemployment benefit in real terms and the benefits budget continued to increase regardless of the self-help rhetoric voiced by the Conservative government (Alcock, 1998; Ditch, 1998). The aim of cutting benefits was not realistic given the economic policies of the Conservative government. Indeed, it could be argued that the free market did not inject enough life into the economy to lessen demands upon the benefits system.

A similar pattern emerged in the United States. The Reagan government was particularly critical of what it perceived to be excesses in the benefits system. It was argued that the provision of benefits had created a disincentive to work because people were cushioned from the harsh realities of having no job or insufficient income. In May 1981, Reagan attempted to introduce legislation to cut the benefits bill and to restrict access to disability benefit. Although Congress rejected these measures, the Reagan administration did cut spending on health and made it tougher for people to qualify for benefits and for food stamps (Mishra, 1990, p. 21). Reagan cut the social services block grant by 20 per cent and by 1983 almost 300,000 people had lost their benefits as a result of tightening the tests for eligibility. The government made savage cuts to the benefits accessed by the poorest sections of the community, particularly Aid to Families with Dependent Children, while reducing taxation for the more prosperous sections of American society (Clarke and Fox Piven, 2001, p. 34; Scaperlanda, 1993). Benefit cuts are often seen as a way to reduce welfare expenditure and thereby make it possible to reward the economically productive with cuts in their tax bills. In this way, neo-liberals and new right conservative administrations seek to reward success and penalise what is often regarded as failure.

The view that poverty arises due to personal failings creates a reluctance to go much beyond a minimal benefits system. If individuals are to blame for their own poverty, why should the taxpayer have to foot the bill? This line of argument was used to dismantle sections of the welfare state during the 1980s. It assumes that people are poor because of laziness, incompetence or lack of moral fibre and that providing benefits will merely add to their sloth and place a burden upon society. It is argued that working people are effectively subsidising the poor and that at least some of the recipients of this help are unworthy of support. This interpretation of poverty leads to harsh social policies that stigmatise the poor and forces them off benefits. The solution to long-term poverty and the economic decline of the nation is thought to lie partly in making it more difficult for people to qualify for unemployment benefits. It is argued that, if deprived of a long-term safety net, the unemployed will be forced to make themselves fit for work and thereby fuel the state with the taxes they pay rather than feed off the state with the benefits they consume.

Housing

Neo-liberals have tended to be very critical of the public provision of housing and have argued consistently in favour of private ownership or giving private landlords opportunities to make profits. Hayek (1960) claimed that the public supply of housing tends to replace, rather than supplement, private rented accommodation and that if the government attempts to provide superior quality housing to that provided by private property owners, then council tenants, who are often among the poorest in the community, will get better housing than those further up the economic ladder. In Hayek's view, extending public provision, which would deprive the private sector of income and make the poor increasingly dependent upon the government, could not rectify this disparity. Hayek (1991) pointed out that although state supply and control of housing might have been useful as an emergency measure following the devastation caused by the Second World War, public provision of subsidised housing cannot be sustained in the long term. Apart from the heavy costs incurred in building properties and in subsidising rents, public provision of housing was thought to divert resources away from productive industry and expand consumption '... at the expense of capital formation' (Hayek, 1991, p. 309). This could be seen as a drain on the nation's resources and as a threat to both the private sector and to the profits that can be accrued from renting out property. It could also be seen as a threat to individual liberty, in that it expands the role of government over one of our most fundamental needs.

This preference for private sector renting and for private ownership of property featured in the policies of new right administrations during the 1980s. The Thatcher governments attacked the provision of social housing and argued in favour of a 'property owning democracy'. By the late 1970s, it was recognised that old style council provision had become unpopular with tenants and that the demand for council housing was in decline. The Thatcher governments seized upon this to introduce its Housing Act of 1980, which gave council tenants the right to buy the property they had hitherto been renting. This was seen in part as a way to raise money for the councils concerned, who were allowed to retain 25 per cent of the revenue for sales and use the remainder to pay off their debts. Private home ownership was also encouraged during the 1980s through the deregulation of building societies, which allowed building societies to offer mortgages to people on relatively low incomes. While housing policy in the early 1980s was characterised by encouraging private ownership, by the late 1980s the Thatcher government relied rather more upon cutting back on building council houses. By placing restrictions upon local authority borrowing, councils were unable to invest in council housing and were forced to increase their rents. The Thatcher governments were unwilling to support the continued maintenance of council housing, so looked for ways to bring the private sector into social housing. The 1985 Housing Act gave local authorities the right to transfer its housing stock to the private sector. This gave rise to the formation of Housing Action Trusts and, following the Housing Act of 1988, council tenants were given the right to choose their own landlord. Within a year, almost half a million council tenants transferred to new social landlords. Since then, local authorities have increasingly abandoned the function of providing council housing and have concentrated far more upon overseeing the provision of housing in their areas (Durden, 2000, pp. 139–143).

The Reagan governments were particularly keen to reduce the role of government in housing ventures. Reagan had inherited the Department of Housing and Urban Development (HUD) from previous (more progressive) regimes but did all he could to limit its power and role in subsidising the construction of housing for people on low incomes. He reduced the size of HUD and appointed leaders who had neither the experience nor interest in developing the activities of the organisation. According to Michael Schaller, HUD '... stood out as a cash cow ripe for plunder' (Schaller, 1994, p. 117). The Reagan government cut federal assistance for new housing programmes by 70 per cent during its first term in office and although it was unable to pull out altogether from housing, the Reagan government remained committed to minimising Federal involvement. This withdrawal by the federal government contributed to rapid increases in the costs of renting private accommodation and to a marked increase in homelessness. On the positive side, however, there was an increase in initiatives for low-income housing such as those programmes led by non-profit making Community Development Corporations (see Hays, 2001, pp. 88, 175–176). It could be argued, indeed, that withdrawing central government from the provision of housing can create a gap for other organisations to fill. Problems can of course occur when this gap is filled by an unrestrained private sector.

According to advocates and disciples of neo-liberalism, the state should keep as far as possible out of the direct provision of housing. Rather than rely upon direct public provision of housing, people are given the choice of renting from the private or voluntary sectors or of buying their own homes. Extending home ownership is definitely regarded in a positive way. Owning your own home can be seen as a way of encouraging people to stake their place in society, to establish roots and assume a greater degree of civic responsibility. It could be argued that once we own property, we are more likely to display the kind of characteristics valued by neo-liberals. In particular, unemployment is, in the majority of cases, no longer an option for people who are buying their own homes. By cutting back on public housing and by pushing people towards the private sector, the government has yet another tool to force people off benefits and to undermine the dependency culture.

Health

Neo-liberals have been extremely active in calling for the provision of health care to be subjected to the discipline exerted by market forces. Just as many conservatives in the 1940s believed that a National Health Service would be a bottomless pit that consumed resources while failing to satisfy all health needs, so neo-liberals have been vocal in their condemnation of 'socialised medicine' and in demanding that people shoulder the financial costs of the health care they receive. Neo-liberals have been critical of socialised medicine for many years. Hayek (1960), for example, was very sceptical about the value of free health care. He argued that those who recommend free health care do so because they assume that health needs can be measured objectively, that all health needs should be satisfied and that a free health care system virtually pays for itself by making more people healthy enough to work and to pay taxes. In Hayek's view, many of our health needs are subjective and should not be satisfied automatically by the state. He was concerned not only with the cost of free health care but also with the power it could conceivably give to the state. Like British conservatives at the end of the Second World War, he argued that the personal bond between medical practitioners and their patients would be undermined by making medics servants of the state and that the government of the day would be given yet another tool it could use to coerce the public. In rather melodramatic terms, he pointed to the way in which the state medical system had been used and abused in the Soviet Union as 'an instrument of industrial discipline' (Hayek, 1960, pp. 297–300). Driven by the perceived need to contain costs incurred in either running or subsidising health care programmes, neo-liberals are inclined to argue that it is inappropriate for the state to intervene too directly in the provision of health care.

Although the Thatcher government in Britain was ideologically in favour of people taking out private insurance to cover their health care, it had also inherited the responsibility of running the National Health Service. Acknowledging that it was unable to gain support for privatising the National Health Service, it devised a number of ways to cut spending on health care by introducing such managerial techniques as the internal market. By introducing market principles into the health service, the customer replaced the patient and services were rationed on a more explicit basis. The internal market made hospitals into financially independent trusts, in which the income they received depended upon the services they provided. GPs also gained control over their own budgets and the money they received depended upon the number of patients on their books. Part of this budget was used to purchase health care from hospitals, which competed for business by attempting to offer the most cost-effective treatment (BBC2, 9.07.1995; Alcock, 1996, pp. 24, 70–71). The introduction of market principles made sense as a cost-cutting exercise. By giving each branch of the health service a budget to work within, health care professionals were told that they would be unable to provide all patients with the health care they needed, especially if this involved a significant transfer of funds from GPs to hospitals. Hospitals, likewise, were taught to devise formulae to help set priorities on quasi-scientific grounds. Health professionals and health managers started to talk about prioritising treatment for people whose quality of life would benefit the most and for the longest period. This formula, which was expressed in terms of Quality Adjusted Life Years, meant that priority was often given to relatively young and healthy members of the community over the elderly who would, almost by definition, benefit for a shorter amount of time from the treatment they receive (Busfield, 2000, pp. 150–169; Taylor and Hawley, 2004). While such measures are consistent with the economic criteria employed by the new right, they certainly fall foul of many of the founding principles of the British National Health Service.

Republican governments in the United States also attempted to reduce state expenditure on health care. During the 1980s, the American government tried to push people towards employment-based health insurance by placing more restrictions on Medicare and Medicaid, thus discouraging health care providers from treating people who relied upon state assistance. Health Maintenance Organisation's initiatives were expanded to provide health care in return for an annual fee and, by the late 1980s, approximately 12 per cent of the American public subscribed to this form of health cover (Clarke and Fox Piven, 2001). Further protection was, however, introduced for the elderly. A reserve fund was established in 1988 that would come into effect to assist the elderly once their original Medicare benefits had been depleted (Moroney and Krysik, 1998, p. 129). Commentators still complain, however, about the lack of a comprehensive health care programme and acknowledge that this stems from the reluctance of political leaders (and deeply ingrained ideological hostility) towards federal government intervention in social and economic life (Levey, 1990). We should remember that private health insurance has always been more important in America than in Britain, largely because the United States lacks a strong social democratic tradition and because the other key ideologies have shied away from 'socialised medicine'.

Government involvement in the provision of health care became quite unpopular during the 1980s. Governments driven in part by neo-liberal ideas attacked state involvement and did what they could to reduce the health budget. Right wing governments in the United States and in Britain attempted to encourage individuals to make sufficient provision to cover the costs of the health care they need and receive. Similar pressures were also exerted on the health systems in Sweden and in New Zealand, where state expenditure was reduced and market mechanisms introduced in the belief that this would make service provision more efficient (Whitehead, Evandrou, Haglund and Diderichsen, 1997; Davey, 2001). Efficiency apart, the case against state involvement is often based upon the belief that health is a personal possession and that we should be responsible for our own health care. From a neo-liberal perspective, it could be argued that assuming this responsibility is in the long-term interests of the individual because the individual would ultimately have to pay the price for engaging in health-damaging behaviour.

Education

The attitudes of neo-liberals towards the education system contain a tension between wanting to revive competition between education providers while turning educators away from the social liberal approaches once deemed essential for a progressive education. For influential theorists like Milton and Rose Friedman, the education system was in severe need of reform because, since the 1930s, governments had played too active a role in financing, manipulating and directing the system rather than listening to the demands made by parents. They believed it was necessary to move away from centralised control and to return control to local bodies that would be far more responsive to the needs of parents (Friedman and Friedman, 1985, pp. 138, 146). Friedman argued that government involvement in education does not necessarily benefit the poorer sections of the community and that government subsidies of higher education in particular tend to benefit middle class families. Instead of subsidising students in higher education, Friedman was in favour of a loan system. For elementary and secondary education, his preference lay in providing vouchers that could be used by parents to purchase or pay towards the education they want for their children (Friedman, 1975, pp. 9, 248, 260–279). For neo-liberals, it is important to free the education system as far as possible from the direct control of the government. Some conservative governments shared this sentiment.

Mrs Thatcher was determined to overturn many of the educational policies of the post-war years and undermine the trend towards egalitarianism in education. She attacked the higher education system and introduced a series of harsh cuts during the early 1980s. Her measures were so savage that Oxford University made a point of refusing to grant her an honorary degree on the grounds that her policies were inflicting 'deep and systematic damage' on the British education system (Evans, 2004, p. 141). The school system was also subjected to radical change. Her government introduced measures to extend parental choice in the education of their children and numerous conservative councils reintroduced grammar schools. Under the provisions of the 1988 Education Reform Act, parents were given more choice in their children's education, schools were given the freedom to opt out of local authority control and standards were formalised and enshrined within the first truly national curriculum in British education. This national curriculum was intended to strip the subjects taught in school of their vague or contradictory nature. History, for example, was to be refocused on British events. 'Facts' were given preference over the importance of appreciating different interpretations (Evans, 2004; Todd, Ware and Taylor, 2002). This approach to education combined greater freedom in the way that schools managed their own affairs, while imposing a set curriculum on state schools. This curriculum allowed relatively little room for the more exotic approaches to education pioneered by progressive educationalists since the 1960s.

The Reagan governments attempted to reduce the managerial roles of central government and empower parents to make constructive choices about the education of their children. During the presidential elections in 1980, Ronald Reagan pledged that his administration would reduce federal control over education by returning control to local communities, introduce tuition tax credits to empower parents in choosing suitable education for their children, abolish the bussing programme which had been set up to combat racial segregation and abolish the Department of Education which had become a powerful political lobby group (Friedman and Friedman, 1985, p. 139). Fellow Republican George Bush senior presented himself in 1988 as the 'education president'. He wanted to introduce a package of education reforms that would include merit pay for teachers, development of new innovative schools financed by the public and private sectors and an education voucher system to assist low- and middle-income families. Bush found, however, that he was unable to gain support for his proposals and that right wing Republicans withheld their support because they objected to the lack of attention paid to discipline and traditional values (Greene, 2000; Mervin, 1996).

Some education systems were transformed during the 1980s under the influence of neo-liberal ideas, mixed with more than a hint of authoritarian conservatism. Whereas many liberals and social democrats had been enthusiastic about the liberating effects of education and about how education could transform the class makeup of society, Conservative and Republican governments during the 1980s attempted to put an end to (or at least suspend) permissive tendencies in the education system. At the same time, there was a greater emphasis upon private provision and upon reducing direct government management and funding of schools. This was a period of cuts, both economically and in terms of the range of the education offered to people. A standardised menu was devised in Britain in the hope of returning the education system to its traditional concerns and away from its apparently brief flirtation with progressive ideas. One thing is for sure, the education system was considered far too important to be left in the hands of those who had taken to heart the social liberal or social democratic ideals of the post-war period.

Conclusion

The economic and social foundations of neo-liberalism concentrate upon liberating the individual from the undue influence of the state. Embracing the competitive ethos and in the firm conviction that the energy and vision of the few can in turn create opportunities for the many, the neo-liberals along with new right administrations throughout the world sought to reduce the economic activities and responsibilities of the state and to rely considerably more upon the operations of the free market. They believed that this would allow for lower rates of taxation and that it would increase efficiency in the economy and in those social services where an internal market could be established. Citizens were told that they should aspire to independence, work hard for their money and provide for themselves and their families rather than rely upon the state. They argued that the welfare state was a threat to the freedom and inititiative of the individual and that it stripped people of their will to succeed. The solutions included making cuts to social provision and making the welfare state a last resort rather than a comfort zone for the citizen body. The neo-liberal world was one where inequalities were recognised as natural, important and invigorating. Social justice had no place in their designs. The new right administrations continued to provide the familiar range of social services, albeit reluctantly and with an eye to making us less dependent upon the state and more willing to invest part of our income in private provision. This was an important turning point in the development of welfare regimes. Fearlessly, the neo-liberals and new right administrations transformed the expectations that many people had of the welfare state and seemed to convince sizeable sections of the electorate that a society based upon self-interest was more efficient, more rewarding and more sustainable than one that pandered to the poor. This view of welfare will no doubt continue to influence those who are looking for ways to cut taxation and to allow for the continuance of inequalities.

6

Third Way

Recoiling from the jolt administered by neo-liberals and the new right, the centre and centre-left had to find their balance once again. The Democratic Party in America had been out of office for 12 years and the Labour Party had been stuck in opposition to the Conservatives for 18 years. There can be little doubt that these parties regained their popularity and sense of direction by reassessing their aims and by devising a 'third way' between their old policy agenda and that of their main opponents. For Bill Clinton, the third way was situated between the old-style social liberalism of the Democratic Party and the new right perspectives of the Republicans. The new cocktail emphasised individual responsibility alongside a commitment to the community. It promised to serve the interests of the rich and poor and establish a new balance between the public and private sectors (Clinton, 2002). For Tony Blair, the third way meant maintaining the social democratic commitment to social justice but combining this with the (neo) liberal faith in the '... primacy of individual liberty in the market economy' (Blair, 2003a, p. 28). In both cases, the third way meant increasing the role of government in economic and social affairs while stopping short of the level of intervention once supported by the Democratic and Labour Parties. The following account of the third way will pay particular attention to the ideas of Anthony Giddens and Will Hutton and to the policy initiatives of the Clinton administrations in the United States and the Blair governments in Britain.

Economy

The economic ideas of the third way can be seen, in many ways, as a reaction to the extremes of the free market economics of the neo-liberals and the interventionist ideas of many social liberals, conservatives and social democrats in the post-war period. Rather than call upon the government to intervene directly to control or manage the economy, supporters of the third way are more likely to talk about government coordinating a variety of sectors and empowering individuals to make the best of themselves and their communities.

Anthony Giddens (1998a), for example, believes that the economy needs to combine the best of the public and the private sectors. Rather than rest upon extensive state intervention or the free market, he claimed that a mixed economy should be established in which people are encouraged to take risks while having support from the state. Indeed, he believed that the state should invest in the infrastructure and in so doing it could help to develop a vibrant entrepreneurial economy in which there exists '... synergy between public and private sectors, utilizing the dynamism of markets but with the public interest in mind' (Giddens, 1998, p. 100). This approach would seem to recognise both the value of capitalism and the limitations of the state.

For those who believe that a third way can be devised and applied in economic affairs, capitalism appears to have a lot to offer. This might apply particularly if capitalism can be harnessed for the public good and made more inclusive. As we have seen, capitalism can be divisive and encourage the pursuit of short-term profit rather than long-term sustainable development. For Will Hutton (1995) (Channel 4, 18.06.1996), the problem with free market economics is that it creates social exclusion and perpetuates adversarial relations between the classes. In his view, working in accordance with the rhythms of the free market allows the business community to treat labour as expendable and unworthy of long-term contracts and suitable training. Hutton's alternative consists in what he calls 'stakeholder capitalism', in which workers and management are encouraged to develop long-term relationships based upon trust rather than market principles and in which workers are involved in making key decisions in the workplace. These kinds of arrangements were deemed necessary for capitalism to function smoothly and to serve a broader range of interests.

Beneath the surface of the third way, and its apparent support for capitalism, lies the belief that it is no longer prudent to be overt in supporting high levels of government intervention in the economy. Even if such intervention does not necessarily lead to a gridlocked command economy, neo-liberals seem to have convinced a generation of voters that using the sate in this way can be both expensive and counter-productive in propping up those who lack the energy, drive and initiative to survive in the market. For supporters of the third way, the era of such high levels of state intervention is in the past. Giddens (1998), for example, points out that the globalised economy is undermining some of the powers of the nation state and that it is unrealistic to expect the state to perform all the functions it had previously carried out during the age of Keynesian economic management (Giddens, 1998, pp. 29–32). The message appears to be clear. Supporters of the third way would argue that the state can and should be used to energise and coordinate individual and communal effort rather than to take on extensive managerial roles in the economy.

The third way approach can be seen in the policies of the Blair government in Britain. Blair (1998a) argued that it is futile to fight against the private sector, as the private sector is the main generator of wealth. Instead of attempting to curtail or circumvent private enterprise, Blair is in favour of the state establishing a partnership with the business sector in which the state helps to educate citizens with appropriate skills and encourages long-term sustainable growth through prudent management of the economy. For Blair, some government intervention in the economy is essential '... to protect the weak and ensure that all gain some of the benefit of economic progress' (Blair, 1998a, p. 11, see also pp. 8–11). It is clear, however, that such intervention would not stretch to nationalising key industries and to the level of intervention championed by many leaders of the Labour Party in the post-war period. To the pioneers of the social democratic state, Blair's third way would probably seem very tame.

Social values

Advocates of the third way have shown a definite interest in combining elements of liberalism and social democracy. This desire to find a new synthesis owes at least something to the belief that social democratic values need to be adapted to suit a more individualist political climate. While Giddens (1998) denies that we live in the 'me generation' and believes that people are certainly aware of moral issues and concerns, he claims that 'new individualism' has taken hold and that it had far more to do with placing value upon individual achievement and entitlement than with ignorance and neglect of each other. For Giddens, we live in an age of 'moral transition' rather than one of 'moral decay' (Giddens, 1998, p. 36). For supporters of the third way, it makes sense to expand our freedom and encourage individual initiative while making sure that citizens are empowered to take advanatge of their freedoms.

According to the third way, freedom and empowerment go hand in hand. The individual is not left to fend for him or herself and it is argued that people need to be helped to realise their potential. The Blair government, for example, declares its commitment to the sovereignty of the individual while maintaining that the state can facilitate personal development by supporting people in the choices they make and by extending the range of opportunities open to the individual through such things as education and training (Department of Health, 2004; Reid, 2004; Civil Renewal Unit, 2005). This view of freedom is considerably more compassionate than the sink-or-swim approach of the neo-liberals, but arguably less prescriptive than the extremes of positive liberty. In this way, supporters of the third way can argue that they are sensitive to the needs of the individual for both personal space and social support.

Like many social democrats, those who support the third way are often concerned with challenging gross inequalities in society. Third way logic states that the problem is not merely the existence and extent of poverty but also the levels of social exclusion. Giddens (1998) warned that large-scale inequalities in society are apt to threaten social cohesion, create widespread conflict and disaffection and harm society by failing to make the most of the skills and abilities at our disposal (Giddens, 1998, p. 40). He was clearly worried about high levels of social exclusion affecting both the rich (who withdraw from society in gated communities or by accessing private education and health care) and the poor (who experience poverty in a variety of ways). Giddens points out that exclusion is about '... the mechanisms that act to detach groups of people from the social mainstream' (Giddens, 1998a, p. 104). For the third way, this social exclusion must be tackled in the interest of social cohesion. In many ways, this echoed the mentality and sense of urgency pervading one nation conservatism because it shows quite clearly that harsh inequalities can have a detrimental impact upon all sections of society, not merely upon the poor.

Rather than focus primarily on the problems of inequality, Giddens argued that it could be more fruitful to clarify our understanding of the meaning of equality. For Giddens, the true meaning of equality rested in a respect for diversity and an understanding that it must contribute towards social inclusion and the cultivation of human potential. Rather than see equality in terms of redistributing resources 'after the event' (perhaps through progressive taxation), Giddens believed that it was more important to 'redistribute possibilities' by making use of deliberately inclusive policies. An inclusive society is one where all citizens have opportunities to be involved in the public sphere and where people have access to education and work (Giddens, 1998, pp. 101–103). For supporters of the third way, equality of opportunity is more important than equality of outcome. This shift in emphasis takes the third way a considerable distance from the ideas and policies outlined by many of the earlier social democrats and it can be detected in a lot of the ideological flavour of Blair's Labour government. According to Blair (1998), true equality of opportunity does not mean 'dull uniformity in welfare provision and public services' but rather the spread of real opportunities throughout society (Blair, 1998a, p. 3). Once again, the emphasis is placed firmly upon empowering individuals.

Theorists and practitioners of the third way are adamant that the promotion of social justice should not been confused with the pursuit of equality of outcome and with a programme of massive public expenditure, financed through imposing a heavy tax burden upon the electorate (Blair and Schroeder, 1999). Third way theorists have argued that social justice can be realised under capitalism. For the Commission on Social Justice (1993), the case for social justice rested upon the recognition that we are all social creatures who rely upon each other and have rights as well as responsibilities. Social justice is thought to rest upon recognising the equal worth of all citizens, the right of everybody to have their basic needs met, that people need access to a wide range of opportunities and that '... unjust inequalities should be reduced and where possible eliminated' (Commission on Social Justice, 1993, p. 62). These sentiments were clearly embraced by Tony Blair (1998a and 2003a) who argued that social justice consists in recognising the 'equal worth of each individual' and that everything should be done to put an end to discrimination and to prejudice. Rather than embrace equality of outcome, which he associates with the stifling policies of the old left, Blair believes in the pursuit of true equality of opportunity (Blair, 2003a, pp. 29–30). Gordon Brown argues likewise that each person should have an equal chance to fulfil his or her potential and that this involves giving people opportunities to find suitable work, to engage in lifelong learning and to have access to culture (Brown, 2003). Equality of opportunity, it should be appreciated, allows for a greater degree of diversity and inequality of outcome. It allows for meritocracy, condemns uniformity and equates progress with the destruction of barriers to social mobility. Because of this, it is an idea associated more readily with liberalism than with social democracy.

The social values of the third way can be viewed as a cogent critique of the uncompromising individualism promoted by neo-liberals. Arguing that neo-liberals went too far in praising the achievements of the few at the expense of the many, supporters of the third way claim that the inequalities common in capitalist societies do considerable damage to the social fabric and to the real lives of communities. Searching for ways to enhance social cohesion, the third way attacks the root causes of social exclusion and attempts to encourage us to view the solutions to social problems in a holistic way. Like some forms of liberalism, the third way promotes equality of opportunity and argues that social justice can be attained under capitalism. For its supporters, individuals must be viewed in social context and be given real opportunities to take advantage of their freedoms. According to this view, true freedom relies upon us being empowered rather than left to our own devices. As we will see, this allows for the state to intervene in a positive way to assist in individual and community development.

State and welfare

For supporters of the third way, it is important to look for ways to retain the welfare state in a modified form while seeking to reduce the extent to which we rely upon the state. The third way seeks to grant to the state a positive role in guiding society towards a more just social and economic system, but it is argued that this role should be to 'steer' rather than to 'row'. Blair, indeed, claims that we must recognise that there are limits to what the state can do and that, instead of relying upon extensive state activity, the state needs to forge partnerships with the voluntary sector. The so-called enabling state would thus strengthen rather than weaken civil society by allowing a variety of groups to make their own distinctive contributions to the social good (Blair, 2003a, p. 131). One of the primary functions of the enabling state is to look at a range of social problems, which had previously come under the remit of the welfare state, and to find new solutions that invite contributions from the state and from other agencies. Instead of expecting the state to solve these problems alone, the enabling state was to act as the prime initiator and coordinator of broader civic activity.

Advocates of the third way believe that they are developing a new theory of the state in which the relative extremes of social democracy and neo-liberalism are avoided. Giddens (1998) claimed that whereas social democrats have traditionally wanted to expand the range of functions performed by the state and neo-liberals have wanted to shrink the state, the third way seeks to reconstruct the state by decentralising decision making and by making the state more responsive to a broader range of influences. For Giddens, the state cannot guarantee social cohesion. Indeed, it was considered more important for individuals to assume more responsibility for their own actions and lifestyles and for us to '... find a new balance between individual and collective responsibility' (Giddens, 1998, p. 37). Blair (1998a) argued likewise that the traditional left and right had overstated the influence of the state in shaping the character of society. Whereas the left argued that true freedom cannot be achieved without a strong state, the right had argued conversely that freedom relied upon dismantling the state. He complained that the old left allowed civil socety to be swamped by the state and that neo-liberals and their conservative followers had retreated too far from using the state on the assumption that the gap would be filled spontaneously with private intiative and 'civic activism'. For Blair, the state is just one of the actors in society. It was argued that it could serve the common interest to a far greater extent by forging links with the private sector and with voluntary organisations. In this way, the state could be used as 'an enabling force' to protect communities and voluntary sector organisations and to encourage their growth.

Theorists and practitioners of the third way have severe reservations about the size and responsibilities of the old welfare state. They recognise that the welfare state, especially in Britain, had been created and maintained by liberals, conservatives and social democrats to alleviate post-war problems and that many of these problems had either been minimised by the welfare state or proved to be impervious to the influence of the state. Giddens (1998) argued that when welfare systems sought to alleviate the problems of the poor without any real regard for other sections of society, these attempts created social divisions rather than social unity. In his view, the welfare system needs to be restructured so that it benefits as much of the population as possible and that this could help to '… generate a common morality of citizenship' (Giddens, 1998, p. 108). For Giddens, a restructured welfare system must incorporate the values of social justice and focus upon investing in people and in encouraging risk-taking. The welfare system, which could be run by the state alongside other agencies in the community, was seen by Giddens as part of a 'social investment state'. He hoped that this system could nurture the potential within us all and encourage constructive risk-taking. He claimed that we are increasingly subject to new forms of risk (largely because of rapid developments in the economy) and that we should be encouraged to take control over our own lives and to advance our own interests and positions rather than look to the state to provide for our needs (Giddens, 1998, pp. 116–128). The vision was one of dynamic individuals working in a vibrant civil society rather than of passive citizens waiting for the state to bestow its favour.

Key figures in the development of the third way have wanted to make sure that they are not mistaken for advocates of extravagant welfare policies. During the presidential election campaign in 1991, Bill Clinton promised to 'end welfare as we know it'. His aim was to convince people that the receipt of welfare benefits should be viewed as a 'second chance' en route to new work rather than as a way of life (Clinton, 1996). Clinton was never a strong supporter of the Roosevelt vision of society. Although the name of Roosevelt appeared in some of his more vacuous speeches, it is clear that he was intent on moving the Democratic Party away from the legacy of Roosevelt-style liberalism. In his 1996 presidential campaign, he promised that his policies were going to be different from his Democratic predecessors and that he was not going to introduce 'wildly liberal measures' on welfare. Liberal concerns were replaced by a more business-friendly policy agenda that, for some commentators, made Clinton the most conservative Democratic president since the 1930s (Leuchtenburg, 1999). For Clinton, the third way exists between the liberalism traditionally associated with the Democratic Party and the neo-liberal or new right policies of the Republican governments of the 1980s. This third way consisted in backing away from the progressive era of Lyndon Johnson in particular and in reminding American citizens that they must recognise and act upon the responsibilities they have for their own welfare and for their own communities.

A similar sense of cautious reformism characterised the third way in Europe. Blair and Schroeder claimed that they were interested in modernising the welfare state and in finding '… new ways of expressing solidarity and responsibility to others without basing the motivation for economic activity on pure undiluted self-interest' (Blair and Schroeder, 1999, p. 7). Blair (1998a) acknowledged that the post-war welfare state in Britain was instrumental in lifting people out of poverty but he argued that it should now respond to changes in the labour market and in family structures. In his view, the future of welfare provision relied upon forging long-term partnerships between the public and private sectors (Blair, 1998, p. 14). Although New Labour envisages a smaller welfare state than many of its social democratic predecessors, and relies to a far greater extent upon the private sector, the Blair government remains committed to eradicating at least some forms of social injustice. New Labour made a commitment in its first term of office to tackle social exclusion and the problems of people being cut off from mainstream society. In *Bringing Britain Together* (1998) the Labour government claimed that social exclusion consisted in a series of linked problems that included unemployment, poor housing, bad health and exposure to high crime rates and that these problems required a comprehensive social programme that dealt with each facet of social exclusion (see also Social Exclusion Unit, 2000). Gordon Brown, for example, acknowledged that a decent social programme should include, at the very least, a '... minimum wage, a tax and benefit system that helps people into work, the best possible level of health and social services for all and the assurance of dignity and security for those who are retired or unable to work through infirmity' (Brown, 2003, p. 136). This is a programme that aims to make people fit to participate fully in the economic, social and political life of the nation. It is not about transforming the foundations of society but about the ways in which we view and interact with other people. This has many similarities with the ideas of the one nation conservatives. Rather than allow society to remain divided, government policy is directed towards creating one nation or a unified community in which we all have a stake and towards which we are all responsible. This is considered preferable to maintaining a costly and extensive welfare state.

It is clear that advocates of the third way are great believers in diversity and that they tend to believe that no single institution is capable of providing adequate economic or welfare services that would suit all people. Rather than rely solely upon the state or upon private initiative, they adopt a far more pragmatic approach and thereby allow for a greater degree of flexibility in economic and social planning. Supporters of the third way, who are willing to use the state when necessary, seem to believe that there are numerous ways to tackle social and economic problems and that approaching these issues in a dogmatic fashion will often reduce the likelihood of success. Those who believe in the third way reject the dogmatism of the more extreme ideologies and are aware of the need to be mindful of the particular requirements of any given situation. They would appear to be concerned in particular with merging compassion and prudence in the hope of convincing people that it is possible to combine sound economic management alongside a well-funded and effective social programme. The third way does not promise to reinstate the welfare state to support people from the 'cradle to the grave'. Instead, it promises to redesign the welfare state for the twenty-first century. This new design allows less room for the state and has greater hopes for the newly empowered individual.

Welfare and social policies

Those who are active in devising a third way are aware of the need to find an appropriate role for the state in social provision. Like many social democrats and social liberals, they understand the social context of employment, housing, health and education and are interested in improving the prospects for the vast majority of people. Whereas neo-liberals and some conservatives are willing to leave social affairs to the distributing mechanisms of the market, supporters of the third way recognise that the state can assist in empowering people and making them less dependent upon the state. Driven by a vision of responsible and active citizenship, the third way seeks to combine the benefits of a lively civil society alongside a state that coordinates and facilitates a range of progressive social policies.

Benefits

The third way's vision of a society of responsible citizens allows little room for dependence upon unemployment benefit. Giddens (1998) warned that the benefits system runs the risk of creating a 'moral hazard' and that high rates of benefits increased the likelihood of this hazard. According to Giddens, a moral hazard could be seen in the way that benefits sometimes have an adverse effect upon behaviour and in the way that benefits designed to counter unemployment can even decrease levels of employment because people might access benefits in order to avoid the responsibilities of work (Giddens, 1998, pp. 114–115). Blair and Schroeder's (1999) claim that prolonged periods of unemployment can demoralise and demotivate people and that, if we want all people to participate fully in the life of society, it is important to find ways to wean the unemployed off benefits and usher them into work. For this to occur, it is argued that the benefits system must be reformed and measures put into place to create new opportunities for gainful employment. By reducing taxation for low-income workers and by introducing new forms of tax credit, it was hoped that unemployed people would be encouraged to take low-paid work (if that was the only work available) in the knowledge that they would not be made worse off as a result of losing their benefits.

Blair's Labour government tends to view the benefit system in fairly negative terms and argues that benefits can promote dependency upon the state and thus deprive society of vigour. For New Labour, the solution is to combine rights and responsibilities. New Labour rejects the view that we have a right to benefits and replaces it with the view that individuals have a contract with the state in which our rights are dependent upon fulfilling our obligations. Blair claims that the British people are in need of a 'clear philosophy of rights and duties' and that the welfare system has to be reformed so that dependency on benefits will no longer be an option. It is argued that people should be 'empowered' (rather than 'penalised') to break out of the benefit culture and attain the skills necessary for gainful employment (BBC2, 23.10.1997). The Labour government has introduced a range of financial pressures and inducements to accelerate this change in culture. A deliberate attempt has been made to limit access to benefits and to reduce the real value of benefits. While taking away with one hand, the Labour government offered something in return. New Deal for Employment increased the training and help available to people looking for work. New Deal for Communities pumped money and opportunities into the poorest neighbourhoods. The government also attempted to make work more financially attractive by introducing a minimum wage, family tax credit to assist working families on low incomes and help with child care to encourage people with young families back into work (Social Exclusion Unit, 2000; Channel 4, 2.02.1999; Rowlingson and McKay, 2005). These measures were introduced in the belief that the benefits system should only be a safety net for those who are unable to work and that the government can help by making work a more viable option.

The Clinton government was also determined to place limits upon the entitlement to benefits and to extol the virtues of self-reliance and hard work in the hope of placating the middle classes, who were becoming more vocal in their opposition to abuses in the benefits system. The Clinton government argued that the benefits system should be there to provide people with a second chance rather than to give them an alternative way of life, free from the responsibilities many assume in paid employment. In attempting to find a third way that would appeal to both liberals and conservatives, Clinton devised a programme that included punitive measures alongside an increase in social spending. He attempted to gain conservative support by placing limits on a person's eligibility for benefits and by threatening action against absentee fathers who failed to maintain their child support payments. Liberals were wooed by the promise that the government would pump more money into health care, job training and child care facilities; though this additional expenditure was to be phased in slowly (Klein, 2002; Campbell and Rockman, 1996; Herrick and Midgley, 2002). In 1996, the Clinton administration introduced the Personal Responsibility Act that placed a two-year limit on eligibility for welfare benefits and instituted a programme of preparing for work. A five-year lifetime limit was placed upon entitlement to benefits and benefits were cut for immigrants. The AFDC, established by the New Deal, was abolished and replaced by a block grant system in which states received a lump sum in the belief that this would encourage state administrators to restrict access to benefits. It has been argued that the Personal Responsibility Act marked '… the end of welfare as we know it, representing the culmination of neo-conservative and neo-liberal attacks on "welfare" that had been developing since the 1980s' (Clarke and Fox Piven, 2001, p. 38; see also Goar, 1996). Without the necessary public investment, however, this piece of legislation offered considerably more to Republicans than to old-style Democrats. Restricting access to benefits might force people to find work, but it does little in itself to provide people with opportunities for advancement. Of course, from a neo-liberal point of view, it is not the responsibility of the government to provide these opportunities. This attitude seems to have influenced the policies of Clinton's third way.

For the third way, access to benefits is restricted to those who fail to fulfil their responsibilities. A person who is able to work and refuses to do so is given a range of options and at least some opportunities for training. Like the neo-liberals, the third way has little time for those who wish to remain dependent upon welfare. Government policy in both Britain and the United States looked for ways to undermine the benefits culture and to reintegrate the socially excluded into the life of the community. This resulted in a blended approach that seemed, in many ways, to resemble the intervention and inducements favoured by social liberals and social democrats alongside the punitive measures usually associated with the political right.

Housing

The third way approach to housing recognises the limitations of relying solely upon either the private sector or social housing. Will Hutton (1996) pointed out that the Conservative Party during the 1980s had legislated in a rapid decline in social housing and that the remaining housing stock was usually in a dilapidated state and in the most socially deprived areas. He launched a sustained critique of Conservative policy, which he claimed was responsible for a marked increase in homelessness, inequality and crime and had '… intensified the breakdown of urban life and with it many of our most cherished notions of community and citizenship' (Hutton, 1996, p. 210). Given the choice, however, many supporters of the third way would not pin their hopes on a large-scale revival of social housing. Recognising that many forms of social housing became unpopular with tenants, the third way acknowledge that there are benefits to be accrued from helping people to own their own homes. According to Gordon Brown (2003), progressive forces on the left should look towards the formation of a property owning democracy in which property is distributed as widely as possible. Like Crosland before him, Brown regards this as a socialist rather than a conservative ideal (Brown, 2003). This is no doubt the case, as long as we subscribe to a fairly narrow definition of socialism. It is clear, however, that it does not correspond in the slightest to Marxism and that only a minority of social democrats would support this view of housing and see socialism in this way.

The Blair government is in favour of a mixed economy of housing. The first Blair government argued that investment in council or social housing was a form of social consumption and that it did not count in any real way as a form of productive investment. The alternative for the Blair government consisted in using the private sector and applying the Private Finance Initiative to housing (Durden, 2000). The Blair government has been particularly keen on promoting home ownership and in looking for ways to increase individual responsibility and encourage people to believe and act as if they have a stake in their communities. Rather than continue with the old system of social housing, the Blair government considered a range of proposals to transfer part ownership of social housing to the tenants concerned. This was described as a form of 'asset based welfare' and was seen as an alternative to the much-discredited benefits culture (Weaver, 2001a, 2001b). It is clear, moreover, that New Labour is committed to making social housing 'more respectable'. Armed with the idea of enhancing community spirit, New Labour has granted the state the right to intrude into what could be seen as the private lives of individuals. Legislation aimed to curb what are deemed to be anti-social activities has been applied in poor areas in Britain. Julian Le Grand uses the example of how council tenants in Oldham were given instructions about how to tend to their gardens, what pets they could raise and how they should care for their children (Le Grand, 2003). In some ways, there is nothing new in this. Victorian philanthropists were famed for visiting the poor and dispensing their wisdom on how to live and, during the early post-war years, access to council housing was restricted to people considered by inspectors to be of good character. What New Labour policy shows, however, is that the idea of community can be used to justify strengthening the authoritarian features of the state. Just because local governments look for ways to cut back on social housing, this does not mean that they are any less intrusive.

Advocates of the third way recognise that housing is of social significance, though they are generally in favour of expanding home ownership. Clinton's policy on housing involved supporting the expansion of home ownership and using more flexible and indirect ways to support the social provision of housing. Like some of his Republican predecessors, he sought to reduce the power and influence of HUD. This organisation had become far too unpopular and discredited. Clinton also wanted to move away from subsidising high-rise housing in poor areas. The preferred alternative consisted in providing low-income families with vouchers, which they could use to rent property from private landlords in more prosperous areas. Clinton was also willing to back affirmative action initiatives to fight discrimination in housing. This was done in part to discourage divisive practices in the allocation of rented accommodation. Although the number of people owning their own homes increased during the Clinton years, inequalities in housing between ethnic groups became more extreme. Non-white sections of American society have tended to prosper less in the housing market and rents have increased, thus making it more difficult for low-income families (Aberbach, 1996; Dreier, 1997; Husock, 1997; Malamud, 1999).

The third way allows for extensive private provision of rented accommodation and for the use of multiple providers of social housing. In both Britain and the United States, third way administrations have turned against monolithic public housing estates. Fearing the spread of ghettos, these governments have tried to break down the barriers between public and private housing and to distance themselves from large-scale public housing ventures. Instead of direct government provision of housing, preference has been given to subsidising greater choice in housing for low-income families. This was set up as a new blend of public and private provision.

Health

Rather than depend upon the state providing all health care, the third way often encourages a mixed economy of care. The third way approach to health care recognises that social factors play an important role in shaping the health we experience and that the state should therefore play some part in tackling health problems. In Britain, the third way rejects the internal market in health care (which had been introduced by the Thatcher government) because it increased competition rather than cooperation. It was recognised, however, that serious problems could arise from attempting to return to excessive state control of health resources and it was argued that a centralised bureaucracy does not provide an attractive alternative to the chaos of market forces. The third way promised to avoid both extremes by facilitating the development of local partnerships, working within the framework of national standards (Department of Health, 2003; Blair, 2003b). In this way, the third way seeks to combine the more centralising tendencies of social democracy with the localism found more often in liberalism and in some forms of conservatism. In this context, the state sets a framework for statutory and voluntary sector organisations to provide a range of services that are monitored and evaluated in accordance with declared targets.

The Blair government has had a reasonable amount of success in applying a third way approach to health care. This government subscribes to the view that health is influenced by a series of socio-economic conditions and that if the government is going to tackle poor health this must be in conjunction with a broad programme of social reform. Poor health is said to stem in part from poverty that in turn rests upon such things as unemployment, poor housing and poor educational standards. The Blair government saw that health policy should be part of a programme that aims to eradicate, as far as possible, the problems of social exclusion and, as such, that it required 'joined-up solutions'. National standards and performance indicators were established and far greater emphasis was placed upon tackling health inequalities and on health promotion campaigns. Rather than see the health service as a purely reactive service that deals with 'illness', the Blair government has been instrumental in transforming the service to deal with 'health'. Multi-disciplinary primary care trusts have been established to deal with the health needs of local areas and to tackle social exclusion in a direct and proactive way. It was argued that this increase in investment in primary care could help policymakers understand the problems that exist on a local level and health practitioners to work in partnership with each other and with other agencies to confront and deal with the socio-economic factors that can often cause poor health (Department of Health, 2000, 2003; North, 2001; Abercrombie and Warde, 2000; Glennerster, 2000). For the Blair government, the third way approach to health care does not consist in privatising the health service but in decentralising control and in prioritising multi-disciplinary work at the community level. While avoiding any notable increases in government control of the health service, New Labour has concentrated upon setting targets and granting additional power and independence to those parts of the health service that excel in the delivery of their care.

Third way ideas on health were not applied to any great extent in the United States because of the size of political opposition to state intervention in such matters. Clinton inherited an under-funded health system. It was estimated that 15 per cent of American citizens lacked health insurance and that the health system was heading towards a crisis because of the increasing costs of health care. The Clinton administration introduced a comprehensive review of health care, headed by Hilary Clinton, which attempted to devise a third way between nationalised and private provision and involved introducing health care insurance for all citizens. Liberals within the Democratic Party pushed for more federal action, while conservatives in his own party and in the Republican Party argued that the government should withdraw as far as possible, decrease the financial burden imposed upon employers to contribute towards health insurance schemes for their workers and rely to a far greater extent upon voluntary activity and personal responsibility. It is evident that the conservative argument won the day and, with active backing from vested interests and from insurance companies, the Republican Party was able to block Clinton's attempts to reform funding of the health care system. Because of this, the third way in America continued to rely upon individual contributions to health insurance packages (Campbell and Rockman, 1996; Clarke and Fox Piven, 2001; Linder and Rosenau, 2002).

Those who believe in a third way often show that they are aware of the social context of health and the social responsibility of government agencies to provide at least some health care for the citizens. Characteristically, the third way is fearful of too much government intervention while at the same time it is critical of relying solely upon market mechanisms or the private sector. For the third way, it is appropriate for the government to embark upon a social mission to reduce health inequalities and to devise ways to extend health care provision to those of limited means. Once again, it is likely that this will entail the government entering into partnership with the private sector and with other agencies in the community.

Education

For those who place their faith in the third way, having witnessed the more instrumental attitudes towards education championed by Conservative and Republican governments, education has special significance in the fight against social exclusion and in adapting to the needs of the twenty-first century. Third way theorists and practitioners (see Giddens, 2000; Blair and Schroeder, 1999) argue that education should not be regarded as a one-off experience we encounter in our formative years and that it is more important to see that education is a lifelong process through which we transform ourselves and adapt to changing conditions. They recognise that education has an important role in fostering social cohesion, civic engagement and economic efficiency. They are therefore willing to see education being provided in a variety of ways and speak in glowing terms about the advantages of partnerships between the state, the private sector, parents and the local community (see, for example, Department for Education and Employment, 2003). The third way does not rely solely upon the state to provide education or to apply its social agenda. Instead, there is a flexible approach to educational provision through which money from the state is passed on to a variety of providers in the community.

The Labour government in Britain has undertaken a widespread reform of the education system. Nursery provision has been extended and literacy and numeracy emphasised in early years education. Those schools that are thought to underachieve have been given extra funds and tougher head teachers and ties with the community have been strengthened. Education Action Zones have been established to target the disadvantaged, to reduce levels of truancy and supplementary schools have been established to help those who are under-achieving. School children have also been taught about their own social and political systems in the hope that this will encourage the next generation of citizens to participate in social and political life. The Blair government has also pledged extra resources for the further education sector, particularly to meet the needs of the business sector and to provide training in new technology. New community learning centres have been created and funds provided for further education initiatives in deprived areas. The Blair government also recognises the importance of mass higher education in breaking down class barriers and equipping the majority with the skills necessary for the modern globalised economy. It is argued that one of the ways of tackling social exclusion is to improve access to higher education. This widening participation programme involves prioritising those groups underrepresented in higher education, pushing the growth of part-time provision and encouraging the development of new teaching strategies to serve the changing needs of higher education students (Frazer, 2000; Kendall and Holloway, 2001). For New Labour, the education system needs to be made more flexible in the education it provides and in the range of providers that are eligible for state funding.

The application of third way ideas on education is limited in the United States largely because education policy tends to be devolved to a large extent to individual states. Clinton, however, was in favour of making the education system more responsive to the needs of the majority. Clinton showed, throughout his political career, that he was in favour of protecting and advancing the educational opportunities of disadvantaged sections of the community (Shull, 2000). It is clear, in addition, that he was committed to developing the public education system. He was particularly interested in creating a system of national standards for schools in the public sector. Although the American right attacked this for giving too much power to federal government, the majority of states have adopted his reform programme. The Clinton government also introduced some extremely generous tax cuts to assist those parents who were helping their children through university. This was packaged as part of his 'national crusade' to widen access to university education (Parker, 1998). Although Clinton had a more limited agenda, there are some similarities between the policies of Clinton and Blair. In particular, both third way premiers have been willing to use the power of national government to enhance social justice and to expand access to higher education. For both Clinton and Blair, the education system is there to be used to extend opportunities to as many people as possible.

The third way aspires to create an education system that adapts to socio-economic changes, encourages lifelong learning and accommodates people from a variety of backgrounds. Education is seen as one of the great socialising influences and as important in promoting social cohesion and the values of responsible citizenship. Rather than concentrate solely upon individual achievement, education is seen as a social good that requires the attention and active intervention of national government. This does not mean that supporters of the third way want the government to provide all education free of charge. Rather, they tend to believe that the government has a key role in distributing resources and opportunities throughout the community so that diverse sections of society can engage creatively with the various levels of the education system.

Conclusion

The third way offers an attractive combination of individual liberty and social justice. Rather than leave everything to the private sector or require the state to manage the economy excessively, the economic foundations of the third way allow for private initiative and for state-coordinated community development. Instead of having to choose between the state and the private sector, the third way seeks to revive the multitude of agencies in civil society and to form a network of partnerships between individuals, social groups, communities, the voluntary sector and the government. In both economic and social affairs, the third way is committed to individual responsibility and community development. Although the welfare state continues to have a role in their vision of society, they seem reluctant to finance an extensive welfare regime. Like neo-liberals and the new right, champions of the third way want to reduce dependency on benefits and divert resources into job creation and training schemes. Rather than tie the state into heavy involvement in housing and health care, the third way promotes a wide distribution of property and a mixed economy of care. The third way does not envisage the continuation or the return of an extensive welfare state. Individuals are called upon to assume more responsibility for their own welfare and, if they need help, these individuals must be willing to fulfil certain obligations. The welfare state provided by the third way is a safety net and a network of resources that responsible citizens can access when necessary. Apart from anything else, the third way is important in showing how resilient the welfare state can be. In spite of attacks from the political right, the idea that the state should have some role in coordinating activities to enhance the common welfare has emerged once more.

7

Radical Critics: Marxism

It is now time to leave behind the political mainstream and to look at some ideas that are often found on the fringes of the Western political system. All of the ideologies and movements dealt with so far have had some degree of electoral success and have been involved in developing, defending or reforming the welfare state. Each, in its own distinctive way, works within the confines of the capitalist system and seems content to compete for control over parliamentary or congressional chambers. The ideologies covered in Chapters 2–6 are democratic and reformist. They compete over the jurisdiction of the state and vary considerably in the scope of their economic and social programmes. The next three chapters, however, are dedicated to those who have yet to secure a significant amount of power in Western systems and who tend to be critical of the political mainstream. We begin by taking a look at the ideas of the Marxists. Rather than argue that capitalism should be saved through prudent economic management and constructive welfare policies, many Marxists believe that capitalism is flawed as an economic system and positively dangerous in the values it promotes. From a Marxist perspective, rights to welfare are given not to secure a fairer system, out of benevolence or in recognition of the importance of advancing some form of equality, but to protect and conceal the selfish interests of the capitalist class. This interpretation of welfare systems will be illustrated by drawing upon the ideas of classical Marxists (Marx, Engels and Lenin) and contemporary Marxist authors (Gough, Ginsburg, Navarro, Miliband and Offe).

Economy

Marxism rests firmly upon economic foundations. The economic theories of Marx and Engels were particularly important in identifying the nature of capitalism and in detecting weaknesses within the system. They argued that the capitalist system is based upon the private ownership of the means of production, which creates a social division between those who own the means of production and those who rely upon selling their labour power. Whereas it could be argued that the feudal system benefited from paternal bonds, something that one nation conservatives applaud, the capitalist system is said to exist because of a simple wage relation between the employer and the employee (Marx and Engels, 1845). For Marx, this wage relation allowed the capitalist class to exploit and even dehumanise workers by depriving workers of control over the product of their own labour (Marx, 1844) and by allowing the capitalist to make a profit from the labour of their workers. Marx pointed out in *Capital* (1867) that this system is too fragile to continue in the long run. He claimed that capitalists have to compete against each other for their market and that this will force them to economise by spending less on wages and more on machinery, thereby increasing levels of unemployment. At the same time, capitalists will attempt to increase their share of the market by expanding and merging with other companies. While the ownership of the means of production falls into fewer hands, the conditions endured by the working class will deteriorate. From a Marxist perspective, capitalism will crumble under conditions of over-production, under-consumption and high unemployment (Marx, 1867, pp. 714–715). As critics of capitalism, Marxists tend to have relatively little interest in finding ways to stabilise the system. It is this all-or-nothing approach that separates many Marxists from those who look for ways to defend capitalism.

It is clear that Marxists have little time for social democrats, who are deemed to be gullible and fooled into believing that their policies have eradicated the horrors of capitalism and have allowed for a peaceful transition to a post-capitalist society. Ralph Miliband (1973) argued that state management in the economy had not transformed the character of the capitalist system significantly. He argued that state planning and coordination serves the interests of capitalism and that the mixed economy was still dominated by private enterprise. For Miliband (1977) capitalism had simply been stabilised by state intervention. These reforms had done little or nothing to change the fundamental character of the capitalist system, because capitalism '... is unable to do without exploitation, oppression and dehumanisation; and that it cannot create a truly human environment for which it has itself produced the material conditions' (Miliband, 1977, p. 39). For Marxists, therefore, it is important to abolish rather than attempt to humanise capitalism.

Marxists want to replace capitalism with a system based upon the common ownership of the means of production. Rather than leave economic power in the hands of a minority, Marxists hope that this power can be transferred to the community. There is certainly no one Marxist blueprint for the running of the economy in a socialist or communist system, but it is clear in discussions on communism that the workers would be expected to have a greater say in the way they worked and in the way that their industries were run (Marx and Engels, 1845, 1848; Marx, 1871b; Lenin, 1917). Whereas social democrats might be willing to support state ownership of the means of production, Marxists are far more interested in looking for ways to empower the working class to increase control over their own lives. This involves, among other things, the workers freeing themselves from the dictates of the capitalist system.

Marxists reject capitalism because they believe that it crushes the spirit of the workers and enslaves people to the cause of maximising profits. For Marxists, anything short of the total abolition of capitalism would fail to free the workers from exploitation and alienation. Whatever the state does to stabilise the capitalist system it does little or nothing to convince Marxists that the long-term welfare of the working class can be improved in a piecemeal way. Because of this, Marxists are often condemning of the efforts and activities of social democrats. Rather than see social democracy as a half-way house between capitalism and socialism, Marxists tend to believe that social democracy is designed to persuade workers that they have no need to confront the capitalist system in a direct and revolutionary way. This belief often manifests itself in prolonged Marxist attacks on 'reformism' and in attempts to poach support from social democratic parties. Groups like the Militant Tendency in Britain campaigned for many years to turn socialists in the Labour Party away from social democratic ideals (see Callaghan, 1989). From a Marxist point of view, the values advanced by social democrats are far too close to the values that protect the interests of the capitalist class.

Social values

For Marxists, individuals are viewed primarily in their economic and social contexts. Rather than see the individual as an abstract entity with rights and responsibilities, Marxists believe that we belong to social classes and that these classes can be defined according to our place in the productive process. Marxists do not begin with the individual and think about what will suit individuals. Instead, they concentrate upon social formations and attempt to grapple with the common good. This approach to economic, social and political affairs owes a lot to the founders of Marxism. Marx (1843) had very little time for the idea of negative liberty, which he associated with the interests of the capitalist class. He complained that this bourgeois notion of freedom, which gave us the right to do whatever we wished as long as we caused no harm to others, saw the individual as isolated from society and made us regard other people as barriers to our own freedom. This scenario saw society as external to the individual rather than as central to our own sense of identity.

For Marx (1845), true freedom is only possible within a community for it is in the community that we develop our gifts. Indeed, the Marxist position states that individuals can only develop if society develops. Freedom is thus gained through association rather than from isolating ourselves from our fellow citizens (Marx, 1845, pp. 54, 83–86).

It could be argued that Marxists are enemies of freedom. It is clear that they have little respect for the freedom of members of the capitalist class to pursue their own interests, largely because Marxists believe that the interests of the capitalist class are often in conflict with the interests of the rest of the society. The existence and implications of this conflict is considered to be far more important than the economic freedom of the minority and thus pushes Marxists away from respecting the negative liberty of the few. Negative liberty is regarded as a dangerous mirage framed in the interests of preserving and legitimising the capitalist system. Marxists have argued that negative (bourgeois) liberty means little more than economic freedom for a select few and that this form of freedom merely creates class inequalities and economic instability (Lukes, 1991, p. 49). This does not mean, however, that Marxists are critical of all forms of freedom. Marxists place far more emphasis upon positive liberty for the collective than upon negative liberty for the individual. It might be the case that some individual freedoms need to be curtailed in the interests of society but, for the majority of Marxists, this would only be legitimate in a society based upon the principles of equality and social justice.

From a Marxist point of view, equality of opportunity would do too little to assist the working class and to lift the workers out of poverty and insecurity. Marxists consider equality of outcome to be a legitimate and noble long-term aim. Marxists have argued, however, that it is unlikely that equality of outcome would be practical during the early stages of a socialist society. Lenin (1917), for example, believed that the transition from a capitalist to a communist society would have to go through two stages. During the first stage, private property would be abolished but inequality in the distribution of resources would continue and workers would still be paid according to the work they did. It would not be until the second stage, when the workers gained complete control over the system, that this form of inequality would be abolished and people would receive what they need rather than a market price for their labour. It is essential, from a Marxist point of view, that the inequalities created by capitalism are challenged and overturned. Marxists want to rid society of exploitative economic relations and they argue that it is these relations that create widespread economic, social and political inequalities. With the fall of capitalism and the undermining of economic exploitation, the prospects for social justice are thought to be enhanced.

Marxists are enthusiastic about social justice but they believe that it is impossible to achieve under capitalism. Marx claimed in 'Critique of the Gotha programme' (1875) that social justice could only be attained under a communist system. For Marx, a communist society would rest upon the principle '... from each according to his abilities, to each according to his needs' (Marx, 1875a, p. 185). Social injustice is thought to exist wherever people are deprived of what they need and where they are given only what the market allows. According to this definition, capitalism is an inherently unjust system because the market, rather than need, dictates how resources are allocated. Capitalism also seems to rely upon the existence and preservation of inequalities. Although social reformers have looked for ways to alleviate the problems of an unequal society, Marxists would argue that they could only ever have limited success because they operate within a value system designed to protect capitalism.

Marxist social values champion the rights of the many rather than the privileges of the few. The values supported by Marxists are the direct opposite of those advanced by classical liberal and neo-liberals. Whereas these liberals support negative liberty, the maintenance of inequalities and argue that social justice is a dangerous illusion, Marxists support positive liberty, equality of outcome and argue that social justice is possible only under communism. Neo-liberals and Marxists make for perfect enemies on many issues. Because their priorities are so different, they would find it very difficult to compromise and to establish common ground. Sitting on the extremes of the conventional political spectrum, they can take shots at each other and condemn each other for being misguided and blind to the realities of life. For many Marxists, it makes no sense to find ways to compromise with the capitalist system. Apart from anything else, the social values they support are inconsistent with capitalism and can only be realised once exploitation and class divisions have been overcome.

Welfare and the state

From a Marxist perspective, little can be achieved by the state in a capitalist society. While the ideologies of the political centre allow for the state to be used to minimise the damage created by the instabilities of capitalism, Marxists argue that the interests of the dominant class contaminate the state. By writing off the capitalist state in this way, Marxists are often confronted with the problem of how to engage with the capitalist political system. Their reliance upon revolutionary methods has made them political outcasts and politically ineffective in most Western states. What they say about the capitalist state is, however, of relevance and importance in discussing the politics of welfare. This is not because Marxist ideas have had a particularly important effect upon Western policymakers, but because they provide an interesting critique of the welfare policies of the political centre and they highlight at least some of the problems that can be encountered if we rely too heavily on the capitalist state.

Marx and Engels were generally quite suspicious towards the capitalist state because they believed that the bourgeoisie use the state to protect their property. In their early writings, they argued that the workers needed to take over the state and use it to seize control of the economy (Marx and Engels, 1848). Over time, however, Marx and Engels became increasingly critical of the state in its handling of the working class and its suppression of radical movements. By the early 1870s, following the smashing of the Paris Commune, Marx became convinced that the working class should avoid using the state. He said that the state (with its army, police, bureaucracy, clergy and judiciary) arose during the closing stages of feudalism to assist the bourgeoisie but then became an instrument of class oppression, used in 'social enslavement'. For Marx, socialism relied upon the abolition of the state and the formation of new communal structures free from the influence of class privilege (Marx, 1871b, pp. 285–291). This general mistrust of the bourgeois state can also be seen in the writings of other Marxists. Lenin, for example, argued in his 'The state and revolution' (1917) that the state could have a useful function in the transition from capitalism to communism but that it would 'wither away' once the workers were able to control their own affairs. For many Marxists, the state is part of the problem rather than part of the solution.

According to the Marxist line of thought, the welfare state could be seen as a capitalist institution designed to reinforce the interests of the capitalist class and placate the working class with a series of welfare measures. By providing the workers with unemployment benefits, health care, subsidised housing and education, it could be argued that the welfare state reduces the need for the capitalist class to pay the workers a decent wage (see Pfaller, Gough and Therborn, 1991; Dearlove and Saunders, 1984). Marxists were aware that the welfare state could only ever offer a temporary respite from the harsh realities of the modern industrial economy and that economic and social policies were not sustainable in the long run if they relied heavily upon the continued operation of the welfare state. Pfaller and Gough (1991) point out that post-war welfare states grew and prospered during periods of economic growth and that the governing class in particular considered the financing of the welfare state to be justifiable and useful on the grounds that it helped to reduce social and industrial conflict and thus represented a sound investment in social peace. They argue that while the economy was buoyant, demands on the welfare state were kept to an acceptable level and the majority paid at least something into the system. Cracks began to appear, however, when the economy entered recession in the 1970s and demands on the welfare state grew. They claimed that once this occurred, the welfare state became a burden (Pfaller and Gough, 1991, p. 42).

For many Marxists, the relationship between capitalism and the welfare state is inherently unstable. It is not simply that the welfare state became too expensive at a certain stage in its development, but that the leaders of welfare systems make promises they cannot keep. Claus Offe, for example, claims that the welfare state has a strange and ultimately destructive relationship with the capitalist system and he has voiced doubts about whether the welfare state can coexist with capitalism in the long term. Offe believes that the welfare state is ineffective and oppressive that it spreads a 'false ideology' and compensates for the instabilities and inadequacies of capitalism rather than eliminating them. It is argued that the welfare state only deals with the symptoms of inequality but does little to reduce the causes of inequality. The expansion of its bureaucracy has, moreover, made it increasingly inefficient. For Offe, its oppressive features can also be shown in the way it demands that people are available for all types of work and in the way it seeks to impose moral codes on society through regulations concerning cohabitation and rights to benefit. Finally, it creates a deceptive ideology by attempting to conceal that the welfare state operates in response to the problems created by the system itself (Offe, 1984, pp. 149–156; George and Wilding, 1994, p. 117).

Offe is aware that attacking the welfare state can play straight into the hands of reactionary forces. What these forces fail to appreciate, however, is that the welfare state protects capitalism by helping to stabilise demand and by helping to secure at least the foundations for social peace (Offe, 1985, p. 84). He claims that the welfare state helps to reduce industrial conflict and thereby gives capitalists the stability they need to plan their businesses. By reducing fluctuations and crises in the capitalist system, the welfare state also deprives capitalism of the slumps it can exploit (Offe, 1984, pp. 195–199). Viewed from a classical liberal perspective, economic crises can be good for the business community because they often allow for capitalists to pick up cheap labour and to be innovative in searching for and adapting to new markets. The welfare state, if coupled with prudent economic management, could preserve an inefficient system and deprive capitalists of the motives they need to change direction. It might seem strange that Marxists should concern themselves with such matters, but we should remember that many Marxists rely upon capitalism entering a period of crisis so that workers will be forced to tackle exploitation and take apart the capitalist system. By alleviating crises, the welfare state helps to shield the true nature of capitalism from the workers and can thus breed complacency and what is often called false consciousness.

Marxists have argued that the state does little to serve the general welfare and that the state exists to protect the interests of the capitalist class. They acknowledge that this might involve policies designed to appease the working class and claim that liberal welfare measures in general serve to protect and give legitimacy to the capitalist system. It is worth remembering that liberals are defenders of capitalism and that they attack only the harsh features or side effects of the capitalist system, rather than the key features of capitalism itself. Indeed, the classical liberals were the original architects of the capitalist edifice. The welfare state is thought to conceal the extent of inequality and allow us to believe that the system is fair and organised in the interests of all. In particular, it has an important part to play in training the future generation of workers and in keeping the workers healthy enough to work. It is thought to cushion society from the instabilities of the economic cycle and thus prolong the life of the capitalist system. The welfare state is therefore seen as a mixed blessing. It can make life bearable for the poorest sections of the community, while preserving the system that makes them poor. From a Marxist perspective, the welfare state can only ever serve the short-term interests of the working class whereas the long-term interests of the working class rely upon overthrowing the system that creates the need for a welfare state.

Welfare and social policies

Marxists doubt whether the long-term welfare of society can be improved through implementing social policies alone. Although defenders of the capitalist system are willing to use social policies to make capitalism more bearable, Marxists believe that such policies merely extend the lifespan of the capitalist system. As we have seen, many Marxists are critical of the welfare state. The existing welfare state, indeed, is thought to serve the capitalist class by perpetuating a market mentality in which people only have rights if they have made sufficient contributions to the economic system. What this fails to take into account is that capitalism creates and perpetuates inequalities that have a negative impact upon our rights as citizens. For Marxists, the long-term welfare of society cannot be enhanced independently of the economic transformation of society.

Benefits

Marxists are generally sceptical about the motives for providing benefits under capitalism. Norman Ginsburg (1979), for example, argued that the benefits system was introduced and endures to reinforce capitalist social relations by giving the impression that capitalism is fair and compassionate and by empowering the state to intervene in the life of the individual. Benefits help capitalists to maintain the unemployed until they are needed by the economic system. Setting benefits at a low level helps to maintain an incentive to work and thus effectively disciplines those in work. Regulations are put in place to make sure that eligibility for benefits is made contingent upon the manner by which workers became unemployed. People who abandon their jobs, for example, are not in the majority of cases entitled to claim benefits. By labelling those who use the system as undeserving or as scroungers, claimants are rendered economically and socially unworthy and this stigma is in turn used to keep other people in work. Ginsburg argues that the '... stigma of being a claimant is an essential ingredient in a system designed to discipline claimants and to promote the values of insurance and individual and family self-help' (Ginsburg, 1979, p. 104, see also pp. 46–49). Ginsburg's assumption is that capitalism is unjust and that the benefits system is part of the ideological apparatus that maintains this injustice. According to this line of argument, the benefits system is not merely a form of social support but a mechanism through which capitalist values are transmitted to society and some of the most vulnerable sections of the community are made to feel ashamed of their own unemployment. If we accept the Marxist analysis of society, unemployment is a natural consequence of fluctuations in the market economy and we should recognise that a person who is made unemployed is more a victim of circumstances than an instigator of a scam.

The Marxist analysis also draws attention to how the conflicting aims of the benefits system create confusion and dysfunction. One of the aims of the benefits system is to alleviate poverty, but this sits uneasily alongside the pressure to limit expenditure on benefits and to operate a system of sanctions against people who claim unemployment benefit. Ginsburg (1979) is convinced that while the benefits system assists some of the poorest sections of contemporary society, it runs counter to the long-term interests of the working class. It is apparent, from a Marxist perspective, that these long-term interests cannot in any real sense be satisfied or guaranteed under a capitalist system that, by definition, exploits the working class and treats the labour of the working class as a disposable factor in production. From this point of view, unemployment benefit maintains workers at the taxpayer's expense until capitalists are ready to employ them. This will mean quite often that workers will remain unemployed until employers can see that taking on more workers will be good for their profits, a measure that is often calculated in the short term. The benefits system can be seen to make it relatively easy for employers to dispense with any labour that is surplus to requirement. Short-term contracts can be used to minimise the commitment of the employer and to allow the employer to make temporary workers unemployed. The cash-nexus, which allows for labour to be bought or rejected according to market conditions, is in this way preserved by the support offered by unemployment benefit.

Marxists are left with the problem of finding an alternative to unemployment benefit. Although benefits help to prop up the capitalist system, withdrawing the right to benefit cannot (in the short- to medium term) be in the interests of workers, especially those who experience insecurity in employment. Even the most optimistic of Marxists acknowledge that the desired revolutionary transformation of society is not an immediate option, partly because capitalism has developed its own set of stabilising mechanisms. If unemployment is an unavoidable feature of capitalism, what can be done to alleviate this problem and, more to the point, minimise its impact upon the working class? Marxists have argued that in the short- to medium term, workers could look for alternatives to being employed by capitalist enterprises. Offe, for example, argues that worker cooperatives could be established and used as 'non-capitalist forms of producing useful things' (Offe, 1984, p. 297). This is not meant to be a long-term solution (though there is no reason why this model could not be used in a socialist society) because these cooperatives would still be operating in a capitalist environment. Still, the formation of worker cooperatives could be instrumental in empowering workers, giving them more control over their own working lives and making them far less dependent upon a dehumanising and intrusive benefits system. It could be argued that under a socialist system, the benefits system (as constituted under capitalism) would no longer be necessary. This is because Marxists would want to see goods and services distributed according to need rather than according to our worth in the market. For Marxists, it is important to recognise that working conditions can and should be improved, both under capitalism and in a future socialist society, and that social rights should not be made contingent upon satisfying the demands of the capitalist class.

Housing

Whereas social democrats have called for the state to take an active role in the provision of housing, Marxists have seen this as another attempt to buy off and control sections of the working class. Ginsburg (1979) argued that the state got involved in housing provision because, for the bulk of the working class, the costs of housing are extremely high in relation to levels of income and this effectively places pressure on many workers to push for higher wages. Taking on its traditional role of defending the interests of the capitalist class, the state was said to intervene to underwrite and encourage the growth of council housing. Ginsburg acknowledged that council housing tended to benefit the poorer sections of society, but he attacked the view that council housing represented something of a 'socialist experiment' in Britain by pointing out that council housing was often built using loan capital and that finance capitalists were still making money from the loan payments due on council property.

The Marxist critique of social housing also points out that this form of housing can be used as a way to control the working class. Ginsburg (1979) argues that local governments often monitor tenants of council housing and there is certainly room for abuses in the way housing providers use their power. This form of social control sometimes includes the direct raiding of properties to check for 'over-crowding' and has often been justified on quasi-moralistic grounds. Divisions and inequalities have also been created within council provision, as some council estates are put aside for those who are deemed 'less respectable'. In this way, slums are created, not only by the people who live there, but also by deliberate (if slightly desperate) policies instituted by local councils. It is argued that council housing has, in a strange way, reinforced class divisions and '... any benevolent welfare aspects of council housing management have been very much secondary to its predominant role as guardian of state property and order in the home' (Ginsburg, 1979, p. 168). Although council provision could appear to be an attractive alternative to accessing accommodation via a private landlord, these coercive features of council housing can turn it into another form of social control. Under the guise of benevolence, the state would appear in this scenario to have too much power over the working class.

If council provision is rejected, there are not many alternatives left for Marxists. Owner-occupation is likely to be of limited appeal to those who believe that it could seduce workers to accept the 'dominant value system' (Ball, 1983, p. 17). There is indeed plenty of evidence to suggest that the spread of home ownership among the working class has a significant impact upon the way that workers behave and the values they hold (Choko, 1993). Other alternatives could include participating in housing cooperatives, though it could be argued that they still have to survive within a framework set by capitalists. For Marxists, the long-term solution relies upon the state or communal control of property and the just distribution of property in accordance with social need. Marxists could justify this on the grounds that the socialist state would not use housing to oppress the workers but to respond to their needs.

Health

From a Marxist point of view, government intervention in the provision of health care is often in the interests of the capitalist class because it repairs the workers and makes them fit for work. One of the key figures in the development of Marxist views on health is Vincente Navarro, who argued in *Class Struggle, the State and Medicine* (1978) that the British National Health Service should be seen in the context of the class relations prevalent under capitalism. He argued that health policies were designed as a system of dividends and rewards for a strong economy and were implemented only on condition that they did not harm the economic prospects of the nation. According to Navarro, the National Health Service was not particularly revolutionary in its inception. Indeed, the working class wanted considerably more than they got in the early post-war years. Navarro claimed that the National Health Service '... has not been an instrument for the self-realization of the masses, whereby they are the agents and not the subjects of change within and outside the health sector' (Navarro, 1978, p. 142). Although it is clear that the National Health Service provides the working class with greater access to health care, Marxists have complained that this concession to the working class is given under certain conditions and can be withdrawn. The state might, for example, want to reduce spending so that it can cut taxes. From a Marxist point of view, this is what prompted the Thatcher governments to reform the health system in the late 1980s and early 1990s.

The National Health Service can also be seen to reflect and reinforce the class composition of society. Navarro (1978) points out that consultants and surgeons have tended to come from aristocratic backgrounds, they have traditionally served the interests of their own class (especially in the old voluntary hospitals) and the Royal Colleges have been instrumental in defending their privileged positions. General Practitioners, who are generally from more modest backgrounds, are often seen to provide health care to the middle class and working class. This class division among health care professionals was not in any real sense challenged by the formation of the National Health Service. Rather than nationalise all health care, Bevan allowed the old hierarchy to continue. This was shown in the way he attempted to woo the consultants rather than develop support among General Practitioners (see Chapter 4). Consultants have maintained their power and this, in part, explains how resources have sometimes been diverted away from General Practitioners and put into hospital care. According to Navarro, the aristocracy and upper middle classes continue to be dominant in the provision of health care. They have the same background and effectively speak the same language as senior civil servants and are therefore able to defend their own interests with relative ease. From a Marxist perspective, the National Health Service protects the existing hierarchy in society by broadening access to health care at the same time as maintaining the class composition of the health care system. It could be argued that, because of this, health care was by no means democratised by the formation of the National Health Service. Indeed, the social democratic policies of the post-war Labour government are deemed partly responsible for the maintenance of the class system and for the continued dominance of bourgeois values.

Although Marxists have been critical of the state provision of health care, it is because they are suspicious of the motives of those who control the capitalist state. From a Marxist point of view, state provision (as long as it is distributed according to need) should be preferred to private practice and to the arguably predatory practices of some health insurance companies. However, some commentators (Ham, 1992) believe that Marxists go too far in their class analysis of the health system. It has been argued that Marxists fail to acknowledge that spending on health can harm the capitalist system because the high levels of taxation necessary to fuel the health system cut into the profits of the capitalist class. Baggott (1998) points out that senior health authority officials do not necessarily collude with the interests of capitalism. For example, the vast majority of health care professionals resisted the internal market, which was a deliberate attempt to apply capitalist values to medicine. For Marxists, however, state intervention in the provision of health care is something of a mixed blessing. Although it undoubtedly serves the short-term interests of the working class, it could be seen as an instrument used by the state to maintain the class system. Although one nation conservatives would applaud this, many Marxists revile it.

Education

Marxists are critical of the education system under capitalism because it helps to prop up the capitalist system. Marx was aware that the needs of the capitalist system stood in the way of the workers having access to a proper and well-balanced programme of education (Marx, 1869). He believed that the class system is perpetuated not only by the unequal distribution of economic and political power, but also by a system of education that limits horizons for the working class. He complained that workers were only given sufficient education to perform their allotted, and limited, functions in the economy. In place of real education, workers were offered an intellectual diet of simplified and constantly reinforced bourgeois values (Marx, 1847). Viewed in this way, the education system can be seen as part of a superstructure that is used by dominant elites to protect their own interests. This can be done by constructing the curriculum in such a way as to ensure that the working class only learn that which is necessary for the capitalist system to function and to flourish.

Marxists are aware that the ideological functions of education go far beyond mere vocational training. Offe (1976), for example, has argued that education is not designed primarily to make us qualified for a particular job (or range of occupations) but to make us fit the broader needs of society. He points out that we are likely to use in the workplace only a fraction of the knowledge we gain through formal education and that employers look more closely at employees' attitudes than at mere technical skills and capabilities. He argues that the education we receive in the West places a heavy emphasis upon adapting to the needs of dominant groups and our abilities to find our place within society. We are said to be categorised according to our educational experience and attainment and placed into a hierarchy to serve the interests of the system. Offe argues that employers in America are particularly interested in where people studied and make judgements based upon '... the cultural peculiarities and the specific traditions of the different institutions' (Offe, 1976, p. 83). This view of education recognises its so-called ideological functions. The values deemed important in a particular society are thus transmitted and constantly reinforced by the education system. According to this view, we are initiated into the values of the dominant class and our success under capitalism relies upon our willingness to adopt and live in line with these values.

Although Marxists are suspicious of the education system under capitalism, they have often been at the forefront of those demanding the expansion of education provision for the working class. Marx and Engels believed that the capitalist state should provide education for the working class. This was justified on the grounds that it would raise the cultural level of the working class (Engels, 1971) and that it would equip people with the skills necessary for industrial life and to make them fit to live in a socialist society (Marx, 1866). Marxists, of course, would have little time for private education as this could be seen as the traditional domain of social and economic elites. There are some alternative providers, like the Workers' Education Association and trade union colleges in Britain, but such provision is focused on adult education rather than schooling for children. Unless there is a socialist transformation of society, it would seem that Marxists are stuck with state provision and are left as radical critics and monitors of the capitalist education system.

Conclusion

Marxists do not appear to be willing to compromise with capitalism or to make capitalism more bearable for the poorer sections of the community. Although some would argue that advances can be made by using the welfare state (see Ferguson, Lavalette and Mooney, 2002), many Marxists see the welfare state as an illusion imposed upon the workers to keep them quiet. For Marxists, capitalism is a flawed, unstable and unjust system and it is argued that the welfare state can do little more than deal with the symptoms of social ills and prolong the life of the capitalist system. They mistrust the concessionary nature of social provision and warn the working class in particular that these concessions can be taken away at the whim of a reactionary government. In the chapter on neo-liberalism (Chapter 5), we saw how this can happen. For Marxists, citizens need a guaranteed social right to material security. In their view, this could not be achieved under capitalism but required a complete economic, social and political transformation of society. Marxists argue that social justice could only be attained under a system of collective provision, in which we contribute what we can and we take what we need. It could be argued, however, that Marxism works better as a critique of the welfare state (and of capitalism) than as a constructive plan for the future. Given that many Marxists are disinterested in working towards social reform and that they are positively hostile to designing blueprints for the future, they tend to leave a lot to fate and to the dynamic energy and vision of active revolutionaries. Regardless of whether we accept their views on the probable demise of capitalism, they make an important contribution to the debate on welfare by pointing out the limitations of both bourgeois freedom (negative liberty) and of social reformism.

8

Radical Critics: Feminism

Whereas Marxists criticise the welfare state for failing to deal adequately with the long-term needs and interests of the working class, feminists believe that the welfare state fails to challenge with any degree of conviction inequalities between men and women. Feminism differs significantly from liberalism, conservatism and socialism because it attempts to cut across class divisions and concentrate upon issues surrounding gender. Feminists investigate the roots of the oppression of women and attempt to suggest ways in which women can liberate themselves from the constraints of patriarchal (male dominated) society. They understand that women are discriminated against because of their sex and that women have specific needs which require fundamental economic, social and political change (Wilford, 1994). For some feminists this involves a policy of equal opportunities, while others want to undo the bonds between men and women, transform the social and economic system or revolutionise our understanding of the environment. As we will see, feminists have some interesting things to say about the character of Western society and about the limitations of the current system of social provision. It is clear that the welfare state, whatever its original intentions, has not liberated women from discrimination and oppression. Although this might be a lot to expect from a system designed primarily to stabilise the status quo and alleviate a relatively narrow band of social problems, feminists have been instrumental in revealing some of the severe limitations of current welfare states. Indeed, many feminists can be viewed as radical critics of the way Western societies approach welfare provision. This can be illustrated by taking a look at a variety of authors including (though by no means confined to) Betty Frieden, Carole Pateman, Kate Millett and Ann Oakley.

Economy

Feminism borrows a great deal from other ideologies. Liberal and socialist feminists, in particular, rest their arguments on familiar foundations. Liberal feminism tends to appeal to women who are searching for fair treatment in their careers because it aims to increase the profile and power of women within the capitalist system, while doing relatively little to challenge the foundations of capitalism itself. Liberal feminism shares with the liberal ideology as a whole the view that the rough edges of capitalism can be made less abrasive through enlightened legislation, formulated and applied by people of good will. It often appears as if liberals regard social problems almost as design flaws in an otherwise efficient and worthy social system. An important part of being a liberal is to accept the permanence of capitalism and to look for ways to make it fairer. For liberal feminists, this means exposing it to the valuable contributions that can be made by women. Brennan and Pateman (1998) argue that although the modern system promises to advance freedom and equality for women, capitalism separated the bulk of economic activity from the majority of households and thereby increased the power of men. In their view, it was not until the late twentieth century that women's rights were given due recognition and that this effectively marked the 'last stage of the bourgeois revolution' (Brennan and Pateman, 1998, pp. 97, 110). From a liberal feminist perspective, women need fair access to the opportunities offered by the capitalist system.

Whereas liberal feminists believe that women can benefit from participating in the competitive capitalist system, socialist feminists have argued that capitalism itself stands in the way of the advancement of women. Socialist feminism attempts to use the Marxist economic critique of capitalism and infuse Marxism with a gender dimension. While not ignoring the importance of class, socialist feminists argue that the traditional Marxist analysis was incomplete because it failed recognise the importance of gender. Although Marx showed little interest in the gender question, Engels produced a tract on 'The origins of the family, private property and the state' (1884), which has become known as a classic statement of socialist feminism. Engels traced the subordination of women to the economic system. He claimed that women originally had control over reproduction, the domestic sphere and men and that this forced men to look for status and power outside of the home. Once out of the home, men were thought to have claimed pieces of land for themselves and, once they had property to hand on, they wanted to ensure that their partners were faithful so looked for ways to exert control over women. The subordination of women is thus traced to the institution of private property and the emancipation of women to the abolition of private property.

Following this logic, socialist feminists have argued socialism is needed as a prior condition for the emancipation of women. They claim that the subordination of women will disappear under socialism and that removing economic divisions between men and women will allow for greater equality and freedom inside marriage. For modern socialist feminists, the problem lies in the nature of the patriarchal system that moulds the economic, social and cultural systems in the interests of men. If the origins of subordination are economic, it makes sense to concentrate upon changing the economic system (Mitchell, 1984; Jardine and Swindells, 1989). Socialist feminists are critical of separatism or women-only campaigns and believe that economic and political change relies upon men and women working together within the socialist movement. Separatism is thought to undermine class unity and alienate both men and women. Feminists in Sweden have been particularly committed to working with men in existing institutions, but it has been argued that this has hampered the development of more radical feminist initiatives (Ginsburg, 1992, p. 57). It is clear, however, that socialist feminists believe that there is little to be gained from extending the rights of women within the capitalist system and that a radical overhaul of the economy is needed before social conditions and social relations can be transformed in any far-reaching and meaningful way.

Just because some feminists have borrowed their economic frameworks from the liberal and socialist traditions, it does not mean that they regard these economic foundations as being unimportant. On the contrary, many feminists recognise that the patriarchal control of the capitalist system subordinates women and that the advancement of women relies upon challenging the injustices of this system. Whereas liberal feminists want greater opportunities for women in the existing system and socialist feminists want to overthrow capitalism, other feminists look for ways to withdraw from the system and create their own economic environments. Radical feminists, in particular, have been active in developing women-only cooperatives as an alternative to working with or for men (Coote and Campbell, 1987; Taylor, 1992). For radical feminists, economic issues should be discussed in the context of sexual politics. Competing ideologies are deemed insufficient because they fail to give sufficient weight to the gender dimension of the economic, social and political systems.

Feminist perspectives on the economy illustrate the importance of gender issues when considering the impact of capitalism on the life of the individual. For feminists, we live in an economy dominated by the interests of men. The harsh economic calculations that are so central to classical and neo-liberalism would appear to be inconsistent with many features of the feminist argument. Whereas conservatives promise compassion and charity, feminists demand justice. The mild reformism of social democracy and the third way is likewise rejected for its failure to challenge patriarchy and for its apparent inability to look beyond rearranging the class balance of society. For feminists, women are too often treated as disposable units of labour, not only by the capitalist class but also by supporters of the mainstream ideologies. For many feminists, capitalism is rejected for failing to accommodate the needs of women. In contrast, feminist economics place gender at the centre of the analysis and relegate issues of class and economic efficiency to the periphery.

Social values

Despite all of the differences in the way that feminists regard the roots of the oppression of women and the source of their liberation, they are united in the belief that the economic, social and political dominance of men must be dismantled. Feminists recognise that power relations between the sexes are socially determined and therefore subject to change. Whereas conservatives will talk about natural inequalities, feminists often side with those who argue that power structures are determined by minority groups seeking to further their own interests. There is no reason to believe that men should always have dominant positions in society. Feminists point out that human nature and power relations are not fixed and that an egalitarian social transformation relies, at least in part, on the desire of people to change. Feminists often speak about 'human potential' rather than 'human nature'. They argue that gender identities and roles are not preordained but depend upon '... the dialectical relationship between the thoughts, feelings and actions of individuals in the web of connections in which we find ourselves' (Rowbotham, 1989, p. 113). Feminists are apt to show us that the subordination of women is not a natural state of affairs but one created by men.

Feminists believe that freedom relies upon having access to the corridors of power, to opportunities in work and to equal civil rights. They have been instrumental in fighting for rights which were denied to women in Western societies until fairly recently and are still denied to women in some cultures. Feminists recognise that in a patriarchal society, men determine social norms. Those who manage to fit in are praised; those who do not are shunned. It would appear that men have granted to themselves the power to limit the roles of women. They define what is sexually attractive (especially through their control of the media) and what is socially and morally acceptable for women to say and do. The freedom of women is often limited not only by the law or economic inequalities but also by the dominance of men. It could be argued that freedom can only be meaningful if it takes into account this gender dimension. If this is the case, the value of feminism extends far beyond what it can offer to women. It can, indeed, have an important place in programmes designed to liberate society from oppressive practices (see Coote and Campbell, 1987; Wilford, 1994).

Feminists do differ in the way they view equality. For liberal feminists, equality of opportunity is of paramount importance and they have had a particularly important role in campaigning against discrimination against women at work (Lewis, 1992, pp. 117–119). Socialist feminists, on the other hand, tend to be critical of equal opportunities legislation because they believe it serves the interests of middle class women and that it does little to undermine the economic roots of women's oppression. For socialist feminists, the capitalist system itself is at fault rather than outdated social conventions. Although reforming pay scales and outlawing discrimination at work might help women in the short term, socialist feminists would argue that this merely prolongs the subordination of women. For socialist feminists, a great deal of harm can be done by those fooled by the illusion of equality under capitalism (Coote and Campbell, 1987, pp. 22–26). While liberal feminists look for equality under capitalism, socialist feminists seem to expect women to wait for equality and work towards the creation of a socialist society. It is clear by contrast that many radical feminists have little interest in equality and are far more interested in preserving and enhancing the uniqueness of women (Rowbotham, 1989, p. 19). This can mean many things. It can mean that women delve into the unique characteristics of their gender, or look for ways to unite with other women to develop new projects free from the unwanted interference of men. Although men control the existing public sphere, in that they tend to dominate politics and the upper levels of the business community, it does not mean that women have to work and play according to the rules set by men.

For many feminists, the creation of social justice relies upon the abolition of the patriarchal system. Kate Millett argued in *Sexual Politics* (1977) that the relationship between the sexes is one of dominance and subordination and that, under the patriarchal system, men dominate women. It was argued that men hold top positions in society and that the dominant religions, cultures and ethics are manufactured by men in the interests of men. One solution to this imbalance, at least according to radical feminists, is to be found in sexual liberation for women and the end to both marriage and the burdens of motherhood. At the very least, this would have to be accompanied by the collective provision of childcare (Millett, 1977, pp. 62–65; Wilford, 1994, pp. 271–273). This shows, among other things, that the liberation of any particular group in society does not rely solely upon how members of this group see themselves. Although a transformation in consciousness, through which members of oppressed groups refuse to remain in a subordinate position and push for social and political change, is a vital ingredient in challenging and reforming dominant social values it often has to be accompanied by tangible policies. The liberation of women can be seen to involve not only women transforming themselves but also having sufficient support for such things as child care, without which many women could feel isolated and restricted in the functions they perform and in the lives they lead.

The social values supported by feminists are framed to liberate women from the dominance of men. When many of the older ideologies talked about freedom of the individual, almost by default this often meant freedom for men. Leaders of the business community, the trade union movement and of political parties have tended to be men. There are of course notable exceptions, but feminists could claim with some justification that women leaders continue to operate in accordance with the conventions established by men. It could be argued that men dominate the old public sphere to such an extent that women have been forced to find alternative ways to mobilise opinion and to campaign for change. While some clearly want equality with men, others have attempted to break free and to devise new ways of living and working that do not rely upon the approval or support of men. It would seem that for many feminists, freedom and equality mean very little within the context of a patriarchal society. Just as Marxists have argued that true freedom and equality cannot be attained for the majority under capitalism, so feminists would argue that patriarchy obstructs women and prevents them from reaching their true potential. The campaign for the liberation of women therefore involves challenging the key social values associated with the patriarchal system.

State and welfare

It could be argued that the political system is controlled by men and operates in accordance with a male agenda. Commentators claim that women are often excluded from political power because of demands of the private sphere and that women should be encouraged to form their own groups to deal with their own issues rather than compete with men for power within patriarchal institutions (Schwarzmantel, 1994, pp. 114–116). Although some feminists are committed to separatist endeavours, others will look to the state for practical legislation to improve the standing of women in the patriarchal system. For these feminists, the state is there to be captured and put to good use.

Feminists tend to hold on to a broad conception of politics, which in turn colours the way that they view the state. A key feature of the feminist argument is to be found in its rejection of the liberal distinction between the public and private spheres. Susan Okin (1991) points out that liberals want to protect the private sphere from social and governmental intervention and that this 'private sphere' is too often equated with 'domestic' life. Women are thought to inhabit this private sphere, while men assume control of the public realms of economic and political life. Given this control, men grant to themselves political rights and the right to control their 'own' household. The feminist response is to declare that the 'personal is political' because personal relationships involve an element of power. Feminists have thus sought to challenge power relations within the family with the aim of transforming gender roles. This refusal to accept the liberal distinction between the public and the private has also led some feminists to argue that the domestic sphere should be open to state intervention (Okin, 1991, pp. 67–90). It is certainly the case that the reluctance of the state to intervene in the 'domestic sphere' can leave many forms of abuse hidden from society and that women have had to fight hard for recognition of their rights within the family. It appears to be in the interests of patriarchy to draw a firm line between public and private actions and, in some cases, allow men the freedom to intimidate and abuse their partners.

Although the feminist dictum that 'the personal is political' might appear to relegate the importance of the state, feminists have argued that we should recognise that governments play an important role in distributing power between the genders (Sapiro, 1998, pp. 78–79). Pringle and Watson (1998), for example, claim that there exists a dynamic relationship between the state and gender and that the state both reflects and reinforces inequalities between the sexes. They point out that the state is far from a stable entity and that it changes constantly as a result of political struggles (Pringle and Watson, 1998, pp. 214–218). If the state does indeed have a fluid nature, it would make sense for liberation movements of all types to do what they can to influence the current and future shape of the state and to undermine its discriminatory features. The state, as we have seen, can have a dramatic impact upon the character and shape of society. So much so that it would seem inadvisable to ignore its operations and to underestimate its power.

Although the state seems to protect the patriarchal system, there are certainly sections of the feminist movement that want to harness the powers of the state and use these powers to advance the welfare of women. During the 1960s and 1970s, many liberal feminists concentrated upon securing equal rights through the welfare state. It was argued that the state had an important role in undermining the power of men and in helping to secure legal and financial independence for women. Liberal feminists fought against stereotypes and attempted to carve out new functions for women. In Britain, they led campaigns to ensure that family allowance was paid directly to women rather than through their husband's pay packet as some form of tax credit (McIntosh, 1981, pp. 119–120). For liberal feminists, it is important that the state removes the barriers to women and, according to this line of thought, the state should ensure equal opportunities, help with child care and provide training for women returning to work after raising a family. The welfare state is thought to have the potential to reduce inequalities and respond to the needs of women because it can offer '… both a possibility and a place for the extension of women's economic and social rights' (George and Wilding, 1994, p. 136). If the root of women's oppression lies in the unfair distribution of economic rewards and opportunities for advancement, then it is clear that the welfare state could be used to assist women to progress both economically and socially. This view suggests that the gender imbalance in economic and social power can, to a certain extent, be redressed through the redistribution of resources and through a well-financed and clearly coordinated welfare state. Fraser (1998), for example, argues that the welfare state allows for 'affirmative redistribution policies' and that it can do at least something to redress inequalities in the economy. In her view, welfare states often rest upon an '… official commitment to the equal moral worth of persons' (Fraser, 1998, p. 449). It would seem, moreover, that welfare states have helped to change gender relations in a number of countries. In Denmark, for example, the welfare state serves to integrate women into the public sphere rather than exclude or marginalise the role of women in society. It is said, indeed, that Scandinavian welfare states are 'women-friendly' in the extensive support they give to families and in the funding they provide for child-care facilities. Liberal feminist ideas are also expressed in many progressive welfare ventures in Australia, where a number of services are delivered by and for women. This has stemmed, in part, from the close ties between the women's movement and the labour movement (Pateman, 1989a, pp. 144–146; George and Wilding, 1994, pp. 136–137, 145; Pringle and Watson, 1998, pp. 209–214).

It has been argued that liberal feminism is flawed by its simplistic view of the state. Liberal feminists assume that the state can be used to redress the balance between the sexes. This can be seen as an over-optimistic view of the neutrality of the state and a superficial view of the subordination of women. Liberal feminists concentrate almost exclusively upon extending the rights and opportunities of women in the public sphere. This fails to take into account that women are also subordinated in the private sphere. Essentially, liberal feminism is a response to the aspirations of predominantly white middle class women (George and Wilding, 1994, pp. 131–132). Liberal feminists, in their push for equal rights, rely upon men and women cooperating and upon their willingness to overlook differences between the sexes. They assume, in true liberal fashion, that women can be emancipated without dismantling the existing economic system and with the blessing of men. Feminists on the left of the conventional political spectrum consider this insufficient and naïve in the extreme.

Socialist feminists believe that the subordination of women and the subordination of the working class stem from the same economic foundations and that, although welfare provision can deal with the symptoms of this subordination, it cannot do anything significant to transform unequal economic relations. While welfare policies can redistribute resources, they can only do so within a framework constructed to serve the needs of the capitalist system. Although socialist feminists tend to be critical of the welfare state, they recognise that it can have some value for women. Dependence upon the welfare state is seen as preferable to dependence upon men and, although the welfare state might be a patriarchal institution, it is considered less damaging than power relations in traditional patriarchal families. Socialist feminists are aware moreover that if they attack the welfare state, they run the risk of finding themselves entangled with reactionary forces (see Clarke, Cochrane and Smart, 1987, pp. 152–154). This ambivalence towards the welfare state owes a lot to the mixed messages found in the Marxist ideology. As we have seen, Marxists recognise that the welfare state can help oppressed groups only at the expense of perpetuating a system that is, by its very nature, oppressive. Socialist feminists find themselves in a similar position. If they reject attempts by welfare states to alleviate the oppression of women, on the grounds that these policies do not go far enough and in the fear that they stabilise an unjust system, there is always a chance that they will be branded as obstructive and blinded by ideology to the prospects of beneficial social reform. It has to be recognised that there are limits to what welfare states can achieve and that critics of the welfare state have different reasons for withholding their support and, quite often, they believe that their political programmes would circumvent the need for the patchwork welfare systems that exist at present.

For some feminists, the liberal and socialist features of feminism fail to deal with roots of patriarchy and concentrate too much on purely economic solutions. Carol Pateman (1989a, 1989b) argues that the welfare state provides no real solution. It is said to have created a two-tier system in which men have rights to welfare and women are often means-tested as dependants. Women are also expected to take on the bulk of care in the home, thus relieving the welfare state of these obligations. Liberals and conservatives are apt to claim that people are entitled to welfare if they pay into the system and that by working we buy into an insurance system administered by the state. What this fails to take into account is that women also make significant contributions to the welfare of the nation as primary carers of the young, sick and elderly. This contribution is rarely (if ever) seen as relevant to the rights of citizenship owed to women who are increasingly marginalised by the patriarchal welfare state (Pateman, 1989a, pp. 138, 140–141; 1989b, pp. 8–10).

Many radical feminists are critical of the welfare state and argue in favour of women taking care of their own welfare needs. They tend to look towards women-only groups as an alternative to centrally controlled welfare services. From a radical feminist point of view, it makes no sense to rely upon the state because the state is a male institution used to perpetuate patriarchy. Nickie Charles (2000) provides numerous examples of how women's groups have set up their own welfare services. Women's groups, for example, established their own network to assist in abortions prior to the legalisation of abortion in the United States. They also set up refuges and rape crisis centres in Britain and the United States to empower women and, in spite of all of the bureaucratic obstacles, women's groups have also run their own day care centres for children. Charles points out that these initiatives have often been '... achieved with support, albeit limited, from the state while, at the same time, retaining autonomy from the state' (Charles, 2000, p. 143). Although some commentators argue that the radical critique leads nowhere, for the idea of providing separate services can do little more than 'provide interesting insights and models' (George and Wilding, 1994, p. 134), the alternative is unthinkable. Even if radical feminists are unable to tend to all their own welfare needs, it does not mean that they should resign themselves to a male-dominated system. Radical feminists are aware that the emancipation of women requires the reduction of the power of men and believe that this cannot be done by cooperating with an agenda set in the interests of the patriarchal system. For such radical spirits, campaigning for reform within the existing structure can be seen as tantamount to collaboration with the enemy.

For feminists, the state provision of welfare services can create real problems for women. Although it is no doubt useful for those who operate within a broadly liberal framework, feminists who are committed to bringing about fundamental and radical change can view the welfare state as a hindrance and as something of a Trojan horse. Just as Marxists argue that the welfare state protects the capitalist system, so socialist and radical feminists are inclined to see the state provision of welfare as one of the many methods designed to maintain the subordinate position of women and to protect patriarchal values. Writing in the 1970s, Elizabeth Wilson pointed out that the welfare state allows the state to influence and control the way that women raise their families and that feminists should seek to establish a welfare system which '... instead of trying desperately to shore up the family in its present inadequacies, would extend the possibilities of social relationships that are more successfully supportive and nurturant' (Wilson, 1977, p. 187). The alternatives for feminists seem to be quite clear. The choice would appear to be between working for incremental change within the existing system or rejecting patriarchal structures and the promise of piecemeal progress. From a feminist point of view, the welfare state could be seen as a concession given in the hope of marginalising, or even silencing, the voices of dissident groups.

Welfare and social policies

Feminists have argued that the welfare state too often consists in a series of measures designed to support the power and position of men in society. Rather than recognise women as having independent rights as citizens, welfare states often assume that women will be dependent upon men. In this way, the welfare state could be seen to have had a part to play in maintaining gender roles and the dependent status of women. Feminist commentators (Williams, 1989; Lewis, 1992) have argued that the British welfare state has done little to eradicate the subordination of women. The welfare state relies upon women taking an active role in caring for the young and the old and it assumes almost by default that the traditional sexual division of labour will continue. For many feminists, this makes it imperative for women to look for alternatives to the welfare state.

Benefits

Many feminists are prepared to support the state provision of benefits because it is preferable to leaving women, especially those who are raising a family, dependent upon men. What feminists object to, however, is the way that the benefits system treats women. For the purpose of entitlement to benefits, women are often regarded as dependent upon their husbands or partners. It could be argued (see Williams, 1989; Lewis, 1992) that the post-war welfare state in Britain was primarily concerned with inequalities between social classes rather than between men and women and this has, to a large extent, continued to be the case. Poverty among women runs higher than among men, and women are often expected to give up their paid work to look after children and sick relatives. Feminists have argued that the welfare state in general and the benefits system in particular is based upon extremely outdated views about the role of women in society and divisions of labour within families. Ann Oakley (1981), for example, argues that the failure of the government to deal with the problem of low pay for women, and to recognise women's rights in access to benefits, stems from the view that men are the primary breadwinners in society. In her view, the benefits system actively discriminates against women (Oakley, 1981, pp. 293–296). Until political leaders respond constructively to the social and economic needs of women, the welfare state is only ever likely to gain limited support among feminists.

Feminist groups have fought hard to win certain rights to benefits. During the First World War, liberal feminists in Britain were active in a campaign for family allowances. In 1917, the Family Endowment Society was formed and it argued that the campaign for a family allowance should be based upon the recognition of the valuable contribution to society made by mothers. Groups like the National Union of Women's Suffrage Societies argued that there needed to be a collective solution to the poverty experienced by women and their families and it called for community nurseries to be formed to allow more women to go out to work (Clarke, Cochrane and Smart, 1987, pp. 67–71). Liberal feminism also had an important impact upon the development of American social policies. Women's groups were active in the United States during the early years of the twentieth century in pushing for child benefits and for protective legislation for women workers. While most of Europe developed paternalist welfare states, resting upon a view of the male breadwinner, the United States is said to have established a more 'maternalist' welfare state which took into account at least some of the needs of women (Lewis, 1998). The Swedish system is even more sensitive to the roles performed by women and recognises care work and raising a family as a basis for entitlement for benefits. (Charles, 2000, p. 124). For liberal feminists in particular, the emphasis is placed upon attaining equal rights. Mary McIntosh (1981), for example, argued in favour of allowing the married woman access to benefits in her own right regardless of the employment status of her partner and, in her view, this form of 'disaggregation' would help to undermine inequalities within marriage (McIntosh, 1981, pp. 127–131). It is clear that for feminists, discrimination in the benefits system can have a catastrophic effect upon the status, identity and power of women.

Feminists are far from happy about the skewed nature of the benefits system. Rather than stick to the male breadwinner model in which rights to benefits are given only to those in paid employment, feminists have argued that benefits should be available for women in recognition of their work in the domestic sphere. It could be argued that the benefits system is sexist in the way it operates in many countries. Without considering the implications for women, benefit systems could be seen as too prone to relegate women to the status of a dependent and thus ignore the multitude of tasks performed by many women in the home. From a feminist point of view, this shows that the welfare state cannot be trusted to respect and deal with the needs of women in a just way.

Housing

Feminist perspectives on housing often concentrate on the problems faced by women when they have to raise a family on their own and, as a result, experience problems associated with living on a relatively low income. Single-parent families often have restricted choices in the world of work because of the need to fit work around childcare. It might also be the case that single-parent families find that training and other out-of-hours work is considerably more difficult to arrange and to complete successfully, thus creating barriers for those lone carers looking to advance their careers. Although some feminists might be willing to support government intervention in housing, others have argued that '... reliance on the state could reinforce women's lesser citizenship in a new way' (Pateman, 1998, p. 264). If feminists do accept state intervention in housing, it is not without recognising that problems can arise from depending upon the state.

Social housing in Britain was originally designed for traditional families. As we saw when discussing social democracy, there was often a vetting process involved and preference was given to people who were employed. The status and reputation of social housing decline considerably in the post-war period and made it relatively easy for the Conservative government to sell off the housing stock. It has been argued that these government policies did positive damage to the experience that women have of social housing. Cuts in the social housing budget in Britain during the 1980s (see Chapter 5) had a particularly harmful effect upon women. Women who are lone parents, divorced and widowed often rely rather more than men on social housing because they often live on lower incomes and are therefore less able to negotiate affordable mortgages. In addition, it has been argued that lesbian women have been discriminated against by local authorities because housing regulations failed to recognise and deal with the homelessness of women following the breakdown of a lesbian relationship (Woods, 1996). From a feminist point of view, it could be argued that social housing fails to deal adequately with the needs of women and with the changing nature of families.

Feminist groups do not always rely upon extensive levels of state support. Women often take an active role in developing alternative forms of accommodation for themselves and there are a number of inspiring examples in Britain. The Women's Pioneer Housing Project was established in London in the early twentieth century to provide housing for women involved in the suffrage movement and now has over 1100 properties. In Scotland, there are a number of important housing projects including Amazon House in Edinburgh and, in Glasgow, Four Walls and Take Root. The latter project encourages women to build their own homes and to use women contractors with an eye to creating female-friendly housing that gives due care and attention to aesthetics, solar energy and security (Chaudhuri, 1999). In Wales, Welsh Women's Aid have run effective campaigns to secure accommodation for those women leaving refuges (Charles, 2000, p. 143). If the welfare state is indeed a patriarchal institution, then it makes sense for women to take the initiative in this way. Separatism can influence not only the way, but also where, women choose to live. For some sections of the feminist movement, it is important to find alternatives to the state provision of housing.

Health

Feminists tend to look at health in its social context. Rather than see health as an individual possession for which we are responsible as individuals, they recognise that both the health and health care we experience are at least in part socially constructed. Ann Oakley (1993) claimed that health is not simply determined by the choices we make as individuals, as these choices are also socially determined. In her view, health is a 'social product' and one that is '... the responsibility of both the governors and the governed to ensure a healthy social environment in which health is no longer something to be striven for, the prerequisite of a few, but everyone's birthright' (Oakley, 1993, pp. 106–107). Feminists have pointed out that access to health care should be regarded as a universal right and that the provision of appropriate health care should be the responsibility of the government (Norsigian, 1996). At least some feminists would place themselves alongside liberals and social democrats in demanding equal rights to health care and active government intervention in the provision and maintenance of the health care system.

Feminists are, however, extremely critical of the way that the health system can discriminate against women. Feminists have argued that health care has been used as a way to control women. This applies in particular to the area of reproduction, which is often treated as a form of illness by the medical profession and is an example of attempts by men to dominate women (Lewis, 1992). Feminists claim that men dominate many health professions. Where women health professionals are in a strong position, in midwifery, for example, the state still intervenes to ensure that the interests of male doctors are not jeopardised. Women are underrepresented in the ranks of doctors and administrators and tend to have relatively subordinate roles in health care (Baggott, 1998). Given that men dominate the upper reaches of the medical profession, it is hardly surprising that the way in which women are treated in the health system reflects this gender imbalance. Feminists claim that medics often fail to understand the medical needs of women and that science, like other systems of knowledge, often has a definite gender bias. Tasmin Wilton (1992) points out, for example, that medical textbooks often treat men's bodies as the norm and talk of the complications arising from dealing with the bodies of women. This would seem to create the illusion that there is 'medicine', which deals with the health of men, and 'special medicine' dealing with the health of women.

Feminists argue that it is important for women to have control over their own health and fertility. This is facilitated by such things as well-women groups and by ensuring that women can choose where they give birth. It has been argued, however, that such measures are sometimes regarded as a threat by vested interests in gynaecology and obstetrics (Abercrombie and Warde, 2000, p. 502). It is argued that the problem of sexism in health care needs to be addressed by shifting power away from doctors, a profession dominated by men, and securing greater autonomy for midwives and nurses given that these professions are usually dominated by women (Baggott, 1998, p. 78). This shift in power, although not enough on its own, could help to undermine at least some of the fallacies about the health needs of women. Feminists are also keen on women taking control of their own health care. They have been active in forming a network of self-help groups for women, especially since the 1970s, and these groups have done a reasonable amount to shake the complacency of the medical establishment (Norsigian, 1996). According to Oakley (1993), women's groups should be willing to take more responsibility for women's health issues and rely to a far less extent upon male medics. Feminists are willing to support these groups within the state system or as alternatives to state provision.

Education

Education plays an important part in the feminist programme because, if gender identities and inequalities between the sexes are socially determined, then the education system must partly be responsible for the subordination of women. If women are to free themselves from the mental slavery perpetuated by men, reviewing the content and purpose of education would seem to be of central importance. Liberal feminists pay particular attention to education, partly because they believe that inequalities between men and women can be overcome by changes in the law and by ensuring that men and women are treated equally. From a liberal feminist perspective, the subordination of women is a cultural phenomenon and, as such, it is open to change. It therefore makes sense for these feminists to pay attention to the education system and to look for ways to make it more open to the needs of women.

Feminists have long argued that many of the differences between men and women are created by the education we receive. Writing in the 1790s, Mary Wollstonecraft claimed that women are enfeebled by education and that if the minds of women were allowed to develop the '... nobler passions and motives will govern their appetites and sentiments' (Wollstonecraft, 1982, p. 179). Liberal feminists in particular have been critical of the education system for keeping women in a subordinate position in society. Betty Frieden (1971) complained that the education given to girls often aimed to cultivate the skills and temperament necessary to serve the interests of men. This was done in part by convincing us that boys and girls (and men and women) are suited to different academic subjects. For liberal feminists, equity is important. They argue that if men and women are to have equal opportunities in society, the education system must be so arranged to nurture all students regardless their gender.

Feminists believe that education can assist in transforming gender relations. For Frieden (1971), the solution lay in expanding educational provision for women and encouraging women to take a broader range of courses that would in turn make them more suited to a wider variety of occupations and roles in society. In her view, there needed to be a national programme in America for educating and retraining women equivalent, in many ways, to the educational opportunities offered to members of the armed forces when they returned home. This programme would have to be financed by the government and it would have to take into account the other commitments that women often have. This would mean expanding opportunities in part-time adult education in particular (Frieden, 1971, pp. 367–375). Feminists are aware that many women want to combine a career and a family. They recognise, moreover, that the advancement of women relies upon opportunities being made available so that they can deal effectively with the multiple roles that many have in the private and public spheres. If women are to take more advantage of opportunities for training and in higher education, it is quite possible that the way further and higher education is delivered must be changed. Feminists have argued for many years that we need to move away from compulsory education and from outdated dependence upon book learning. Looking forward to the future development of cybertechnologies, Shulamith Firestone (1979) claimed that it should be possible to find more efficient ways to transmit information in ultra-modern learning centres (Firestone, 1979, pp. 218–220). To a certain extent, such methods have become a reality with the spread of distance learning programmes.

Conclusion

Feminists hold a variety of views on the economy. Whereas socialist feminists are critical of capitalism, liberal feminists are content to work within the confines of the capitalist system and to use economic and social policies to enhance the welfare of women. Like many liberals, they defend the welfare state and expect a great deal from the social policies instituted by the state. It could be argued, however, that the welfare state is part of the patriarchal system and that it caters primarily to the welfare needs of men. Services tend to be geared around equipping people with the skills and health necessary to work and with providing financial relief for the unemployed. Other needs such as child support, family allowance and child-care facilities seem to be marginalised in many welfare states and have only been introduced as a result of active campaigning by women's groups. Although many feminists recognise that the welfare state can provide support for women, they are often sceptical of relying too heavily upon the state and often doubtful about the future of the welfare state and its role in the liberation of women from the constraints of patriarchal society. Like many Marxists, feminists argue that the capitalist state is too limited in the interests it supports and that the state needs to be more inclusive in its social remit. For many feminists, this involves stripping the state of its patriarchal bias. Feminists are also aware that the prospects for an inclusive welfare society or welfare state rely upon transforming power relations in the welfare sector and that more women need to be involved in the management and delivery of social services. For radical feminists in particular, women should take control over their own welfare needs. Rather than rely upon the benevolence of a welfare state, they ask women to rely more upon each other. In so doing, they illustrate further the limitations of the welfare state.

9

Radical Critics: Greens

In the final chapter on the radical critics, we will take a look at the ideas of the greens. Often strange, but rarely dull, the greens question the core foundations of the industrial capitalist system. Unlike the ideologies covered in Chapters 2–6, the greens do not want to tinker with the distribution of the national product or promise to reward their supporters with tax cuts or increments to social provision. The greens, like the Marxists and some sections of the feminist movement, believe that society needs to be completely transformed and organised according to a different set of values. Having more in common with the political left than with the political right, the greens are often critical of capitalism and argue that the profit motive can and does have a disastrous effect upon the environment and that some form of public regulation is necessary to limit the damage caused by private companies. The greens also ask us to reconsider how we view ourselves and our relations with each other and with the planet. It is clear that they want us to transform the way we think and abandon the common preoccupation with material gratification. Like the other radical critics, they argue that there are definite limits to what the welfare state can achieve and that we should look elsewhere for our salvation. This chapter on the greens will draw upon the ideas of a range of theorists including Murray Bookchin, Andre Gorz, Fritjof Capra, Jonathan Porritt and will also include something on the policies of the Green Parties in Britain, the United States and in Australia.

Economy

The greens share with other radicals a distinct mistrust of capitalism. It could be argued indeed that the greens have reformulated socialist thought and added an extra layer to our understanding of the destructive features of the capitalist system. Seabrook (1988) argued that socialists of the nineteenth century absorbed the capitalist faith in industrialism in a largely uncritical way and that they had hoped to hijack capitalist wealth and apply it to '… more benign and humane ends than private profit' (Seabrook, 1988, p. 3). Lambert (1988) has argued that whereas the socialist analysis suited the nineteenth century, with its emphasis upon tackling the problems of poverty, this analysis is unsuited to the age of industrial decline and environmental destruction. Some greens, like Martin Ryle (1988) for example, believe that socialists and the greens are involved in a 'converging critique' of the wasteful nature of capitalism and are equally concerned about the ways in which capitalism creates (or at least exacerbates) inequalities (Ryle, 1988, p. 192). Notwithstanding these similarities, the greens can still argue that they have something reasonably distinctive to say about the dominant economic arrangements of the modern age. This distinctiveness stems from their conviction that the solution to the majority of modern social and economic ills does not lie solely in redistributing wealth between the classes, but in challenging the very foundations of the industrial capitalist system.

For the greens, the industrial capitalist system is repugnant because it is wasteful, destructive and unsustainable. Premised on the belief that we can produce whatever we want, it is thought to feed on human greed and encourage the use of destructive technology. The greens point out that infinite production is impossible to achieve and sustain because resources are finite. It is argued that we will eventually have to curtail our consumption, regardless of whether we want to, because the existing system is inherently unstable and continues as if there are no real limits to the resources we can consume. The greens believe that if we reduce our consumption of energy sources, we can reduce levels of production and the amount we consume. Alternative sources of energy (wind, water and sun) can be tapped without depriving future generations of their supply of natural resources. These forms of energy might be less efficient, but they are considered to be capable of satisfying our needs even if they cannot satisfy all of our wants. Many greens are adamant that recycling is not enough and that we must replace consumer society with a more sustainable system in which we pay more attention to spiritual fulfilment. Greens have argued that we need to rediscover our links with the earth and that without this spiritual change it is impossible to create a sustainable society (Dobson, 1990, pp. 16–18, 104). A sustainable society is one that works within the confines of available resources and one that is constructed to last in the long term rather than to satisfy short-term desires. For many greens, we must look to the future rather than concentrate upon satisfying our fleeting consumer desires.

The greens believe that placing restrictions upon the growth of the economic system will have a beneficial impact upon our sense of community and upon the social system as a whole. The American economist Herman Daly claims that the idea of pursuing growth is put forward because people doubt the practicality of sharing existing resources. This is thought to illustrate that modern society exists in a spiritual void. He claims that communities can benefit from scarcity because scarcity encourages greater degrees of sharing and cooperation. Middle class suburbs are displayed as examples of areas combining affluence and a poor sense of community (Daly, 1977, p. 149). The greens argue that affluence divides communities and harms the human spirit. By cutting back upon our material sides, it is hoped that the spirit of community could be revived. It is argued that people cooperate more when they have less and the greens believe that local communities should be able to assume control over many of the services currently provided by the state. Ted Trainer, for example, claimed that responsibilities would have to be shared out in a local area for '... care of small children, maintenance of the windmill, care for the old and of convalescents' (Trainer, 1985, p. 89). However rustic this might sound, the greens are sincere in their belief that affluent lifestyles and values of the middle class, which are praised in particular by liberals, the neo-liberals and advocates of the third way, are fragile, unsustainable and are often at the expense of the community. The greens point out, with some justification, that many of the social problems we experience in the West can be traced to the decline of community. If we are encouraged to live as isolated individuals or families and to pursue our own interests, it is unlikely to create a harmonious and well-coordinated society in which the welfare needs of all are considered to be of social importance. Within the context of the current economic system, individualism can do little to guarantee the common good. The greens, like many radicals, seem to understand this. Where they differ is in showing how this is symptomatic of a system that places value upon affluence and upon the pleasure we seem to derive from consuming material goods.

For the greens, it makes little sense to attempt to humanise the capitalist system because capitalism is inherently unjust, unstable and harmful to the natural environment. Because of this, the role of the state in a capitalist economy will only be of marginal significance. The state might be able to do something to reduce pollution by setting targets or by using taxation to penalise polluters, but such interventions would fail to address the root causes of environmental destruction and would do relatively little to reduce the damage caused by the industrial system. Whereas environmentalists might be happy to promote recycling and energy conservation, many in the green movement look for more radical and fundamental change in the way we organise our lives and in the way we produce the means of our subsistence. For these radical spirits, the capitalist economy needs to be replaced by an economy that deals with our needs rather than with our wants.

Social values

Green social values ask us to reassess our place in the natural order and to elevate the welfare of the planet over all other concerns. Whereas conventional politics is often concerned with economic issues, the green's case tends to rest upon a broader base in which we are asked to recognise that the natural and human worlds are interconnected and that we have been sidetracked from our true selves by a heartless and destructive economic system (Lambert, 1988, pp. 137–138; Parkin, 1988, p. 178). Jonathan Porritt (1988) claimed that there is a need for a more 'holistic' view of the world in which 'spiritual values' are given at least equal importance as the 'spur of materialism'. In his view, this is a '… precondition for the emergence of a genuinely sustainable system of wealth creation' (Porritt, 1988, p. 203). For this reason, the greens often assign secondary importance to those purely human values designed to make our lives more bearable.

The greens are certainly interested in forming a free society and in resisting authoritarian measures. This is shown in the way that they view the state (this will be covered in the next section) and in the way they tend to run their own organisations in a non-hierarchal and cooperative manner. For the greens, it is important that individuals have both freedom and autonomy. Consider, for example, the contribution made by the green economist Philippe Van Parijs (1997) who argued that the distinction between negative and positive liberty was less than useful and should be replaced by one between formal and real freedom. Van Parijs argues that formal freedom can be associated with the ideas of the neo-liberals and that it rests upon the belief that freedom is gained through ownership and control of private property and through ensuring that these property rights are not infringed. He claims that the problem with this view of freedom is that it seeks to maximise the freedom of (fortunate) individuals but it fails to extend freedom to all people. He warns, however, against opting for positive liberty because it can impose moral values and undermine the autonomy of the individual. According to Van Parijs, real freedom contains elements of both positive and negative liberty. It recognises that individuals should have autonomy and a range of opportunities, while at the same time it attacks unacceptable inequalities and promotes social justice (Van Parijs, 1997, pp. 4–19). For those who accept this line of reasoning, freedom and inequality are not compatible. A free society is therefore one that has, at the very least, found an effective way to deal with the inequalities created in the modern industrial capitalist system.

The greens are aware that resources need to be distributed in a fairer way and they argue that without this it would be impossible for all basic needs to be satisfied. For some, this means establishing a more frugal society while for others it entails concentrating upon needs rather than wants (Kenny, 1994, pp. 231–232, 240). They point out that the cause of poverty can be traced to inequalities in the way that goods are distributed. Andre Gorz argued in *Ecology as Politics* (1980) that poverty is caused by the rich monopolising resources and because the affluent consume in wasteful ways. Gorz claimed that simply increasing production would do little to eliminate poverty because '... poverty will only disappear if the inequalities of power and rights, which are its principal source, are also eradicated' (Gorz, 1980, p. 31). In order to achieve equality in what we consume, a new social and political system would need to be formed in which old hierarchies are abolished and the principles of social equality embraced. Material inequalities, according to Gorz, stem from other forms of inequality and they have symbolic value that would fade in significance in an egalitarian economic, social and political system (Gorz, 1980, pp. 28–32). It is clear that Gorz owes a great deal to the political left and that his ideas are important in illustrating the connection between consumerism and inequality. Consumerism, it should be noted, fuels the capitalist system and contributes towards our increased reliance upon industrial production and the perpetuation of an economic system that creates wants rather than satisfies needs. Consider the amount of money spent on advertising; the primary function of which is not to inform but to influence the way we spend our money. From a green point of view, the dreams we are sold of a consumer paradise help to conceal the extremes of inequality.

If Western society is to move away from its preoccupation with consumer satisfaction, it is clear that something has to take its place and that people need to reassess their priorities. The greens believe that individuals need to pay more attention to their spiritual sides and that this could help to reduce the appeal of material plenty. They argue that we need to concentrate less upon economic betterment and more upon spiritual growth and that happiness is said to reside in the heart not in the pocket. It is argued that if we learned to concentrate a little more upon our spiritual sides, we could gain a better understanding of our place in the world, we might become more willing to make some of the material sacrifices which the greens demand and we would have the mentality necessary to challenge the industrial order. The greens tend to have a non-materialist view of the world. They recognise that the pursuit of material wealth pays no spiritual dividends and that quality of life is of far greater intrinsic value than financial gain. For many greens, self-development and the development of nurturing relationships with each other (and with the natural world) are of fundamental importance in the construction of new political alternatives. According to John Barry, the '... philosophical basis of green political theory involves the redefinition of central concepts such as "human welfare", "development" and ultimately the whole idea of progress' (Barry, 1998, p. 189). Among other things, this relies upon our willingness to engage with a radically different way of viewing ourselves. For many greens, simply tinkering with the causes of environmental damage will do little to save the planet. Humans are asked to reassess their lives and redirect their energies away from seeking material plenty, for only in this way can the natural environment and human society survive in the long term.

Green social values clearly have more in common with the views of liberals and social democrats than with the ideas expressed by the majority of conservatives and neo-liberals. The greens have little interest in maintaining traditional patterns of authority or with giving free reign to the self-interest of the capitalist class. For many greens, capitalism has created too many problems to be left to grow continually. Rather than support negative liberty and the maintenance of inequalities, the greens seem more interested in creating a society in which people are given a greater range of opportunities and where inequalities are addressed with an eye to maximising social justice and moderating consumer demand. The greens are evidently interested in reviving a spirit of community and in eradicating as far as possible the alienation and divisiveness prevalent in modern urban and industrial society. For the greens, we need to pay more attention to quality of life and open our eyes and hearts to the fellowship of others. Their vision is one of cooperation resting upon shared responsibility for our communities and for our planet.

Welfare and the state

The attitude of the greens towards the state provision of welfare is heavily influenced by their conviction that the industrial capitalist system is destructive on a number of levels. While industrialism and capitalism destroy the natural environment and corrode the human spirit, the welfare state panders to our needs and keeps us functioning in what could be seen as an unhealthy and unsustainable system. For the greens, it is important to question the expectations that we have of the state and whether granting the state such power over our social and economic lives is in our best interests. Like other radical critics of the welfare state, the greens regard both the state and the welfare state as mechanisms by which the minority maintains control over the majority.

Greens tend to be extremely critical of the centralised state. For some, it is clear that the state helps to preserve all that is bad in the present system. Murray Bookchin (1990), for example, claimed that the state is the 'institutional apex of male civilization' and that it is primarily concerned with social coercion rather than with social administration. Bookchin is particularly critical of the centralisation of state power because it leads to greater levels of bureaucracy, erodes civic virtues and our sense of social responsibility and turns citizens into passive recipients of services. Under these conditions, people are thought to disengage from the political process and politics becomes '… degraded into statecraft, an art practised by cynical, professional manipulators of power' (Bookchin, 1990, p. 182). From a green perspective, this centralisation of state power helps to maintain the industrial capitalist system and deprive individuals and communities of effective power over their own affairs.

When considering alternatives to the centralised state, the greens look favourably upon local and community-based initiatives. Many greens want the nature of decision-making in politics to be changed. Most of them want decisions to be taken on a lower level unless there are good reasons for centralised decision-making (Dobson, 1990, p. 185). Fritz Schumacher, for example, believes that society should be organised as a network of small groups, coordinated at a national and even international level (Schumacher, 1974, p. 113). For Murray Bookchin (1990), power needs to be removed from the central state and relocated in the community. He applauds moves made by citizen groups in Germany, the United States and in France to recapture social and economic power and he argues that these initiatives provide '... evidence of popular attempts to achieve reempowerment over social life' (Bookchin, 1990, p. 183). From a green point of view, local activity can engage the attention and energy of a broader range of people and convince us of the importance of participation in our local communities. By participating in issues that affect us directly, we are more likely to understand the relevance of politics for our lives and the importance of assuming some responsibility for the welfare of both our communities and the planet.

Many greens have severe reservations about the modern welfare state. It is argued that the welfare state deals with the symptoms rather than the causes of social problems and that social problems often stem from the nature of industrial society. The greens want to reduce public spending because high public expenditure perpetuates the existing system. The welfare state is thought to rely too heavily upon professionals who do little to improve the self-reliance of their clients. It also often relies upon high levels of technology and upon bureaucratic methods. Like some of the Marxists, the greens have argued that the welfare state is too bureaucratic and too intrusive to be of positive and long-term value in building responsible and socially engaged citizens (Green Party, 1997; George and Wilding, 1994, pp. 170–171; Cahill, 1998, pp. 100–101). Although the welfare state helps to lessen the evils of capitalism, it does so by preserving the need for industrialism and for continued economic growth. This cannot be sustained in the long run because a '... welfare state which depends upon growth, and which largely fuels demands for more, is helping to exhaust the very resources upon which it depends' (Fitzpatrick, 2001, p. 346). For the greens, the long-term solution lies in dismantling the industrial system and in redesigning the social system.

The greens are in favour of a non-economic conception of welfare that takes into account social well-being and social capital. It is argued that welfare services should be decentralised and based as far as possible upon self-help and mutual aid. Achterberg (1996) believes that if people can get involved in governing their local schools and in providing a range of services on a local level, this can help us to '... develop a real identity, find a meaning in life, have an ordered set of values and be proud of our own achievements and those of the community' (Achterberg, 1996, p. 172). This could involve shifting power from the state to associations set up 'from below' and allowing these associations to assume some responsibility for service delivery in such areas as social security, education, health care and the care of the elderly (Achterberg, 1996, p. 182). For the greens, moreover, the current welfare state needs to be replaced by a system that views work in a different light. The greens believe that all work should be valued, not only paid work. Non-employment work, indeed, is an essential component of a sustainable society. They argue that all people should be paid a basic income by right and that local employment and trading systems (LETS) could be used to exchange skills and services. This system relies upon us dissociating our personal worth from our standard of living and upon our willingness to go beyond materialism. The greens recognise, however, that it would be 'cynical and unrealistic' to expect people who lived with intense material insecurity to embrace this message and that it was therefore necessary to ensure that a welfare system (however constituted) exists to give people the foundations from which to develop and to realise their potential (Green Party, 1997; Fitzpatrick, 2001, pp. 349–351). Although the greens tend to be critical of the welfare state, they recognise that welfare services still need to be provided.

For the greens, the future welfare of the planet relies upon changing the ways in which we produce and consume commodities. Although some form of welfare provision would be necessary in order to establish a greater degree of equality and social justice, this does not have to be provided by a centralised state. It is clear, moreover, that the greens want people to expect less in terms of material goods and considerably more from their own communities. Through the cultivation of social capital, it is assumed that our broad social needs will be tended to at the community level. Rather than expect the centralised state to provide for us, the greens want us to participate with other members of the community in providing for ourselves and for our neighbours. They urge us to abandon the idea that we are isolated members of the community and embrace our responsibilities towards each other and to the environment. In this way, human welfare and planetary welfare can go hand in hand.

Welfare and social policies

Like many radical critics of the welfare state, the greens believe that there is a limit to what social policies can offer. It is clear that for many greens the welfare of the planet is considerably more important that the welfare of humans and that the problems created by industrial capitalism can only be rectified to a very small degree by social policies. For those who are willing to bide their time and plan for the final collapse of industrial capitalism, social policies covering benefits, housing, health and education could be seen as an unnecessary distraction and one that will only prolong the agony of living in a destructive economic and social system. Not all greens would agree with this. Some sections of the green movement show considerably more interest in finding ways to limit the impact of industrial capitalism on their own lives and in finding practical ways to live an alternative lifestyle.

Benefits

Although the benefits system has become increasingly unpopular since the neo-liberal and conservative attacks during the 1980s, the greens have developed an extremely challenging argument in favour of access to benefits. The Green Party in Britain, for example, argues that we are all interdependent and that many people will need support at various stages in their lives. According to the Green Party, we have equal rights to the basic necessities of life and to benefits (Green Party, 2006). Even if the greens are critical of the current composition of (and rationales used by) existing welfare states, they seem to adopt many of the aims of traditional welfare regimes and recast them in a more cooperative and less judgemental manner. Rather than see the benefits system as a concession, for the greens it is a right.

The greens are critical of the existing benefits system because they believe that it is counter-productive. They argue that the benefit trap encourages idleness and makes unemployment the only economically viable option for those who can only find low-paid work. For many at the bottom of the occupational scale, paid work is often less lucrative than the range of benefits lost on taking a job. This has disastrous economic and spiritual consequences and it is thought to place a severe strain on the benefits system. Those in insecure work could be dissuaded from saving so as not to disqualify themselves from benefits in the near future, on the grounds that they have too much in savings. It can lead to depression, alienation and the feeling of being invaded by an intrusive welfare state (Green Party, 2000a; Elkins, 1986, pp. 152–155). In its *Green Party Platform* document of 2000, the Green Party in the United States argued that injustice creates instability in the social and political system and that it is necessary to take a holistic view of society, which sees any reform of the benefit system in terms of its long-term impact on future generations (Green Party US, 2000). For the greens, there are definite economic and spiritual reasons why the existing benefits system is flawed. Part of this must surely be due to the stigma attached to the receipt of benefits and to the argument that the benefits system is a concession made by the government and taxpayers to the unemployed.

The solution for the greens is not to cut back on the benefits system but to make it open to all people. Some greens argue that we need to work less, give up the pretence of full employment and make sure that all citizens are entitled to have their basic needs met. Technology could be used to reduce the working day and to free up time for leisure and for communal service. According to Andre Gorz, reducing the working week would free people to assume greater responsibility for taking care of the young, the sick, the elderly and for passing on skills. Reducing the working week would make a society based upon mutual aid a practical option (Gorz, 1983, pp. 96–98) and alleviate some of the strain placed on the welfare state. The provision of a basic income, referred to as a Citizen's Income by the Green Party in Britain, would be an unconditional right and could therefore not be withdrawn. It would provide all citizens with enough to meet their basic needs and it would not be lost by those moving from unemployment to paid work. It is argued that a basic income should contribute towards more flexible work patterns and open up the range of work that people will do. Under this system, people would be encouraged to participate in paid, unpaid and voluntary work. The Green Party argues that this would allow for the existing 'welfare state' to move closer to a 'welfare society' in which the citizens were allowed and encouraged to take on more satisfying and 'socially useful' types of work (Green Party, 2000a; Elkins, 1986, pp. 152–155). It argued that benefits should be given as a right and seen as an investment in future generations and as a recognition of the caring functions that take place in the family. This extension of the benefits system could be financed by raising taxes, by cutting expenditure on the military and by reducing subsidies for corporations. Some form of negative income tax, which would top up the incomes of the poorest sections of the community, could be used to fight poverty. This was deemed to be preferable to systems of workfare that, according to the Green Party in the United States, constitute forms of 'slave labour' (Green Party US, 2000). The greens do not, of course, want to create a benefits culture. Instead, they are interested in finding ways to encourage a more flexible approach to work. A green society would not be a land of material plenty, but one where we could develop as individuals and contribute in numerous ways to the good of the community.

Housing

Many greens in Britain tend to favour maintaining some element of social or public housing. Apart from anything else, it fits quite neatly with their commitment to spread security beyond the privileged few and with their general critique of excessive consumption. Greens have argued that it is important that government bodies oversee planning and housing construction, though some believe that this role should be decentralised and financed at a local rather than national level (Spretnak and Capra, 1985). It could be argued that the advancing of home ownership, especially in conditions of scarcity and inequality, is not necessarily the best policy to pursue and that there should be some room for other forms of ownership and tenancy. In many ways, at least some of the greens restate the broad preoccupations of centre-left theorists and practitioners, who recognise that housing should be of social (not merely individual) concern. Public and private provision of housing is deemed compatible with the broader aims of the green movement. What is important is that the government assumes responsibility for environmentally sensitive planning so as to ensure that self-seeking corporations do not damage the physical environment unnecessarily.

It is recognised, however, that the interests of the business community are often given precedence over the housing needs of citizens. George Monbiot claimed in *Captive State* (2001) that business interests have hijacked the planning process in local government and that politicians are far more interested in courting the business community than in developing a sensible and environmentally friendly housing policy. He claims that companies are being given permission to build on greenfield sites, rather than upon poorer quality brownfield areas, because it is cheaper for them to develop this land. Monbiot argues that the Blair government has shown relatively little interest in the solving the problem of homelessness. By giving rebates on council tax, the government has made it easier for people to own second homes. He complains that new housing developments are being seen as sources of investment, many of which are being purchased by people and companies in the Far East, rather than as housing to be bought by local people. In Monbiot's view, planning permission is more likely to be given for the building of luxury homes and for private fitness and leisure clubs than for affordable housing projects (Monbiot, 2001, pp. 157–161). The greens point out that the priorities held by contemporary governments do little to inform an environmentally sound housing policy.

Greens have put forward a number of alternatives to existing policies. Kemp and Wall (1990) argue that any money raised in Britain from selling council properties, a policy advanced with such zeal by the Thatcher governments, should be reinvested into social housing and into improving the existing housing stock. While they are sceptical about the motives and track record of private landlords, particularly those who make it their business to purchase slum properties and do little to improve them, they argue that councils should form closer relationships with housing associations and housing cooperatives that promise to increase the security of the tenant (Kemp and

Wall, 1990, p. 90). Housing cooperatives are favoured by greens because they avoid many of the trappings of capitalism and they are often the result of community activity rather than the impersonal activity of government agencies. This does not mean that the government can have no role. It has been pointed out, for example, that the state can help by paying for architecture and planning services because many of these community groups often operate with very few resources (Ferris, 1995). For the greens in the United States, the government should play a key role in developing environmentally sensitive housing policies rather than provide housing itself. Far more reliance is placed upon the private sector, alongside non-profit community ventures, while public housing is only supported in as far as it encourages the growth of home ownership over time (Green Party US, 2000). This difference reflects broader cultural divisions over the importance of private property and land. The liberal tradition has had a major impact on green thinking in America, while the British greens seem to owe rather more to social democratic ideas.

Health

The greens are not necessarily averse to the state providing health care but they often want the power of central bureaucracies to be curtailed. Porritt (1984), for example, was critical of the overcentralised and paternalistic nature of the British National Health Service which, unintentionally or not, he claimed had allowed individuals to avoid taking responsibility for their own health. By assuming responsibility for the nation's health, the National Health Service is thought to disempower people and it is argued that it runs the risk of imminent collapse because of the strain placed upon it by a dependent and, in some ways, irresponsible public (Porritt, 1984, pp. 82–84, 168). The greens in Britain have been particularly critical of the internal market, established by the Conservative government, because it is bound to lead to more inequalities in health care, be inefficient and lead to further privatisation of the health service (Green Party, 2000b). The Green Party in Britain has argued that health care should be decentralised and that it should be funded and controlled at a local level and be situated, as far as possible, in the community. Such a system could make extensive use of community and district nurses rather than rely upon patients travelling to large and impersonal hospitals and clinics (Kemp and Wall, 1990, p. 156; Green Party, 2000b). The greens in the United States, while not advocating the nationalisation of health care, call for a universal national insurance programme that would cover all people, whether working or not, and use public funds to purchase private health care (Green Party US, 2000). Regardless of these differences, greens in Britain and in the United States believe that the government should be active in promoting the health of the citizens and that, given the environmental causes of poor health, it should not be left to individuals to provide for themselves.

According to the greens (Gorz, 1980; Kemp and Wall, 1990), existing provision of health care pays too much attention to illness and not enough to health. From a green point of view, current health care policies, whether developed by the right or the left, create long-term problems by failing to appreciate the true nature of health and well-being and by financing a system that concentrates too exclusively on the artificial suppression of health problems through the heavy use of conventional medication. For many greens, a sensible health policy should begin with recognising the importance of environmental factors in determining the health we experience. Jonathan Porritt (1984) claimed that our environment and behaviour have a far greater impact on our health than the health care system. Although it is often believed that the growth in medical science during the nineteenth century improved the health of the population, Porritt counters this by claiming that improvements in hygiene, nutrition and sanitation had far greater effects (Porritt, 1984, p. 168). The greens are aware of health inequalities and that the economically disadvantaged tend to suffer in particular from overcrowded housing and poor diets. Greens in Britain have argued that the poor are often housed in polluted areas, where the more affluent sections of the community would not like to set up their homes, and often live in damp conditions which irritate and exacerbate many respiratory diseases (Kemp and Wall, 1990). For the greens, the current emphasis upon treating illness prevents the health service (and the government) from doing anything significant to transform the long-term health of the nation.

According to the greens, if the state wants to enhance the health of the nation it needs to tackle the environmental roots of poor health and put more resources into health promotion and alternative therapies. Environmental factors could be addressed by investing in better housing, reducing levels of pollution and changing the ways in which we work so as to reduce the stress levels associated with work in advanced industrial societies. Greater attention could also be given to subsidising healthy leisure pursuits. Rather than wait for people to visit the doctors, the greens believe that a great deal can be done to promote good health through community health campaigns and to encourage people to take more responsibility for maintaining themselves in good health. Alternative therapies are also favoured because they take a more holistic approach to health, which takes into account the way that patients experience and understand their own state of health and illness (Green Party, 2000b; Porritt, 1987; Kemp and Wall, 1990; George and Wilding, 1994). For the greens, the government has a responsibility to promote good health by targeting environmental factors and by financing health initiatives. This does not mean that we can avoid responsibility for our own health. The greens certainly want us to regulate and change our own behaviour so that we can reduce the damage that we do to ourselves and to the environment.

Education

The greens are reluctant to endorse the expansion of public education, especially if this is at the expense of other more experimental forms of education. They argue that benefits would be accrued from backing smaller schools and that room should be made for both private and alternative schools, partly because they are likely to be more innovative in the education they provide and in the '... hope that the educational experiments in those schools will affect the public schools' (Spretnak and Capra, 1985, p. 113). The greens have a holistic view of education. They emphasise the importance of education to assist people in reaching their potential and to encourage people to serve the community. The greens are particularly critical of narrow career-focussed education. Murray Bookchin, for example, claims that the contemporary education system is flawed because it '... surrenders its civic orientation to a curriculum designed to train the young for financially rewarding skills' (Bookchin, 1990, p. 71). According to the Australian Greens, education should seek to enhance the well-being of both the individual and the community and that it should not be restricted to serving the immediate interests of the current competitive society (Australian Greens, 2000).

Greens in Britain have been critical of the modern state education system for promoting a standardised, uniform and environmentally unaware approach to life and there is certainly the feeling that '... a monolithic comprehensive system is not necessarily the only way, let alone the best way, to promote the educational interests of children, nor indeed to work towards a more egalitarian, less divisive society' (Porritt and Winner, 1988, p. 57). It has been argued that the modern British education system feeds people the false belief that the aim of education is primarily to prepare us to take our place within the capitalist system rather than to develop as individuals. Because capitalism is based upon a command structure, the school pupil in particular is taught to be subservient. This is thought to place severe limits on our love of learning and damage our sense of self-worth (Kemp and Wall, 1990, pp. 159–161). The Green Party in Britain argues that the British education system was established to equip people with the skills necessary to function in an industrial capitalist society and that this fed into a long heritage of standardised and limited curricula and disregard for using a variety of styles of teaching and learning. The true ends of education are in this way hijacked by the needs of a destructive economy (Green Party, 2000c).

It is believed that education in a green society should aim to assist the individual in self-development and that it should be holistic and avoid the problems of overspecialisation. Children would be given a greater degree of freedom and encouraged to question, challenge and learn the skills necessary to cooperate as equals rather than to serve as subordinates (Kemp and Wall, 1990, pp. 161–163). The Green Party in Britain argues that green education would focus more upon social skills than upon mere academic knowledge and that the aim should be to help students become self-directed learners. Educators are asked to adapt to the needs of students rather than attempt to make students conform to existing inflexible structures. It is argued that there should be a range of properly funded options for children and that these would include such things as Steiner education, flexi-schooling and home education. Like the Blair government, the Green Party is in favour of widening access to higher education and to promoting distance learning degrees, but unlike the Blair government, the Green Party is in favour of restoring student grants for all students (Green Party, 2000c). While the Green Party in America shares this commitment to lifelong learning, it makes a point of emphasising the value of cultural diversity in education and of countering the increasing role of commercial corporations in the American education system (Green Party US, 2000). These different priorities are in themselves quite instructive. While the British greens think primarily about making better use of state funding, the American greens are concerned about curtailing the power and influence of the private sector in education. This reflects the different expectations that British and American groups have towards the state.

Conclusion

The economic and social foundations of the green argument make it clear that reformist palliatives merely prolong the life of the industrial capitalist system and consequently cause more harm to the environment. Many greens are critical of capitalism and argue that the state sides too frequently with the interests of the capitalist class. In their view, the current chaotic economic arrangements need to be dismantled and replaced by a sustainable system based upon renewable energy. It is believed that this new system should work in harmony with the environment rather than in an exploitative way. The greens attack extreme inequalities and argue that a green society would need to aspire to social justice and provide the conditions under which all citizens have opportunities for self-development. The greens rely upon the willingness of people to revisit their spiritual sides and to change their lifestyles. A green world would be cooperative and non-exploitative. Rather than being passive recipients of state social provision, they ask people to become active in their communities and to recognise that we share responsibility for the common welfare. Apart from anything else, the greens teach us that the choice is not merely between individual responsibility and the state provision of welfare services. In their view, our long-term welfare relies upon a revival in community and the spread of a radically different system of values.

10

Conclusion

In reviewing ideological perspectives on welfare, special attention has been paid in this volume to the role of the state in the provision of social services and to at least some of the alternatives to state provision. We have seen that theorists and practitioners both comment upon existing provision and discuss possibilities for the future development of human welfare. Responsibility for the advancements of welfare is given to different sections of society by the various ideologies. Ultimate responsibility could lie with individuals, the state, self-help groups, the voluntary sector or with a mixed economy of provision. The various ideologies also differ in the value they place upon charity, social rights, freedom, equality and social justice. It is hoped that the ideologies selected will provide readers with a range of ideas, from which they can pick and mix and use to evaluate their own ideas of welfare. An attempt has been made to include those ideologies that helped to form the welfare state (liberalism, conservatism and social democracy), those that have been instrumental in reforming the welfare state (neo-liberalism and the third way) and those that cast doubt upon the value of the welfare state (Marxism, feminism and the greens). While it is acknowledged that this list is by no means comprehensive, it is hoped that enough variety is provided to suit most political tastes. In this final chapter, an attempt will be made to draw together some of this material and to identify some of the ways in which ideologies can assist us in understanding issues of welfare.

Economy

Ideologies can be divided according to their views on capitalism. To argue that there is no alternative to the free market capitalist system would ignore the contribution to social and political debate made by many of the ideologies covered in this volume. It is clear that very few ideologies consider unfettered capitalism a suitable foundation for their social and political designs and that the majority of the ideologies covered herein argue that capitalism needs to be reformed or even abolished.

For supporters of capitalism, the capitalist system can seem to be part of a natural order and be consistent with good sense and with the essentials of the human makeup. Supporters of capitalism include the classical and neo-liberals. For such theorists, economic progress relies upon there being winners and losers and upon the prospect of personal gain. Making their primary appeal to the self-interest of the individual, they argue that it is wrong to criticise the workings of the market because these markets operate according to economic laws and almost always struggle when interfered with. They tend to be critical of those who base their arguments upon benevolence or abstract theories of social justice for failing to face up to the realities of economic life. Supporters of capitalism will point out that capitalism can provide us with a vast array of opportunities and the prospects of considerable material wealth and that it is down to the individual to take advantage of these opportunities. According to this line of thought, those who participate successfully in the capitalist system will in turn provide employment and opportunities for other members of society.

For those who wish to reform capitalism, the free workings of the market are viewed with some suspicion. These reformers include social liberals, some conservatives, social democrats and those who argue that there must be a third way between neo-liberalism and state control. Rather than appeal to individual self-interest, these reformers are apt to show us that we are all interconnected and that our welfare as individuals is tied up with the welfare of the whole. They point out that the harsh inequalities created by capitalism are either intolerable or unsustainable in the long run and that something needs to be done to humanise or stabilise capitalism. This relies upon the state taking an active role in regulating the system and in providing a range of services that allow individuals to live well within the system. If governments fail to intervene to prevent suffering and to promote the common good, this would be interpreted as these governments failing to fulfil their obligations to the people.

For radical critics of capitalism (including many Marxists, socialist feminists and greens) the system itself is fundamentally flawed and requires far more than the tinkering that can be performed by well-intentioned governments. These radical critics point out that governments that operate within the capitalist state are hemmed in by the interests of the capitalist system and that they are unlikely to do anything of note to challenge the foundations of capitalism. They argue that capitalists often support state intervention in the economy because it helps their system to run more smoothly and that it is indeed in the interests of capitalism for the state to play an active role in economic and social affairs. Rather than rely upon the state to reform capitalism, radical critics often argue that the long-term interests of the majority of the population rely upon capitalism being overturned and replaced with a new non-exploitative economic system.

The economic foundations of political ideologies are extremely important. They show, among other things, that unregulated capitalism creates a certain type of social system in which inequality is largely accepted. Arguments in favour of reforming capitalism often attempt to disrupt the free flow of market forces and to focus our attention upon the need to redistribute resources, even if this means increasing the power of the state in the economy and in society. It is clear that, for some, the capitalist system will never provide suitable foundations for maximising the general welfare and that alternatives to state intervention in the economy and in society have to be found. As social theorists, commentators or students of ideas, we need to ask ourselves whether capitalism can serve the general interest. From what has been said so far, it should be clear that there exists a variety of interpretations of capitalism and that our attitudes towards the capitalist system will in turn influence the way we view society and the activities of the state. Armed with at least some understanding of these economic alternatives, we can move on to consider the importance of social values in the construction of political ideologies and in the myriad of designs created for the provision of welfare services.

Social values

Social values, like economic theory, provide foundations for many ideologies and they are often considered by faithful advocates as non-negotiable. Consider, for example, the ideological makeup of a classical liberal. Are people attracted to this stream of thought because they believe passionately in the free market and in the virtues of supply and demand, or is it because they attach some overwhelming importance to the freedom of the individual? The thirst for social justice is in a similar way liable to be one of the most important factors in drawing people to social democracy, Marxism or even to the third way. Social values tap into our dreams and fears in a profound way. Is freedom more important than equality? Is social justice possible under capitalism? Do we live in a patriarchal society? Can the balance between our material and spiritual sides be changed for the better? When dealing with social values, we express something quite close to the core of ourselves and invite others to share their own philosophies of life.

Many ideologies use the notion of freedom and attempt to make a significant contribution to the way we interpret this most elusive concept. For those who believe that freedom depends upon the absence of restraint, the power and authority of the state is of fundamental importance. These theorists and movements would argue that the more the state intervenes, the less free we become. The alternative position asks us to consider freedom as the possession of something, such as a realistic chance to make the best of ourselves. For those who see things in this way, the state can potentially create the foundations for freedom by intervening in the economy and through the constructive use of social policies. For some ideologies, freedom is of paramount importance. Liberals of all varieties dedicate a significant part of their economic and social agenda to maximising individual freedom. Traditional conservatives are less convinced of its value, while many of the more radical voices warn of its illusory nature under capitalism. This does not deny, however, the importance of freedom. As individuals, we are called upon constantly to adjudicate between our own freedoms and those of other people. It is clear that some people fear freedom (both for themselves and for others) and wish to place limits upon it. In their attempts to do so, they still have to understand the nature of freedom and at least some of the ways that our thirst for freedom can manifest itself.

For those who believe that freedom is the most important social value, the search for equality could be seen as a threat to the core of their beliefs. Classical and neo-liberals in particular may well draw this conclusion and argue that equality or egalitarianism is neither possible nor desirable. Those who support equality of opportunity are often considered less of a threat than those who support equality of outcome. Equality of opportunity can be grafted onto the capitalist system quite successfully, whereas equality of outcome involves embracing a completely different value system. Marxists and at least some social democrats, greens and feminists would argue that a new non-capitalist social and economic system should at least aspire to equality of outcome. Mechanisms would no doubt need to be put in place to protect the common good from the unscrupulous, but the assumption underlying many of these radical streams of thought is that humans will adapt to their new economic and social surroundings with justice in their hearts. Under such circumstances, equality could prevail.

When looking at the contending merits of freedom and equality, it is possible to see at least the beginnings of a pattern emerging. Defenders of negative liberty are inclined to believe that freedom and equality of outcome are incompatible. This form of liberty, it could be argued, would be threatened and undermined by an interventionist state intent upon reshuffling the life chances that we have and imposing egalitarian measures upon society. Negative liberty relies upon us having the freedom to pursue our own interests without being constrained or hindered by redistributive policies. But this would seem to be a rather extreme position. Most of the ideologies considered in this volume recognise that freedom and at least some form of equality can be compatible. In defending equality of opportunity, social liberals and third way theorists could argue that freedom and this form of equality are perfectly compatible. It might be suggested that inequalities stifle freedom and that equality of opportunity is essential if freedom is to be maximised in society. Freedom can also be viewed as being compatible with equality of outcome. For those who believe in positive liberty, some form of economic redistribution (even if it stops short of equality of outcome) is often deemed essential for true freedom.

Some of the ideologies included in this volume would prioritise freedom or equality above everything else. Whereas liberals champion freedom, social democrats anchor much of what they have to say on their beliefs in equality. For other ideologies, freedom and equality might be important but alongside other values. Social justice is particularly important for Marxists and for theorists of the third way. Conservatives often display paternalist attitudes. For feminists, the idea of patriarchy looms large. While for the greens, spiritual values are often in evidence. Although important in themselves, these values often serve as a context for discussing the relative importance of freedom and equality. Even if freedom or equality is not prioritised above everything else, they continued to play an extremely important role in establishing the character of modern political ideologies.

By looking at social values, we gain further insight into the character of an ideology and into some of the key differences between ideologies. Just as theorists and practitioners can be categorised according to their attitudes towards capitalism, the social values they hold are of equal importance in identifying their place on the ideological spectrum. Each ideology has its own distinctive flavour and this flavour is determined in part by the social values it contains. Although these values are to some extent interchangeable and they certainly develop over time, it would be difficult to find a conservative who is primarily concerned with undermining the patriarchal system, a liberal who wants to establish equality of outcome or a social democrat who is willing to defend the full force of negative liberty. Each ideology draws from its own particular range of values. Although some of these values will cross over into other ideologies, there are some boundaries. Once a supporter rejects these values and goes beyond these boundaries, it would appear that this person is in need of a new ideological home.

State and welfare

The ideologies covered in this volume view the state and its role in the advancement of welfare in a variety of ways. While some ideologies clearly rely heavily upon an interventionist state, others seek to limit what the state does. We should note at this point that our attitudes towards the state will more often than not be reflected in our attitudes towards social provision. Although each ideology will have its own distinctive way of looking at the state and of evaluating its role in the advancement of welfare, it is possible to draw connections between some of these ideologies and to suggest that there are a number of views of the welfare state expressed by the ideologies contained herein.

The idea of a *limited welfare state* can be seen quite clearly in the views of classical liberals and neo-liberals. For those who support these ideologies, the state is approached with suspicion. This is mainly because the state is regarded as a potential threat to the freedom of the individual and as a barrier to innovation and independence. The *limited welfare state* could provide some basic social services, but individuals would be left as far as possible to provide for themselves. The *limited welfare state* might provide a safety net for those who were unable to provide for themselves. It is clear, however, that the majority would be expected to tend to their own needs and not rely upon the state.

Conservatives, social liberals and those who believe in the third way are more likely to support a *mediating welfare state*. For these ideologies, the state is not necessarily menacing. They often argue that individual freedom can be enhanced through state activity and that the state has at least some responsibility to limit some of the harsh injustices of the capitalist system. Driven by compassion or by notions of social justice, they argue that the state can mediate between the demands of different groups in society and do significant work to promote equal opportunities and social unity. Although the *mediating welfare state* would intervene to a greater extent than the *limited welfare state*, it would certainly not attempt to do everything at the expense of smothering the private sector.

The *egalitarian welfare state* can be discerned in the ideas and policies of social democrats. Social democrats tend to rely quite heavily upon the state to reform society and to create a more egalitarian system. Rather than simply tinker with extreme inequalities, social democrats often believe that the state can be used to introduce a socialist system in a peaceful and gradual way. Forming an *egalitarian welfare state* is an important part of this process. By providing a range of essential social services, the *egalitarian welfare state* could transform the fabric of society and give people the respect, stability and skills necessary to prosper in a socialist system. This form of welfare state is highly interventionist and can often operate in direct conflict with the private sector.

The final view could be described as the *illusory welfare state*. For many Marxists, feminists and greens, the state protects a malevolent economic and social system. This system is described in a variety of ways. Marxists talk about capitalism. For feminists, the problem is often thought to lie in patriarchy, whereas it is the industrial nature of capitalism that worries the greens. Although there are differences in the terminology they use, they often argue that the welfare state is of fairly limited value. They claim that the policies of the welfare state might benefit people in the short term, but they are convinced that more radical change is needed to create a just world. For these theorists and movements, the welfare state is often regarded as an illusion designed to protect vested interests and to blunt the demand for radical change.

But ideologies do not have to operate at this level of abstraction. The ideologies contained in this book not only have views of the state and of the welfare state, but also have some interesting things to say about distinct areas of social policy. It is argued that by looking at these areas of policy, we can gain further understanding of the ideological tapestry and the insight it provides to the development of human welfare.

Welfare and social policies

As we have seen, social policies provide governments with an effective and immediate way to attend to the welfare of the individual and society. Although for radical spirits it is tempting to claim that such measures merely get in the way of dealing with the root causes of social problems, there are many things that governments (and indeed individuals) can do to alleviate some of the flaws in our system. Looking at these social policies provides us with another way to appreciate the contribution made by political ideologies to our understanding of the social world.

The term welfare is almost automatically associated with the benefits system. This volume has only really dealt with unemployment benefit, though other benefits (like pensions, child allowance and maternity benefits) could have been included. One of the reasons for choosing to concentrate on unemployment benefit is that the perspectives outlined by different ideologies are often quite extreme. For some, most notably the classical liberals and the neo-liberals, access to unemployment benefit should be limited because it threatens the capitalist system and saps the individual of independence and initiative. For those who believe that society is an organism of interdependent parts, the benefits system is needed to ensure the health of the social body. Social democrats, social liberals and even some conservatives would go along with this. In recent years, however, supporters of the third way have argued that access to benefits should not be seen as a universal right but one attached to certain responsibilities. For the radical critics, there are far too many regulations that get in the way of a fair benefits system. They are apt to argue that a satisfactory solution is not likely to evolve independently of far-reaching social, and in many cases economic, change. Arguments for and against the benefits system will often make use of at least some of these ideological perspectives.

We have seen also that housing is a deeply political issue. Those who attack state provision of unemployment benefit are also likely to be critical of the state provision of social housing. For classical liberals and neo-liberals, it is important that individuals assume as much responsibility for their own lives as possible. Supporters of these ideologies defend private property and consider it superior in many ways to public property. Ideologies that recognise the ways in which we are interdependent, however, will tend to support state intervention in the provision of housing. This applies in particular to social democracy but also, to a lesser degree, to social liberalism and to some forms of conservatism. For the radical critics, social housing is only a short-term solution that can sometimes create a new batch of problems for sections of the population. Given this, these radical critics are often more open to supporting participation in housing cooperatives.

Questions about the legitimate role of government in the provision of health care can also be viewed in an ideological light. Those who attack unemployment benefit and the state provision of housing are also likely to believe that health is an individual possession and that we should assume responsibility for paying for our own health care. Social democrats, alongside their liberal and conservative allies, are far more likely to view health as a social product and to call upon the state to invest in public health care. The radical critics are also likely to be aware of the social context of health, but they often have severe misgivings about the way that the state provides health care. Because of this, feminists and greens in particular are inclined to believe in the importance of alternative health care systems that give far more attention to the long-term needs of the patient than the state health care system.

On the issue of education, the ideological divide is often between those who see education as a way to conserve and those who see its liberating potential. Those who defend capitalism and the unequal social system it creates will often see education as something possessed by the individual that can be used to further his or her own interests. For classical liberals, neo-liberals and to some extent conservatives, education is valued for the skills that it can pass on to the workforce and for conserving the dominant value system and social hierarchy. Marxists have attacked this use or abuse of education vociferously. Education can also be seen as a way to transform the values and structure of society. Social democrats, feminists, greens and those who believe in the third way will often value the transformative powers of education.

Some knowledge of political ideologies allows us to see some of the key ideas that are captured and expressed in social policies. The meaning and significance of social policies is not found only in the detail or in the budgets of government departments, but in the ideological character and flavour they contain. Whereas some policies are designed to preserve, others are designed to challenge and to transform. Viewed in terms of their ideological content, we gain at least some understanding of the political implications of the social policies that surround and impact upon our lives.

Conclusion

It has been argued throughout this volume that if we are to understand ideological perspectives on welfare we need to pay some attention to the economic and social foundations of the ideologies concerned. The economic foundations are particularly important because they address the nature of capitalism and its impact upon society. Even the most committed of its defenders recognise that capitalism creates inequalities. Rather than ignore this, we are asked to consider whether these inequalities are justified and the impact that they have upon the welfare of the society. Following on from the way they view capitalism, ideologies will often discuss whether the state needs to intervene to stabilise the system and even to what extent the existing system needs to be overturned and replaced by a new economic framework. It should be noted that those who believe that the state should stabilise the capitalist system will also tend to want the state to provide a range of social services. Indeed, this is one of the key ways that stability can be brought to capitalism.

A reasonable amount of attention has also been given to social values. We have seen that ideologies differ in the values they advance or attack. While some make a case for negative liberty, others discuss what can be done to create a more equal society. Those involved in developing ideologies are often engaged in piecing together a conceptual jigsaw in which they consider the implications of accepting or rejecting a certain combination of values. Those who make a case for equality of outcome, for example, will need to consider how this equality can be established and how it will affect the economic system, the provision of social services, the powers of the state and the freedom of the individual. The same would apply to the other ideologies. The values we hold are often central to our political core and generally far more important than any sense of attachment to a particular economic or social policy. Policies and policy recommendations allow us to promote or undermine certain values. It is argued that by taking note of these values, we can gain some insight into the broad aims and implications of policies and policy recommendations circulating in the political environment.

Although the way that many people engage with the political system is certainly changing, there is no reason to believe that ideological debate has no future. An attempt has been made in this volume to show how ideologies have influenced the development of welfare states and how these ideologies helped to shape the range of tasks performed by a variety of governments. This influence did not end in the 1970s with the problems faced by welfare capitalism. Ideologies continue to influence the development of social services and ideological perspectives on welfare have in no way lost their relevance. Even if the state plays a decreasing role in the provision of our welfare needs, ideologies continue to pose serious questions about the nature of freedom, the implications of inequality and the prospects for social justice and, unless we take into account such issues, we risk being dragged along by mere expedience. It must surely be the case that human welfare cannot be left to the free play of market forces and that the welfare needs of society deserve the attention of social and political theorists, political parties and new social movements. Old welfare states might be in decline, but important debates on the future of welfare continue.

Bibliography

Aberbach, J. (1996) 'Clinton's legal policy and the courts', in C. Campbell and B. Rockman (eds), *The Clinton Presidency*, Chatham House: New Jersey, pp. 126–162.

Abercrombie, N. and Warde, A. (2000) *Contemporary British Society*, Polity: Cambridge.

Achterberg, W. (1996) 'Sustainability, community and democracy', in B. Docherty and M. de Geus (eds) *Democracy and Green Political Thought*, Routledge: New York, pp. 170–187.

Adams, I. (1993) *Political Ideology Today*, Manchester University Press: Manchester.

Adams, I. and Jones, B. (1992) *Political Ideas in Britain*, Pavic: Sheffield.

Alcock, P. (1996) *Social Policy in Britain*, Macmillan: London.

Alcock, P. (1998) 'Poverty and social security', in R. Page and R. Silburn (eds) *British Social Welfare in the Twentieth Century*, Macmillan: Houndmills, pp. 199–222.

Alcock, P. (2000) 'Welfare policy', in P. Dunleavy, P., Gamble, A., Holliday, I. and Peele, G (eds) *Developments in British Politics 6*, Macmillan: Houndmills, pp. 238–256.

Arnold, M. (1867) *Culture and Anarchy*, Cambridge University Press: Cambridge (1935 reprint).

Ashford, D. (1986) *The Emergence of the Welfare States*, Blackwell: Oxford.

Aughey, A. et al. (1992) *The Conservative Political Tradition in Britain and the United States*, Pinter: London.

Australian Greens (2000) *Australian Greens Online: Services* http:// www.greens.org.au/policy/services.html (last accessed 6.06.2001).

Baggott, R. (1998) *Health and Health Care in Britain*, Macmillan: Houndmills.

Bailey, C.J. (2002) 'Economic policy', in G. Peele, C. Bailey, B. Cain and B.G. Peters (eds) *Developments in American Politics 4*, Palgrave: Houndmills, pp. 163–180.

Ball, M. (1983) *Housing Policy and Economic Power: The Political Economy of Owner Occupation*, Methuen: London.

Barker, E. (1915) *Political Thought in England from Spencer to Today*, Williams and Northgate: London.

Barry, J. (1998) 'Green political thought', in A. Lent (ed.) *New Political Thought*, Lawrence and Wishart: London, pp. 184–200.

Barry, N. (1990a) *Welfare*, Open University Press: Milton Keynes.

Barry, N. (1990b) 'Ideology', in P. Dunleavy, A. Gamble and G. Peele (eds) *Developments in British Politics 3*, Macmillan: London, pp. 17–41.

Beer, S. (1965) *Modern British Politics*, Faber and Faber: London.

Behrens, R. (1989) 'The centre: Social democracy and liberalism', in L.Tivey and A. Wright (eds) *Party Ideology in Britain*, Routledge: London, pp. 74–97.

Beland, D. and Hansen, R. (2000) 'Reforming the French welfare state: Solidarity, social exclusion and the three crises of citizenship', *West European Politics*, 23, 1, 47–64.

Bell, D. (1962) *The End of Ideology*, Free Press: New York.

Benn, T. (1980) *Arguments for Socialism*, Penguin: Harmondsworth.

Berki, R. (1970) *Socialism*, Dent: London.

Berlin, I. (1969) 'Two concepts of liberty', in D. Miller (ed.) *Liberty*, Oxford University Press: Oxford, 1991, pp. 33–57.

Bevan, A. (1952), *In Place of Fear*, William Heinemann: London.

Beveridge, W. (1942) *Social Insurance and Allied Services*, Her Majesty's Stationary Office: London.

Beveridge, W. (1944) *Full Employment in a Free Society*, George Allen and Unwin: London.

Birch, A.H. (1993) *The Concepts and Theories of Modern Democracy*, Routledge: London.

Blair, T. (1998a) *The Third Way*, Fabian Society: London.

Blair, T. (1998b) 'Foreword' to *Bringing Britain Together*, http://www.cabinet-office.gov.uk/seu/1998/bbt/nrfore.htm (last accessed 10.09.2000).

Blair, T. and Schroeder, G. (1999) *Europe: The Third Way*, http://www.socialdemocrats.org/blair andschroeder6-8.99.html (last accessed 7.11.2003).

Blair, T. (2003a) 'The third way: New politics for the new century', in A. Chadwick and R. Hefferman (eds), *The New Labour Reader*, Polity: Cambridge, 2003, pp. 28–33.

Blair, T. (2003b) 'The third way: New politics for the new century', in A. Chadwick and R. Hefferman (eds), *The New Labour Reader*, Polity: Cambridge, 2003, pp. 131–133.

Bochel, H. (2005) 'Education', in H. Bochel, C. Bochel, R. Page and R. Sykes (eds), *Social Policy: Issues and Developments*, Pearson: Essex, 2005, pp. 87–108.

Bookchin, M. (1990) *Remaking Society: Pathways to a Green future*, South End Press: Boston, MA.

Bowle, J. (1954) *Politics and Opinion in the Nineteenth Century*, Cape: London.

Brenkert, G. (1991) *Political Freedom*, Routledge: London.

Brennan, T. and Pateman, C. (1998) 'Mere Auxilliaries to the Commonwealth: Women and the origins of liberalism', in A. Phillips (ed.) *Feminism and Politics*, Oxford University Press: Oxford, pp. 93–115.

Briggs, A. (1969) 'The welfare state in historical perspective', in C. Pierson and F. Castles (eds) *The Welfare State Reader*, Polity: Cambridge, 2000, pp. 18–31.

Brookman, J. (2001) 'German inequality grows', *The Times Higher Education Supplement*, 27.07.2001, p. 10.

Brown, A. (1986) *Modern Political Philosophy*, Penguin: Harmondsworth.

Brown, G. (2003) 'Equality – Then and now', in A. Chadwick and R. Hefferman (eds), *The New Labour Reader*, Polity: Cambridge, 2003, pp. 134–136.

Bryson, L. (1992) *Welfare and the State*, Macmillan: London.

Burke, E. (1774) 'Speech to the electors of Bristol', in B.W. Hill (ed.) *Edmund Burke on Government, Politics and Society*, Fontana: Glasgow, 1975, pp. 156–158.

Burke, E. (1791) 'An appeal to the new from the old Whigs', in B.W. Hill (ed.) *Edmund Burke on Government, Politics and Society*, Fontana: Glasgow, 1975, pp. 360–374.

Burns, J. M. (1970) *Roosevelt the Soldier of Freedom*, Weidenfeld and Nicolson: London.

Busfield, J. (2000) *Health and Heath Care in Modern Britain*, Oxford University Press: Oxford.

Bush, G.W. (1998) 'On the issues', http://www.issues2000.org/Celeb/ George_W_Bush_Education.htm.

Bush, G.W. (2000) http://www.issues2000.org/2004/George_W_Bush_ Welfare_+_Poverty.htm.

Bush, G.W., 'State of the Union Address, 2004' http://www.whitehouse.gov/ news/releases/2004/01/20040120-7.html.

Cabinet Office (2000) *National Strategy for Neighbourhood Renewal*, HMSO: London.

Cahill, M. (1998) 'The green perspective', in P. Alcock, A. Erskine and M. May (eds) *The Student's Companion to Social Policy*, Blackwell: Oxford, pp. 98–103.

Cairncross, A. (1992) *The British Economy Since 1945*, Blackwell: Oxford.

Carlyle, T. (1843) *Past and Present*, J.M. Dent: London, no date.

Callaghan, J. (1989) 'The left: The ideology of the Labour Party', in L. Tivey and A. Wright (eds) *Party Ideology in Britain*, Routledge: London, pp. 23–48.

Campbell, C. and Rockman, B. (eds) (1996), *The Clinton Presidency*, Chatham House: New Jersey.

Castels, S. and Wustenberg, W. (1979) *The Education of the Future*, Pluto: London.

Charles, N. (2000) *Feminism, the State and Social Policy*, Macmillan: Houndmills.

Chaudhuri, A. (1999) 'Idealistic homes', *The Guardian*, 2.08.1999, p. 6.

Choko, M. (1993) 'Homeownership: From dream to materiality', in R.A. Hays (ed.), *Ownership, Control and the Future of Housing Policy*, Greenwood Press: Westport, CT.

Christoff, P. (1996) 'Ecological citizens and ecologically guided democracy', in B. Docherty and M. de Geus (eds) *Democracy and Green Political Thought*, Routledge: New York, pp. 151–169.

Christoph, J.B. (1965) 'Consensus and cleavage in British political ideology', *American Political Science Review*, 59, 629–642.

Civil Renewal Unit (2005), *Together We Can*. London: HMSO.

Clarke, J., Cochrane, A. and Smart, C. (1987) *Ideologies of Welfare*, Hutchinson: London.

Clarke, J. and Fox Piven, F. (2001) 'United States: An American welfare state?', in P. Alcock and G. Craig (eds) *International Social Policy*, Palgrave: Houndmills, pp. 26–44.

Clarke, J. and Langan, M. (1993) 'Restructuring welfare', in A. Cochrane and J. Clarke (eds) *Comparing Welfare States*, Sage: London, pp. 49–76.

Clasen, J. (2000) 'Motives, means and opportunities: Reforming unemployment compensation in the 1990s', *West European Politics*, April 2000, pp. 89–113.

Clinton, B. (1995) 'Remarks by the president by satellite to National Education Association', *M2 Presswire*, 7.07.1995.

Clinton, B. (1996) *Between Hope and History*, Random House: New York.

Clinton, B. (2002) 'New Labour and the third way works', Speech to Labour Party Conference October 2002, http:www.labour.org.uk/clintonconfspeech (last accessed 4.12.2003).

Cole, G.D.H. (1953) *A History of Socialist Thought: Volume 1*, Macmillan: London.

Commission on Social Justice (1993) 'What is Social Justice?', in C. Pierson and F. Castles (eds) *The Welfare State Reader*, Polity Press: Cambridge, 2000, pp. 51–62.

Conroy, C. and Litvinoff, M. (1988) 'Sustainable development', in A. Dobson (ed.), *The Green Reader*, Andre Deutsch: London, 1991, pp. 133–137.

Coole, D. (1988) *Women in Political Theory*, Wheatsheaf: Sussex.

Cooper, T. (1988) 'Liberal roots to a green future', in F. Dodds (ed.), *Into the 21st Century*, Green Print: Basingstoke, pp. 119–136.

Coote, A. and Campbell, B. (1987) *Sweet Freedom*, Basil Blackwell: London.

Crosland, A. (1956) *The Future of Socialism*, Jonathan Cape: London.

Crosland, A. (1957) *The Future of Socialism*, Macmillan: New York.

Crosland, A. (1974) *Socialism Now and Other Essays*, Jonathan Cape: London.

Crosland, S. (1982) *Tony Crosland*, Jonathan Cape: London.

Cross, C. (1963) *The Liberals in Power (1905–1914)*, Barrie and Rockliff: London.

Crossman, R. (1952) 'Towards a philosophy of socialism', in R. Crossman (ed.), *New Fabian Essays*, Turnstile Press: London, pp. 1–32.

Crowther, C. (2000) 'Crime, social exclusion and policing in the twenty first century', in *Crime Prevention and Community Safety*, 2, 37–49.

Cruikshank, R.J. (1948) *The Liberal Party*, Collins: London.

Dale, I. (ed.) (2000) *Labour Party General Election Manifestos 1900–1997*, Routledge: London.

Daly, H. (1977) 'The steady-state economy', in A. Dobson (ed.) *The Green Reader*, Andre Deutsch, London, 1991, pp. 145–151.

Damms, R. (2002) *The Eisenhower Presidency*, Pearson Education: London.

Davey, J.A. (2001) 'New Zealand: The myth of egalitarianism', in P. Alcock and G. Craig (eds) *International Social Policy*, Palgrave: Houndmills, pp. 85–103.

D.C.E.C (Delegation of the Commission of the European Communities) (2000) *Berlin: Aging Population Creates Critical Situation* (Lexis-Nexis – last accessed 10.08.2003).

Department for Education and Employment (2003) 'Excellence in schools', in A. Chadwick and R. Hefferman (eds) *The New Labour Reader*, Polity: Cambridge, 2003, pp. 144–148.

Department of Health (2000) *The NHS Plan: A Summary*, Department of Health.

Department of Health (2003) 'The new NHS: Modern and dependable', in A. Chadwick and R. Hefferman (eds) *The New Labour Reader*, Polity: Cambridge, 2003, pp. 149–154.

Department of Health (2004) *Choosing Health*, London: HMSO.

Dearlove, J. and Saunders, P. (1984) *Introduction to British Politics*, Polity: Cambridge.

Dietz, M. (1998) 'Context is all: Feminism and theories of citizenship', in A. Phillips (1998) (ed.) *Feminism and Politics*, Oxford University Press: Oxford, pp. 378–400.

Ditch, J. (1998) 'Income Protection and Social Security', in P. Alcock, A. Erskine and M. May (eds) *The Student's Companion to Social Policy*, Blackwell: Oxford, pp. 273–279.

Dobson, A. (1990) *Green Political Thought*, Unwin Hyman: London.

Dobson, A. (1991) *The Green Reader*, Andre Deutsch: London.

Dodds, F. (1988) *Into the 21st Century: An Agenda for Political Realignment*, Green Print: Basingstoke.

Doherty, B. (2002) *Ideas and Actions in the Green Movement*, Routledge: London.

Doling, J. (1997) *Comparative Housing Policy*, Macmillan: Houndmills.

Dreier, P. (1997) 'The new politics of housing', *Journal of the American Planning Association*, 63, 5–27.

Duncan, G. (1987) 'Understanding ideology', *Political Studies*, 35, 649–659.

Dunleavy, P. and O'Leary, B. (1987) *Theories of the State*, Macmillan: London.

Durden, P. (2000) 'Housing policy', in S. Savage and R. Atkinson (eds), *Public Policy under Blair*, Palgrave: Houndmills, pp. 139–153.

Durham, M. (1989) 'The right: The Conservative Party and conservatism', in L. Tivey and A. Wright (eds) *Party Ideology in Britain*, Routledge: London, 1989, pp. 49–73.

Dutton, D. (1991) *British Politics since 1945*, Blackwell: Oxford.

Dyson, A.E. and Lovelock, L. (1975) (eds) *Education and Democracy*, Routledge, London.

Eatwell, R. (1999) 'Conclusion: The end of ideology', in R. Eatwell and A. Wright (eds), *Contemporary Political Ideologies*, Pinter: London, pp. 279–290.

Ebenstein, W. and Fogelman, E. (1980) *Today's Isms*, Prentice Hall: New Jersey.

Eccleshall, R. (1984a) 'Introduction: The world of ideology', in Eccleshall, R., Geoghegan, V., Jay, R. and Wilford, R (1984), Geoghegan, V., Jay, R., Kenny, M., MacKenzie, I. and Wilford, R (1994), *Political Ideologies*, Unwin Hyman: London, 1984, pp. 7–36.

Eccleshall, R. (1984b) 'Conservatism', in Eccleshall, R., Geoghegan, V., Jay, R. and Wilford, R (1984), *Political Ideologies*, Unwin Hyman: London, 1984, pp. 79–114.

Eccleshall, R. (1994a) 'Liberalism', in Eccleshall, R., Geoghegan, V., Jay, R., Kenny, M., MacKenzie, I. and Wilford, R (1994), *Political Ideologies*, Routledge: London, 1994, pp. 28–59.

Eccleshall, R. (1994b) 'Conservatism', in Eccleshall, R., Geoghegan, V., Jay, R., Kenny, M., MacKenzie, I. and Wilford, R (1994), *Political Ideologies*, Routledge: London, 1994, pp. 60–90.

Eisenhower, D. (1954) 'Special message to the Congress on old age and survivors insurance and on Federal grants-in-aid for public assistance programs, January 14, 1954', www.ssa.gov/history/ikestmts.html (last accessed 1.12.2003).

Eisenhower, D. (1960) 'State of the Union address to Congress, January 7, 1960', www.polsci.edu/projects/presproject/idgrant/sou_pages/eisenhower8su.html (last accessed 1.12.2003).

Eisenhower, D. (1963) *Mandate for Change 1953–1956*, Heinemann: London.

Elkins, P. (1986) 'The basic income scheme', in A. Dobson (ed.), *The Green Political Reader*, Andre Deutsch: London, 1991, pp. 152–155.

Engels, F. (1872) 'On authority' (The Marx-Engels Internet Archive – last accessed 6.10.1999).

Engels, F. (1884) 'The origins of the family, private property and the state', in K. Marx and F. Engels, *Selected Works*, Lawrence and Wishart: London, 1977, pp. 461–583.

Engels, F. (1935) *Socialism: Utopian and Scientific*, in K. Marx, *Selected Works*, Co-operative Publishing Society: Moscow, pp. 135–188.

Engels, F. (1971) *The Condition of the Working Class in England*, Blackwell: Oxford.

Erickson, R.J. (2000) 'Compulsory education in Sweden', *Education*, 120, 506–512.

Esping-Andersen, G (1985) *Politics against Markets: The Social Democratic Road to Power*, Princeton University Press: New Jersey.

Esping-Andersen, G. (1990a) 'Three worlds of welfare capitalism', in C. Pierson and F. Castles (eds) *The Welfare State Reader*, Polity: Cambridge, 2000, pp. 154–169.

Esping-Andersen, G. (1990b) *The Three Worlds of Welfare Capitalism*, Polity: Cambridge.

Evans, E. (2004) *Thatcher and Thatcherism*, Routledge: New York.

Fargion, V. (2001) 'Italy: moving from the southern model', in P. Alcock and G. Craig (eds), *International Social Policy*, Palgrave: Houndmills, pp. 183–202.

Ferguson, I., Lavalette, M. and Mooney, G. (2002) *Rethinking Welfare*, Sage: London.

Ferris, J. (1995) 'Ecological versus social rationality: Can there be green social policies?', in A. Dobson and P. Lucardie (eds) *The Politics of Nature*, Routledge: New York, 1995, pp. 145–160.

Festenstein, M. (1998) 'Contemporary liberalism', in A. Lent (ed.), *New Political Thought*, Lawrence and Wishart: London, pp. 14–32.

Fielding, S. (2000) 'A new politics', in P. Dunleavy et al. (eds), *Developments in British Politics 6*, Macmillan: Houndmills, pp. 10–28.

Firestone, S. (1979) *The Dialectic of Sex*, The Women's Press: London.

Fitzpatrick, T. (1998a) 'Democratic socialism and social democracy', in A. Lent (ed.), *New Political Thought*, Lawrence and Wishart: London, pp. 33–52.

Fitzpatrick, T. (1998b) 'The implications of ecological thought for social welfare', in C. Pierson and F. Castles (eds) *The Welfare State Reader*, Polity: Cambridge, pp. 343–354.

Fitzpatrick, T. (2001) *Welfare Theory*, Palgrave: Houndmills.

Fitzpatrick, T. (2005) *New Theories of Welfare*, Palgrave: Houndmills.

Fleisher, W. (1956) *Sweden, the Welfare State*, John Day: New York.

Foley, M. (1991) *American Political Ideas*, Manchester University Press: Manchester.

Foot, M. (1973) *Aneurin Bevan 1945–1960*, Davis-Poynter, London.

Forder, A. (1984) 'Two theories of social justice', in A. Forder, T. Caslin, G. Ponton, and S. Walkgate (eds) *Theories of Welfare*, Routledge: London, 1984, pp. 182–201.

Foucault, M. (1980) *Power/Knowledge*, Harvester: Hemel Hempstead.

Fourier, C. (1971) *Harmonian Man*, Doubleday: New York.

Fraser, N. (1998) 'From redistribution to recognition? Dilemmas of justice in a post-socialist age', in A. Phillips (1998) (ed.) *Feminism and Politics*, Oxford University Press: Oxford, pp. 430–460.

Frazer, E. (2000) 'Citizenship and culture', in P. Dunleavy, P., Gamble, A., Holliday, I. and Peele, G (eds) *Developments in British Politics 6*, Macmillan: Houndmills, pp. 203–218.

Freeden, M. (2003) 'The ideology of new labour', in A. Chadwick and R. Hefferman (eds) *The New Labour Reader*, Polity: Cambridge, 2003, pp. 43–48.

Fried, A. and Sanders, R. (1964) *A Documentary History of Socialist Thought*, Edinburg University Press: Edinburgh.

Frieden, B. (1971) *The Feminine Mystique*, Victor Gollancz: London.

Friedman, M. (1962) *Capitalism and Freedom*, The University of Chicago Press: Chicago.

Friedman, M. (1975) *There's No Such Thing as a Free Lunch*, Open Court: La Salle, Illinois.

Friedman, M. and Friedman, R. (1985) *The Tyranny of the Status Quo*, Penguin: Harmondsworth.

Fukuyama, F. (1992) *The End of History and the Last Man*, Penguin: Harmondsworth.

Galbraith, J.K. (1980) *American Capitalism*, Basil Blackwell: Oxford.

Gamble, A. (1981) *Introduction to Modern Social and Political Thought*, Macmillan: London.

Gamble, A. (1988) *The Free Economy and the Strong State*, Macmillan: London.

Gelb, L. (1989) *Feminism and Politics*, University of California Press: Berkeley.

George, V. and Wilding, P. (1994) *Welfare and Ideology*, Harvester: Hemel Hempstead.

Giddens, A. (1998a) *The Third Way: The Renewal of Social Democracy*, Polity Press: Cambridge.

Giddens, A. (1998b) 'Positive welfare' in C. Pierson and F. Castle (eds), *The Welfare State Reader*, Polity: Cambridge, 2000, pp. 369–379.

Giddens, A. (2000) *The Third Way and its Critics*, Polity Press: Cambridge.

Gilmour, I. (1978), *Inside Right*, Quartet Books: London.

Gilmour, I. (1992) *Dancing with Dogma*, Pocket Books: London (1993 reprint).

Ginsburg, N. (1979) *Class, Capital and Social Policy*, Macmillan: London.

Ginsburg, N. (1992) *Divisions of Welfare*, Sage: London.

Ginsburg, N. (1993) 'Sweden: The social democratic case', in A. Cochrane and J. Clarke (eds), *Comparing Welfare States*, Open University Press: Milton Keynes, 1993, pp. 173–203.

Glennerster, H. (2000) *British Social Policy since 1945*, Blackwell: Oxford.

Goar, C. (1996) 'Clinton poised to terminate 61 year old welfare system', *Toronto Star*, 1.08.1996, p. 13.

Goodwin, B. (1987) *Using Political Ideas*, John Wiley: Chichester.

Gorz, A. (1980) *Ecology as Politics*, Pluto Press: London.

Gorz, A. (1983) 'A possible utopia', in A. Dobson (ed.), *The Green Reader*, Andre Deutsch, London, 1991, pp. 94–99.

Gough, I. (1991) 'The United Kingdom', in A. Pfaller, I. Gough and G. Therborn (eds), *Can the Welfare State Compete?*, Macmillan: Houndmills, pp. 101–152.

Gould, A. (1993) *Capitalist Welfare Systems: A comparison of Japan, Britain and Sweden*, Longman: London.

Green, T.H. (1888) 'Liberal legislation and freedom of contract', in D. Miller (ed.), *Liberty*, Oxford University Press: Oxford, pp. 21–32.

Greenleaf, W. (1983) *British Political Tradition: Volume 2*, Methuen: London.

Green Party (1997) *Manifesto for a Sustainable Society: Social Welfare*, http://www.greenparty.org.uk/policy/mfss/welfare.html (last accessed 6.06.2001).

Green Party (2000a) *Manifesto for a Sustainable Society: Economy*, http://www.greenparty.org.uk/policy/mfss/economy.html (last accessed 6.06.2001).

Green Party (2000b) *Manifesto for a Sustainable Society: Health*, http://www.greenparty.org.uk/policy/mfss/health.html (last accessed 6.06.2001)

Green Party (2000c) *Manifesto for a Sustainable Society: Education*, http://www.greenparty.org.uk/policy/mfss/education.html (last accessed 6.06.2001).

Green Party (2006) *Manifesto for a Sustainable Society: Social Welfare*, http://policy.greenparty.org.uk/mfss/socwelf.html (last accessed 12.04.2006).

Green Party US (2000) *Green Party Platform*, http://www.gp.org/platform-index.html (last accessed 6.06.2001).

Greene, J. (2000) *The Presidency of George Bush*, University of Kansas Press: Kansas.

Hailsham, L. (Lord) (1975) *The Door Where in I Went*, Collins: London.

Hailsham, V. (Viscount) (1959) *The Conservative Case*, Penguin: Harmondsworth.

Ham, C. (1992) *Health Policy in Britain*, Macmillan: Houndmills.

Harrison, J.F.C. (1968) *Utopianism and Education: Robert Owen and the Owenites*, New York, 1968.

Hay, J.R. (1975) *The Origins of Liberal Welfare Legislation 1906–1914*, Macmillan: London.

Hayek, F. (1944) *The Road to Serfdom*, University of Chicago Press: Chicago.

Hayek, F. (1959) 'The meaning of the welfare state', in C. Pierson and F. Castles (eds) *The Welfare State Reader*, Polity: Cambridge, 2000, pp. 90–95.

Hayek, F. (1960) *The Constitution of Liberty*, Routledge and Kegan Paul: London.

Hayek, F. (1991) *Economic Freedom*, Blackwell: Oxford.

Hays, R.A. (2001) *Who Speaks for the Poor: National Interest Groups and Social Policy*, Routledge: New York.

Held, D. (1987) 'From stability to crisis in post-war Britain', *Parliamentary Affairs*, 40, 218–237.

Hencke, D. (2006) 'Cameron drops pledge on private operation costs for NHS patients', *The Guardian*, 2 January 2006, p. 5.

Herrick, J. and Midgley, J. (2002), 'The United States' in J. Dixon and R. Scheurell (eds) (2002) *The State of Social Welfare*, Praeger: Westport, pp. 187–216.

Herrstein, R. and Murray, C. (1995) *The Bell Curve: Intelligence and Class Structure in American Life*, Free Press: New York.

Heywood, A. (1992) *Political Ideologies*, Macmillan: London.

Hindess, B. (1990) (ed.) *Reactions to the Right*, Routledge: London, 1990.

Hobhouse, L.T. (1893) *The Labour Movement*, Fisher Unwin: London.

Hobhouse, L.T. (1911) *Liberalism*, Williams and Northgate: London.

Hobsbawm, E.J. (1969) *Industry and Empire*, Penguin: Harmondsworth.

Hobson, J.A. (1974) *The Crisis of Liberalism*, Harvester: Sussex.

Hobson, J.A. (1998) *Democracy after the War*, Routledge: London.

Hogg, Q. (1947) *The Case for Conservatism*, Penguin Books: Harmondsworth.

Hornsey, R. (1996) 'Postmodern critiques: Foucault, Lyotard and modern political ideologies', *Journal of Political Ideologies*, 1, 239–259.

Husock, H. (1997) 'Broken ladder: Government thwarts affordable housing', *Policy Review*, no 82 http://www.policyreview.org/mar97/husock.html (last accessed 10 April 2006).

Hutton, W. (1995) *The State We're In*, Vintage: London.

Inglehart, R. (1990) 'Values, ideology and cognitive mobilization in new social movements', in R. Dalton and M. Kuechler (eds) *Challenging the Political Order*, Polity: Cambridge, pp. 43–66.

Issel, W. (1985) *Social Change in the United States 1945–1983*, Macmillan: Houndmills.

Izbicki, J. (1989) 'Education: Echoes from across the channel, as France forges new reforms', *The Independent*, 19.01.1989, p. 17.

Jacques, M. (1983) 'Thatcherism: Breaking out of the impasse', in S. Hall and M. Jacques (eds), *The Politics of Thatcherism*, Lawrence and Wishart: London, 1983, pp. 40–62.

Jagger, G. and Wright, C. (1999) *Changing Family Values*, Routledge: London.

Jardine, L. and Swindells, J. (1989) *What's Left?*, Routledge: London.

Jeffries, A. (1993) 'Freedom', in R. Bellamy (ed.), *Theories and Concepts of Politics*, Manchester University Press: Manchester, pp. 16–42.

Jeffries, A. (1996) 'British conservatism: Individualism and gender', *Journal of Political Ideologies*, 1, 33–52.

Johnson, L.B. (1971) *The Vantage Point*, Weidenfeld and Nicolson: London.

Johnson, N. (1998) 'State welfare', in P. Alcock, A. Erskine and M. May (eds), *The Student's Companion to Social Policy*, Blackwell: Oxford, pp. 147–153.

Kavanagh, D. (1990) *Thatcherism and British Politics*, Oxford University Press: Oxford.

Kavanagh, D. (1994) 'A major agenda', in D. Kavanagh and A. Seldon (eds), *The Major Effect*, Macmillan: London, pp. 3–17.

Keohane, N. (1982) *Feminist Theory*, Harvester: Brighton.

Kemeny, J. (1992) *Housing and Social Theory*, Routledge: London.

Kemp, P. and Wall, D. (1990) *Green Manifesto for the 1990s*, Penguin: London.

Kendall, I. and Holloway, D. (2001) 'Education policy', in S. Savage and R. Atkinson (eds), *Public Policy under Blair*, Palgrave: Houndmills, pp. 154–173.

Kendall, W. (1963) *The Conservative Affirmation*, Henry Regnery: Chicago.

Kennedy, C. (2001) *The Future of Politics*, HarperCollins: London.

Kenny, M. (1994) 'Ecologism', in R. Eccleshall et al., *Political Ideologies*, Routledge: London, pp. 218–251.

Keynes, J.M. (1936) *The General Theory of Employment, Interest and Money*, Macmillan: London (1967 reprint).

Kirk, R. (1953) *The Conservative Mind from Burke to Santayana*, Henry Regnery: Chicago.

Klein, R. (2001) *The New Politics of the National Health Service*, Prentice Hall: London.

Klein, J. (2002) *The Natural: The Misunderstood Presidency of Bill Clinton*, Hodder and Stoughton: London.

Kleinberg, S. (1991) *Politics and Philosophy*, Blackwell: Oxford.

Kooijman, J. (1999) 'Just forget about it: FDR's ambivalence towards National Health Insurance', in R.A. Garson and S. Kidd (eds) *The Roosevelt Years*, Edinburgh University Press: Edinburgh, pp. 30–40.

Kymlicka, W. (1990) *Contemporary Political Philosophy*, Clarendon: Oxford.

Lambert, J. (1988) 'Moves towards a green future', in F. Dodds (ed.), *Into the 21st Century*, Green Print: Basingstoke, pp. 137–152.

Lawton, D. (2004) *Education and Labour Party Ideologies 1900–2001 and Beyond*, Routledge Falmer: New York.

Leach, R. (1987) 'What is Thatcherism', in M. Burch and M. Moran (eds), *British Politics: A Reader*, Manchester University Press: Manchester, pp. 157–165.

Le Grand, J. (2003) 'The third way begins with CORA', in A. Chadwick and R. Hefferman (eds) *The New Labour Reader*, Polity: Cambridge, 2003, pp. 137–138.

Leisering, L. (2001) 'Germany: Reform from within', in P. Alcock and G. Craig (eds) *International Social Policy*, Palgrave: London, 2001, pp. 161–182.

Lenin, V.I. (1917) 'The state and revolution' in *Selected Works*, Progress: Moscow, 1968, pp. 263–348.

Lent, A. (1998) (ed.) *New Political Thought*, Lawrence and Wishart: London.

Lee, P. and Raban, C. (1988) *Welfare Theory and Social Policy*, Sage: London.

Leuchtenburg, W. (1999) 'The Clintons and the Roosevelts', in R.A. Garson and S. Kidd (eds), *The Roosevelt Years*, Edinburgh University Press, Edinburgh, pp. 190–204.

Levey, S. (1990) 'A Paralysis of Leadership?', *Foundation of the American College of Healthcare Executives* (Lexis-Nexis – last accessed 10.08.2003).

Lewis, J. (1992) *Women in Britain since 1945*, Blackwell: Oxford.

Lewis, J. (1998) 'Feminist perspectives', in P. Alcock, A. Erskine and M. May (eds), *The Student's Companion to Social Policy*, Blackwell: Oxford, pp. 85–90.

Liberal Democrat Party (1992) *Changing Britain for Good*, Liberal Democrat Publications: Dorset.

Liberal Democrat Party (1994) *Unlocking Britain's Potential: Making Europe Work for Us*, Liberal Democrat Publications: Dorset.

Liberal Democrat Party (1997) *Make the Difference*, Liberal Democrats: London.

Lichtheim, G. (1970) *A Short History of Socialism*, Fontana: Glasgow.

Linder, S. and Rosenau, P. (2002) 'Health Care Policy', in G. Peele, C. Bailey, B. Cain and B.G. Peters (eds) *Developments in American Politics 4*, Palgrave: Houndmills, pp. 222–233.

Lindsay, A.D. (1969) *The Modern Democratic State*, Oxford University Press: Oxford.

Lloyd, M. (1998) 'Feminism', in A. Lent (ed.), *New Political Thought*, Lawrence and Wishart: London, pp. 163–183.

Lukes, S. (1991) 'Equality and liberty: Must they conflict?', in D. Held (ed.), *Political Theory Today*, Polity: Cambridge, pp. 48–66.

Lund, B. (2005) 'Housing policy', in H. Bochel, C. Bochel, R. Page and R. Sykes (eds) *Social Policy: Issues and Developments*, Pearson: Essex, pp. 171–192.

MacDonald, J.R. (1905) *Socialism and Society*, ILP: London.

MacKenzie, I. (1994) 'Introduction: The arena of ideology', in Eccleshall, R., Geoghegan, V., Jay, R., Kenny, M., MacKenzie, I. and Wilford, R (1994), *Political Ideologies*, Routledge: London, pp. 1–27.

Macmillan, H. (1966) *The Middle Way*, Macmillan: London.

Macmillan, H. (1969) *Tides of Fortune 1945–1955*, Macmillan: London.

Malamud, R. (1999) 'Home ownership leaps in U.S', *Chicago Sun-Times*, 22.06.1999, p. 47.

Marquand, D. (1988) *The Unprincipled Society*, Jonathan Cape: London.

Marquand, D. (1993) 'After socialism', *Political Studies*, xii, 43–56.

Marshall, T.H. (1949) 'Citizenship and social class', in C. Pierson and F. Castles (eds), *The Welfare State Reader*, Polity: Cambridge, 2000, pp. 32–41.

Marshall, T.H. (1970) *Social Policy*, Hutchinson University Library: London.

Marx, K. (1843) 'On the Jewish question', in D. McLellan (ed.), *Karl Marx: Selected Writings*, Oxford University Press: Oxford, 1977, pp. 39–62.

Marx, K. (1844) 'Economic and philosophical manuscripts', in D. McLellan (ed.), *Karl Marx: Selected Writings*, Oxford University Press: Oxford, 1977, pp. 75–112.

Marx, K. (1845) *The German Ideology*, Lawrence and Wishart: London.

Marx, K. (1847) 'Wages', in S.K. Padover (ed.), *The Essential Marx*, Mentor: New York, p. 205.

Marx, K. (1866) 'Instructions for the delegates of the provisional General Council', in S.K. Padover (ed.), *The Essential Marx*, Mentor: New York, pp. 394–396.

Marx, K. (1867) *Capital: Volume 1*, Lawrence and Wishart: London, 1954.

Marx, K. (1869) 'Minutes of the General Council of the First International, 10 August 1869', in S.K. Padover (ed.) *The Essential Marx*, Mentor: New York, pp. 224–225.

Marx, K. (1871a) interviewed by R. Landor, *New York World*, 18 July 1871 (The Marx–Engels Internet Archive).

Marx, K. (1871b) 'The Civil War in France', in *Selected Works*, Lawrence and Wishart: London, 1977, pp. 271–307.

Marx, K. (1875a) 'Critique of the Gotha programme', in P.M. Stirk and D. Weigall (eds), *An Introduction to Political Ideas*, Pinter: London, 1995, pp. 182–185.

Marx, K. (1875b) 'Critique of the Gotha programme', in K. Marx and F. Engels, *Selected Works*, Lawrence and Wishart: London, 1968, pp. 311–326.

Marx, K. and Engels, F. (1845) *The German Ideology*, Lawrence and Wishart: London, 1970.

Marx, K. and Engels, F. (1848) 'The manifesto of the Communist Party', in *Selected Works*, Lawrence and Wishart: London, 1977, pp. 31–63.

McAuley Institute (2003) *Women and Housing: A Status Report*, www.mcauley.org (accessed January 2004).

McBriar, A.M. (1962) *Fabian Socialism and English Politics 1884–1918*, Cambridge University Press.

McIntosh, M. (1981) 'Feminism and social policy', in C. Pierson and F. Castles (eds), *The Welfare State Reader*, Polity: Cambridge, 2000, pp. 119–132.

McSweeney, D. (2002) 'Political parties', in G. Peele, C. Bailey, B. Cain and B.G. Peters (eds), *Developments in American Politics 4*, Palgrave: Houndmills, pp. 35–52.

Mead, L. (1991) 'The new politics of the new poverty', in C. Pierson and F. Castles (eds), *The Welfare State Reader*, Polity: Cambridge, 2000, pp. 107–117.

Mervin, D. (1996) *George Bush and the Guardianship Presidency*, Macmillan: Houndmills.

Mitchell, J. (1984) *Women: The Longest Revolution*, Pantheon: New York.

Miliband, R. (1973) *The State in Capitalist Society*, Quartet: London, 1973.

Miliband, R. (1977) *Marxism and Politics*, Oxford University Press: Oxford, 1977.

Mill, J.S. (1836) 'On the definition of political economy and the method of investigation proper to it', in J.S. Mill, *Philosophy of Scientific Method* (edited by E. Nagel), Hafner: New York, 1950, pp. 407–440.

Mill, J.S. (1852) *Principles of Political Economy*, Longman: London, 1921.

Mill, J.S. (1859) 'On liberty', in S. Collini (ed.), *On Liberty and Other Writings*, Cambridge University Press: Cambridge, 1989, pp. 1–116.

Mill, J.S. (1869) 'The subjection of women', in S. Collini (ed.) *On Liberty and Other Writings*, Cambridge University Press: Cambridge, 1989, pp. 117–218.

Mill, J.S. (1879) 'Chapters on Socialism', in S. Collini (ed.) *On Liberty and Other Writings*, Cambridge University Press: Cambridge, 1989, pp. 219–279.

Millett, K. (1977) *Sexual Politics*, Virago: London.

Mishra, R. (1984) *The Welfare State in Crisis*, Wheatsheaf: London.

Mishra, R. (1990) *The Welfare State in Capitalist Society*, Harvester: London.

Monbiot, G. (2001) *Captive State*, Pan Books: London.

Moore, B. and Bruder, K. (1996) (eds) *Philosophy*, Mayfield: California, 1996.

Morgan, K. (1992) *The People's Peace*, Oxford University Press: Oxford.

Moroney, R.M. and Krysik, J. (1998) *Social Policy and Social Work*, Aldine de Gruyter: New York.

Mullard, M. and Spicker, P. (1998) *Social Policy in a Changing Society*, Routledge: London.

Murray, C. (1982) 'The two wars against poverty', in C. Pierson and F. Castles (eds) *The Welfare State Reader*, Polity: Cambridge, 2000, pp. 96–106.

Murray, C. (1984) *Losing Ground: American Social Policy 1950–1980*, Basic Books: New York.

Navarro, V. (1978) *Class Struggle, the State and Medicine*, Martin Robinson: Oxford.

Nixon, R. (1971a) 'Special message to the Congress proposing a National Health Strategy, February 18, 1971', (www.nixonfoundation.org/Research_Center/PublicPapers.cfm?BookSelected).

Nixon, R. (1971b) 'Special message to the Congress on higher education, February 22, 1971', (www.nixonfoundation.org/Research_Center/PublicPapers.cfm?BookSelected).

Nixon, R. (1971c) 'Letter to the Chairman and Ranking Member of the House Committee on ways and means about the welfare reform bill, March 31, 1971', (www.nixonfoundation.org/Research_Center/PublicPapers.cfm?BookSelected).

Nixon, R. (1971d) 'Statement about the approval of the welfare reform and social security by the House Committee on ways and means, May 18, 1971', (www.nixonfoundation.org/Research_Center/PublicPapers. cfm?BookSelected).

Nixon, R. (1971e) 'Statement about Federal policies relative to equal housing opportunity, June 11, 1971', (www.nixonfoundation.org/ Research_Center/PublicPapers.cfm?BookSelected).

Nixon, R. (1971f) 'Statement on signing a bill amending the Social Security Act, December 28, 1971', (www.nixonfoundation.org/Research_Center/ PublicPapers.cfm?BookSelected).

Nixon, R. (1978) *The Memoirs of Richard Nixon*, Book Club Associates: London.

Normann, G. and Mitchell, D.J. (2000) 'Pension reform in Sweden: Lessons for American policymakers', Heritage Foundation Reports.

Norsigian, J. (1996) 'The Women's Health Movement in the United States', in K.L. Moss (ed.) *Man-Made Medicine: Women's Health, Public Policy and Reform*, Duke University Press: Durham, NC.

North, N. (2001) 'Health policy', in S. Savage and R. Atkinson (eds) *Public Policy under Blair*, Palgrave: Houndmills, pp. 123–138.

Nozick, R. (1980) *Anarchy, State and Utopia*, Blackwell: Oxford.

Oakeshott, M. (1962) 'On being conservative', in *Rationalism in Politics*, Methuen: London, pp. 168–173.

Oakley, A. (1981) *Subject Women*, Martin Robertson: Oxford.

Oakley, A. (1993) *Essays on Women, Medicine and Health*, Edinburgh University Press: Edinburgh.

O'Brien, M. and Penna, S. (1998) *Theorising Welfare*, Sage: London.

Okin, S.M. (1991) 'Gender, the public and the private', in D. Held (ed.), *Political Theory Today*, Polity: Cambridge, pp. 67–90.

Okin, S.M. (1998) 'Gender, the public and the private', in A. Phillips (1998) (ed.) *Feminism and Politics*, Oxford University Press: Oxford, pp. 116–141.

Offe, C. (1976) *Industry and Inequality*, Edward Arnold: London.

Offe, C. (1984) *Contradictions of the Welfare State*, Hutchinson: London.

Offe, C. (1985) *Disorganised Capitalism*, Polity: Cambridge.

Olsen, G.M. (1999) 'Half empty or half full? The Swedish welfare state in transition', *The Canadian Review of Sociology and Anthropology*, 36, 241–267.

Owen, R. (1813) *A New View of Society* (edited by G.D.H. Cole), London, 1927.

Pach, C. and Richardson, E. (1991) *The Presidency of Dwight D. Eisenhower*, University of Kansas Press: Kansas.

Paci, M. (1987) 'Long waves in the development of welfare systems', in C.S. Maier (ed.), *Changing Boundaries of the Political*, Cambridge University Press: Cambridge, pp. 179–199.

Paine, T. (1792) 'The first welfare state?', in C. Pierson and F. Castles (eds), *The Welfare State Reader*, Polity: Cambridge, 2000, pp. 11–16.

Parker, J. (1998) 'Education policy', in G. Peele, C.J. Bailey, B. Cain and B. Peters (eds), *Developments in American Politics 3*, Chatham House: London, pp. 277–291.

Parkin, S. (1988) 'Green strategy', in F. Dodds (ed.), *Into the 21st Century*, Green Print: Basingstoke, pp. 163–179.

Partridge, P.H. (1971) *Consent and Consensus*, Pall Mall: London.

Pateman, C. (1989a) 'The patriarchal welfare state', in C. Pierson and F. Castles (eds), *The Welfare State Reader*, Polity: Cambridge, 2000, pp. 133–150.

Pateman, C. (1989b) *The Disorder of Women*, Polity: Oxford.

Pateman, C. (1998) 'The patriarchal welfare state', in J.B. Landes (ed.), *Feminism, the Public and the Private*, Oxford University Press: Oxford, pp. 241–276.

Pearson, B. and Williams, G. (1984) *Political Thought and Public Policy in the Nineteenth Century*, Longman: London.

Peele, G. (1990) 'Parties, pressure groups and parliament', in P. Dunleavy, A. Gamble and G. Peele (eds) *Developments in British Politics 3*, Macmillan: London, pp. 69–95.

Pemberton, W.E. (1998) *Exit with Honor: The Life and Presidency of Ronald Reagan*, Armonk: New York.

Perry, M. (1993) *An Intellectual History of Modern Europe*, Houghton Mifflin: Boston.

Pfaller, A. and Gough, I. (1991) 'The competitiveness of industrialised welfare states: A cross country survey', in A. Pfaller, I. Gough and G. Therborn (eds) *Can the Welfare State Compete?*, Macmillan: Houndmills, pp. 15–43.

Pfaller, A., Gough, I. and Therborn, G. (1991) 'The issue', in A. Pfaller, I. Gough and G. Therborn (eds) *Can the Welfare State Compete?*, Macmillan: Houndmills, pp. 1–14

Phillips, A. (1998) 'Introduction', in A. Phillips (1998) (ed.) *Feminism and Politics*, Oxford University Press: Oxford, pp. 1–22.

Pierson, C. (1994) *Beyond the Welfare State*, Polity: Cambridge.

Pierson, C. (1998) 'Contemporary challenges to welfare state development', in *Political Studies*, 46, 777–794.

Pierson, C. and Castles, F. (2000) (eds) *The Welfare State Reader*, Polity: Cambridge.

Pierson, P. (1996) 'The new politics of the welfare state', in C. Pierson and F. Castles (eds) *The Welfare State Reader*, Polity: Cambridge, 2000, pp. 309–319.

Pilkington, E. and Gumbel, A. (1994) 'Leading ecologist to address far right', *Guardian*, 25.11.1994, p. 9.

Plant, J. (1989) 'Ecofeminism', in A. Dobson (ed.) *The Green Reader*, Andre Deutsch, London, 1991, pp. 100–103.

Plant, R. (1991) *Modern Political Thought*, Blackwell: Oxford.

Porritt, J. (1984) *Seeing Green*, Blackwell: London.

Porritt, J. (1987) (ed.) *Friends of the Earth Handbook*, Macdonald Optima: London.

Porritt, J. (1988) 'Postscript', in F. Dodds (ed.), *Into the 21st Century*, Green Print: Basingstoke, pp. 195–203.

Porritt, J. and Winner, D. (1988) *The Coming of the Greens*, Collins: Glasgow.

Preston, P. (1999) 'In this unholy war, it's William the Conquered', *Observer*, 25 April 1999, 8.

Pringle, R. and Watson, S. (1998) 'Women's interests and the post-structuralist state', in A. Phillips (1998) (ed.) *Feminism and Politics*, Oxford University Press: Oxford, pp. 203–233.

Pym, F. (1984) *The Politics of Consent*, Hamish Hamilton: London.

Raphael, D.D. (1976) *Problems of Political Philosophy*, Macmillan: London.

Rawls, J. (1996) *Political Liberalism*, Columbia University Press: New York.

Rawls, J. (1999) *A Theory of Justice*, Oxford University Press: Oxford.

Reid, J. (2004) *Choosing Health-closing the Gap on Inequalities*, Department of Health: London.

Rimlinger, G.V. (1971) *Welfare Policy and Industrialization in Europe, America and Russia*, John Wiley: New York.

Rodger, J. (2000) *From a Welfare State to a Welfare Society*, Macmillan: Houndmills.

Roosevelt, F.D. (1932) 'To promote the general welfare', in G. Stourzh and R. Lerner (eds) *Readings in American Democracy*, Oxford University Press: New York, 1959, pp. 293–304.

Ross, F. (2002) 'Social Policy', in G. Peele, C. Bailey, B. Cain and B.G. Peters (eds) *Developments in American Politics 4*, Palgrave: Houndmills, pp. 202–221.

Rowbotham, S. (1989) *The Past is Before Us*, Pandora: London.

Rowlingson, K. and McKay, S. (2005) 'Income maintenance and taxation', in H. Bochel, C. Bochel, R. Page and R. Sykes (eds), *Social Policy: Issues and Developments*, Pearson: Essex, 2005, pp. 39–65.

Ruskin, J. (1862) 'Unto this Last', in J. Ruskin, *Unto this Last and Other Essays on Political Economy*, Ward Lock|: London, 1912, pp. 121–203.

Ryan, A. (1984) 'Liberty and Socialism', in B. Pimlott (ed.) *Fabian Essays in Socialist Thought*, Heinemann: London, pp. 100–116.

Ryle, M. (1988) 'Ecosocialism', in A. Dobson (ed.) *The Green Reader*, Andre Deutsch: London, 1991, pp. 138–141.

Salonen, T. (2001) 'Sweden: Between model and reality', in P. Alcock and G. Craig (eds) *International Social Policy*, Palgrave: Houndmills, pp. 143–160.

Sandel, M. (1996) *Democracy's Discontent*, Belknap Press: Cambridge Massachusetts.

Sapiro, V. (1998) 'Feminist studies and political science', in A. Phillips (ed.) *Feminism and Politics*, Oxford University Press: Oxford, 1998, pp. 67–92.

Saunders, P. (1995) *Social Theory and the Urban Question*, Routledge: London.

Scaperlanda, A. (1993) 'Transfer spending, taxes and the American welfare state', *Review of Social Economy*, 51, 118.

Schaller, M. (1994) *Reckoning with Reagan: American and its President in the 1980s*, Oxford University Press: New York.

Schlesinger, A. (1964) 'Sources of the new deal', in A. Schlesinger and M. White (eds) *Paths of American Thought*, Chatto and Windus: London, 1964, pp. 372–391.

Schumacher, E. (1974) 'Small or appropriate', in A. Dobson (ed.) *The Green Reader*, Andre Deutsch: London, 1991, pp. 112–115.

Scruton, R. (1990) *The Philosopher on Dover Beach*, Carcanet: Manchester

Schwarzmantel, J. (1994) *The State in Contemporary Society*, Harvester: Hemel Hempstead.

Schwarzmantel, J. (1998) *The Age of Ideology*, Macmillan: Houndmills.

Seabrook, J. (1988) 'Green values', in F. Dodds (ed.) *Into the 21st Century*, Green Print: Basingstoke, pp. 1–10.

Shaw, G.B. (ed) (1889) *Fabian Essays in Socialism*, Walter Scott: London.

Shull, S. (2000) *American Civil Rights Policy from Truman to Clinton*, Sharpe: Armonk, New York.

Siciliano, R. (2002) 'The Nixon Pay Board – A public administration disaster', *Public Administration Review*, pp. 368–373.

Silver, H. (1969) (ed.) *Robert Owen on Education*, Cambridge University Press: London.

Sked, A. and Cook, C. (1984) *Post-War Britain*, Penguin: Harmondsworth.

Small, R. (1982) 'Marx and state education', *History of Education*, 1, 207–218.

Smith, A. (1776) *The Wealth of Nations*, Bantam Classic: New York (2003 edition).

Social Exclusion Unit (2000), *National Strategy for Neighbourhood Renewal* (http://www.cabinet-office.gov.uk/seu/2000/nat-strat-cons/01.htm) (last accessed – 1.03.2001).

Spencer, H. (1884) *Man Versus the State*, Liberty Fund: Indianapolis (1982 edition).

Spretnak, C. and Capra, F. (1985) *Green Politics: The Global Promise*, Paladin: London.

Spulber, N. (1989) *Managing the American Economy, from Roosevelt to Reagan*, Indiana University Press: Bloomington.

Stapleton, J. (1991) 'Localism versus centralism in the Webb's political thought', *History of Political Thought*, xii, 147–165.

Stephen, A. (2000) 'There is a welfare state here, too', *New Statesman*, 26.6.2000, p. 25.

Stephens, M., Burns, N. and MacKay, L. (2003) 'The limits of housing reform', *Urban Studies*, 40, April 2003, 767.

Stirk, P.M. and Weigall, D. (1995) (eds) *An Introduction to Political Ideas*, Pinter: London.

Sylvester, C. (1998) 'Homeless in international relations ?', in A. Phillips (1998) (ed.) *Feminism and Politics*, Oxford University Press: Oxford, pp. 44–66.

Tatchell, P. (1988) 'Ecological sustainability', in F. Dodds (ed.) *Into the 21st Century*, Green Print: Basingstoke, pp. 39–51.

Tawney, R.H. (1931) *Equality*, Unwin: London (1975 edn).

Taylor, C. (1979) 'What's wrong with negative liberty ?', in A. Ryan (ed.) *The Idea of Freedom*, Oxford University Press: Oxford, pp. 175–193.

Taylor, G. (1994) 'The material and spiritual sides of life', *Contemporary Review*, July 1994, pp. 11–15.

Taylor, G. (1999) *The State and Social Policy*, Sheffield Hallam University Press: Sheffield.

Taylor, G. (2001a) 'Media review: The major government', *Contemporary Review*, 278, January 2001, 6–14.

Taylor, G. (2001b) 'Media review: The transformation of labour', *Contemporary Review*, 278, February 2001, 65–74.

Taylor, G. and Spencer, S. (2002) 'Introduction', *Social Identities*, Routledge: London, pp. 1–13.

Taylor, G. and Hawley, H. (2003) 'Freedom of religion in America', *Contemporary Review*, 282, June 2003, 344–350.

Taylor, G. and Hawley, H. (2004) 'The construction of arguments over the rationing of health care', *The Social Policy Journal*, 3(3), 45–62.

Taylor, J.K. (1992) *Reclaiming the Mainstream*, Prometheus Books: Buffalo, New York.

Teles, S. (1997) 'Beware the Clinton welfare trap', *New Statesman*, 6.6.1997, p. 22.

Thompson, S. (1998) 'Postmodernism', in A. Lent (ed.) *New Political Thought*, Lawrence and Wishart: London, 1998, pp. 143–162.

Thomson, D. (1981) *England in the Twentieth Century*, Penguin: Harmondsworth.

Tivey, L. (1989) 'Introduction', in L. Tivey and A.W. Wright (eds) *Party Ideology in Britain*, Routledge: London, 1989, pp. 1–20.

Todd, M., Ware, P. and Taylor, G. (2002) *Markets and the Welfare State*, Sheffield Hallam University Press: Sheffield.

Trainer, T. (1985) 'Abandon affluence', in A. Dobson (ed.) *The Green Reader*, Andre Deutsch: London, 1991, pp. 84–90.

Thorne, M. (1990) *American Conservative Thought since World War Two: The Core Ideas*, Greenwood Press: New York.

Tucker, R.C. (1978) (ed.) *The Marx–Engels Reader*, Norton: New York.

Turner, B. (1999) 'Social housing finance in Sweden', *Urban Studies*, 36, April 1999, 683.

Turner, B. and Whitehead, C. (2002) 'Reducing housing subsidy: Swedish housing policy in an international context', *Urban Studies*, 39, February 2001, 201.

Uzuhashi, T.K. (2001) 'Japan: Bidding farewell to the welfare society', in P. Alcock and G. Craig (eds), *International Social Policy*, Palgrave: Houndmills, pp. 104–123.

Van Parijs, P. (1997) *Real Freedom for All*, Clarendon Press: Oxford.

Wallace, W. (1997) *Why Vote Liberal Democrat?*, Penguin: Harmondsworth.

Weaver, M. (2001a) 'Proposals look to give social housing tenants part ownership of homes', *Guardian Unlimited*, 14.05.2001, (http://society.guardian.co.uk/housing/news/0,8366,490874,00.html).

Weaver, M. (2001b) 'Labour looks to boost home ownership', *Guardian Unlimited*, 2.08.2001, (http://society.guardian.co.uk/housing/news/0,8366,531320,00.html).

Webb, S. (1889) 'Historic', in G.B. Shaw (ed.) *Fabian Essays in Socialism*, Walter Scott: London, pp. 30–61.

Weiler, P. (1982) *The New Liberalism*, Garland: New York.

Whitehead, M., Evandrou, M., Haglund, B. and Diderichsen, F. (1997) 'As the health divide widens in Sweden and Britain, what's happening to access to care?: Part 3', *British Medical Journal*, 18.10.1997, 1006–1009.

Wilding, P. and Mok, K. (2001) 'Hong Kong: Between state and market', in P. Alcock and G. Craig (eds) *International Social Policy*, Palgrave: Houndmills, pp. 241–256.

Wilford, R. (1994) 'Feminism', in R. Eccleshall et al., *Political Ideologies*, Routledge: London, pp. 252–285.

Williams, F. (1989) *Social Policy: A Critical Introduction*, Polity: Cambridge.

Williams, F., Popay, J. and Oakley, A. (1999) *Welfare Research: A Critical Review*, UCL Press: London, 1999.

Williams, G. (1991) *Political Theory in Retrospect*, Elgar: Aldershot.

Wilson, E. (1972) *To the Finland Station*, Fontana: Glasgow.

Wilson, E. (1977) *Women and the Welfare State*, Tavistock Routledge: London.

Wilson, M. (1993) 'The German welfare state: A conservative regime in crisis', in A. Cochrane and J. Clarke (eds) *Comparing Welfare States*, Open University Press: Milton Keynes, pp. 141–171.

Wollstonecraft, M. (1982) *Vindication of the Rights of Woman*, Penguin Books: Harmondsworth.

Woodhouse, C.M. (1966) *Post-War Britain*, Bodley Head: London.

Woods, R. (1996) 'Women and housing', in C. Hallett (ed.), *Women and Social Policy: An Introduction*, Harvester Wheatsheaf: Hemel Hempstead, 1996, pp. 65–83.

Wolfe, W. (1975) *From Radicalism to Socialism*, Yale University Press: New Haven.

Audiovisual material

ITV, 13.05.1987, *Victorian Values*.

BBC1, 20.10.1993, *Thatcher: The Downing Street Years Part 1*.

BBC1, 27.10.1993, *Thatcher: The Downing Street Years Part 2*.

BBC1, 3.11.1993, *Thatcher: The Downing Street Years Part 3*.

BBC1, 10.11.1993, *Thatcher: The Downing Street Year Part 4*.

BBC2, 5.02.1994, *Neil Kinnock's Tomorrow's Socialism Part 1*.

BBC2, 12.02.1994, *Neil Kinnock's Tomorrow's Socialism Part 2*.

BBC1, 12.06.1995, *Thatcher: The Path to Power*.

BBC2, 9.07.1995, *New Jerusalem: Safe in their Hands*.

BBC2, 3.12.1995, *The Wilderness Years Part 1*.

BBC2, 11.12.1995, *The Wilderness Years Part 2*.

BBC2, 18.12.1995, *The Wilderness Years Part 3*.

BBC2, 24.03.1996, *Wheeler on America*.

BBC2, 16.04.1996, *The Economics Collection*.

Channel 4, 4.06.1996, *False Economy Part 1*.

Channel 4, 11.06.1996, *False Economy Part 2*.

Channel 4, 18.06.1996, *False Economy Part 3*.

BBC2, 11.09.1997, *Leviathan*.

BBC2, 28.09.1997, *Alan Clark's History of the Tory Party, Part 3*.

BBC2, 5.10.1997, *Alan Clark's History of the Tory Party Part 4*.

Channel 4, 5.10.1997, *Bye, Bye Blues*.

BBC2, 23.10.1997, *Newsfile 3: Politics and Economics*.

BBC2, 5.12.1997, *Earth and Life*.

Channel 4, 14.06.1998, *Pennies From Bevan*.

Channel 4, 18.04.1998, *A Night to Remember*.

BBC2, 1.08.1998, *The People's Century: Breadline*.

Channel 4, 2.02.1999, *Blair's Way*.

BBC1, 11.10.1999, *The Major Years Part 1*.

BBC1, 18.10.1999, *The Major Years Part 2*.

BBC1, 25.10.1999, *The Major Years Part 3*.

BBC2, 30.1.2000, *Blair's Thousand Days*.

Index

For enquiries or renewal at
Quarles LRC
Tel: 01708 455011 – Extension 4009

For enquiries or renewal at
Quarles LRC
Tel: 01708 455011 – Extension 4009